MEXICAN ENOUGH

Also by Stephanie Elizondo Griest

Around the Bloc: My Life in Moscow, Beijing, and Havana

100 Places Every Woman Should Go

MEXICAN ENOUGH

My Life between the Borderlines

Stephanie Elizondo Griest

Washington Square Press
New York London Toronto Sydney

Washington Square Press
A Division of Simon & Schuster, Inc.
1230 Avenue of the Americas
New York, NY 10020

Portions of chapter 1 originally appeared as "Borderlines" in *Bookmark Now: Writing in Unreaderly Times,* edited by Kevin Smokler (Basic Books, 2005), and in *Around the Bloc: My Life in Moscow, Beijing, and Havana,* by Stephanie Elizondo Griest (Villard, 2004).

Portions of chapter 9 originally appeared in *Around the Bloc: My Life in Moscow, Beijing, and Havana,* by Stephanie Elizondo Griest (Villard, 2004).

Chapter 11, "The Ambassador," was published as "La Mentirosa: The Liar," in issue no. 4 of *The Los Angeles Review.*

First Washington Square Press trade paperback edition August 2008

Designed by Nancy Singer

1 3 5 7 9 10 8 6 4 2

Library of Congress Cataloguing-in-Publication Data

Griest, Stephanie Elizondo, 1974–
Mexican enough : my life between the borderlines / Stephanie Elizondo Griest.
p. cm.
Includes bibliographical references and index.
1. Griest, Stephanie Elizondo, 1974– 2. Journalists—United States—Biography. 3. Mexican American journalists—Biography. I. Title.
PN4874.G747A3 2008
070.92—dc22
[B]
2008017394

ISBN-13: 978-1-4165-4017-5
ISBN-10: 1-4165-4017-2

FOR MY SISTER AND BROTHER,

BARBARA AND ALEX,

CON TODO MI CARIÑO

CONTENTS

Se llevaron nuestros frutos, cortaron nuestras ramas, quemaron nuestro tronco, pero no pudieron arrancar nuestras raíces.

They stole our fruit, they cut off our branches, they burned down our trunk, but they could not unearth our roots.

—*Popol Vuh*

AUTHOR'S NOTE

I ventured to Mexico in 2005 with two intentions: to learn Spanish and to gain a deeper sense of my cultural heritage. History had other plans, and I found myself documenting a burgeoning social movement that shook parts of the nation to the core. At no point in these travels did I officially work as a journalist for a news agency. The stories that follow are largely unverified, cultivated over conversations and interviews conducted in Spanish, a language I came to speak fluidly but not fluently. I deeply regret any contextual errors or facts missed in translation. Literary license has been taken with the timing and chronology of certain events. For narrative's sake, some stories that developed over weeks are relayed as having occurred in a single afternoon.

Terminology is tricky. Everyone from South, Central, and North America is an "American," but—for lack of a better alternative—I occasionally use the term to describe people from the United States. Apologies! When referencing U.S. citizens of Latin American ancestry, I use the word "Latino." "Mestizo" refers to Mexicans of both Spanish and indigenous ancestry; "indigenous" to those descending directly from the ancients: the Mayans, the Zapotecs, and so on.

As for the remarkable people you are about to meet, I refer to most by their first name only to protect their privacy and—in some instances—to ward off possible reprisals. I have changed the names of a few parties, as per their request. A heartfelt thanks goes to these heroines and heroes for welcoming me into their lives and entrusting me with their stories. I hope that I've portrayed them justly.

Drop me a line via my website, www.mexicanenough.com. I'm happy to do call-ins for book clubs and classrooms. ¡Gracias!

MEXICAN ENOUGH

CHAPTER ONE

LEGACIES

Arizona/Mexico Border and Brooklyn,
April 26–June 6, 2004

Once, when I was six, I leaped in front of a moving car. My lip split halfway to my ear. As a doctor stitched my cheek, I decided that motor vehicles were death machines and should be avoided. This is why I live in New York City: subways. On the rare occasion I find myself in the driver's seat, I'm haunted by visions of children darting across the road—perhaps images of my former self. I grip the steering wheel at eleven and one o'clock, lurching and braking.

Like now. I'm sputtering down Interstate 10 in a '92 Mazda, en route from Los Angeles to my parents' house in Corpus Christi, Texas. Today is the Tucson–El Paso leg. I veer off the highway onto an isolated farm road curving along the Mexican border and wind up in a desert choked with cactus and brush. This is my ideal driving scenario: no one to hit. The air conditioner has perished, so it is hot as blazes. I roll down the windows and contemplate my thirtieth birthday, which is a month away. My twenties were consumed by my first book, a memoir about traveling around the Communist Bloc. During the decade it took to research, write, and publish it, I grew keenly aware that I was living backward, more in my past than in my present. It is time to move on, but where? To what?

When asked this on my book tour, I had a ready reply: learn Spanish. Despite being third-generation Mexican-American (on my mother's side) and growing up 150 miles from the Texas-Mexico border, my Spanish is best described as Tarzan Lite: a primitive vocabulary spoken entirely in the present tense. My mom faced so much ridicule for her accent growing up that she never taught my sister or me how to speak the language properly. I mostly picked up curse words in school (¡pendejo!) and opted to learn Russian in college. Studies show that only 17 percent of third-generation Mexicans can speak Spanish fluently, but it riddles me with guilt—especially now that I've entered the publishing world. I'm turning down invitations to speak to groups I supposedly represent because I literally can't communicate with them.

A logical life plan would be to venture across this desert and explore the land and tongue of my ancestors. Yet the very notion terrifies me. Ask any South Texan. To us, Mexico means kidnappings and shoot-outs in broad daylight in Nuevo Laredo, or the unsolved murders of young women in Juárez. It means narco-traffickers in every cantina and explosive diarrhea from every comedor. When I was in high school, a college student got snatched off the street while partying in Matamoros during spring break. Bound and gagged, he was driven to a ranch run by a satanic cult. Next thing you know, he was menudo. One worshipper wore a belt made of his victims' spinal cords.

So go to Mexico? Thanks, but I'd rather return to Moscow and track down my old mafiosi boyfriend.

I'm cresting a small hill now. Glistening pools of water appear on the road up ahead, then evaporate. It is dizzyingly hot. I glance down at the gas gauge. It's nearly empty. Cell phone: roaming. Not a soul has passed me on this road. If the

Mazda breaks down, I'm toast. Better turn around and rejoin the main highway. My foot hovers above the brake as I grasp the clutch.

Something appears in the distance. Objects in the middle of the road. Moving sluggishly, then quickly. Bears? What kind of bear prowls around the Arizona desert? No. They must be wild dogs, big ones, standing on their hind legs and . . . running?

No. They are people. One figure seems to be a child. My lifelong phantom has actualized. I slam the brakes. They must be Mexicans fleeing the border. I blare the horn.

"¡Agua! ¡Tengo agua!" I scream out the window.

They must need water. I have two bottles. I must give one to them.

But . . . what if water isn't all they need? What if they ask me to take them somewhere? Of course I will say yes. How can I deny a ride to people in the middle of the desert?

But what if they don't just want a lift? What if they want my car?

Or what if they take it? Toss me into the cactus and roar away? That is what I would do, if the tables were turned: throw out the gringa and go.

The irony here is immediate. Nearly every accolade I have received in life—from minority-based scholarships to book contracts—has been at least partly due to the genetic link I share with the people charging through the snake-infested brush. What separates us is a twist of geographical fate that birthed me on one side of the border and them on the other. They are "too Mexican." I am just enough.

The Mazda has slowed to a crawl, but the border crossers have vanished. Water shimmers where they once stood. I pause a moment, wondering what to do, then slowly begin to accelerate. As I look off into the desert hills from which they descended, a surprising thought flashes through my mind: *I want to go to Mexico.*

By the time I've dropped off the car in Texas and flown home to Brooklyn, I've regained my senses. I can't go to Mexico. That would entail quitting my day job, cramming everything I own into storage, and ravaging my savings account. It's just too easy—and I've done it too many times before. It's why I'm nearly thirty and still sleeping (alone) on a futon in a cramped apartment with multiple roommates while my friends have wandered off, bought houses, married, and procreated. Besides. What if I did learn Spanish—and nothing changed? For years, this has been my pipe dream: *If I only spoke Spanish, I would be more Mexican.* But what if it isn't possible to *become* a member of an ethnic or cultural group—to will yourself into it, to choose? What if you can only be born and raised into it?

That would rule me out. I made a conscious choice to be white like my dad one day in elementary school. Our reading class had too many students, our teacher announced, and needed to be split in two. One by one, she started sending the bulk of the Mexican kids to one side of the room and the white kids to the other. When she got to me, she peered over the rims of her glasses. "What are you, Stephanie? Hispanic or white?"

I had no answer to this. Both? Neither? Either? My mother's roots dwelled beneath the pueblos of northern Mexico; my father's were buried in the Kansas prairie. I inherited her olive skin and caterpillar eyebrows, and his indigo eyes.

But in South Texas, you are either one or the other. Searching the classroom for an answer, I noticed my best friend, Melida, standing over by the brown kids. "I'm Hispanic," I announced. The teacher nodded, and I joined the Mexicans. A few minutes later a new teacher arrived and led us to another room, where she passed around a primer and asked us to read aloud. That's when I realized the difference between the other students and me. Most of them spoke Spanish at home, so they stumbled over the strange English words, pronouncing *yes* like *jess* and *chair* like *share.* When my turn came to read, I sat up straight and said each word loud and clear. The teacher watched me curiously. After class ended, I told her that I wanted to be "where the smart kids were." She agreed and I joined the white class the following day.

For the next eight years, whenever anyone asked what color I was, I said white. It was clearly the way to be: everyone on TV was white, the characters in my *Highlights* magazine were white, the singers on Casey Kasem's American Top 40 were white (or black). White people even populated my books: there were runaways who slept in imperial chambers at the Metropolitan Museum of Art, Sweet Valley High twins who roared around California in convertibles, and girls named Deenie who rubbed their Special Places with a washcloth until they got a Special Feeling. (I sat in the bathtub for hours trying to find this Special Place. Was it that spot behind my elbow? Or just beneath my toe?)

True, I often wondered when their primos would burst onto the scene in their lowriders. And how come nobody ever ate barbacoa or cracked piñatas or shopped for empanadas at HEB?* But I took no offense at these absences. White people's stories just seemed worthier of being told. And so I grew closer to Grandma, in Kansas, because she resembled the feisty Jewish grandmothers in my books more than Abuelita, who lived on a ranch thirty miles out of town. I used to beg Grandma for stories about life on the prairie as she baked me vats of macaroni and cheese. She regaled me with the adventures of my great-great-uncle Jake, a hobo who saw America with his legs dangling over

---

* You're not from Texas, are you? Otherwise, you'd be shopping here too. With more than three hundred stores, HEB is practically the only place to buy groceries in the Lone Star State. The name derives from the initials of the founders' son, Howard E. Butt.

the edge of a freight train. When I wound up across the kitchen counter from Abuelita hand-rolling tortillas, however, I'd sit in silence—and not just because of the language barrier. I simply couldn't fathom she had anything interesting to say. I'd watch her flip the masa on the burner and wish she'd whip up something like Are-You-There-God-It's-Me-Margaret's grandma would instead. Like matzo ball soup. I'd never tried this dish before, but it sounded like minimeatballs floating in cheese sauce.

I switched back to being Mexican my senior year in high school. I was thumbing through the college scholarship bin in the Career Center when my guidance counselor called me into her office and asked a familiar question: "What are you, Stephanie? Hispanic or white?"

Before I could respond, she offered that my SAT scores weren't high enough for funding if I was considered white. If I was Hispanic, she predicted, doors would swing open. "Think about it," she said.

I did for about three seconds, then changed the little *W* on my transcript to a big fat *H*. Suddenly, I qualified for dozens of additional scholarships. I applied for them all, and acceptance letters poured in. Not only was my freshman year at the University of Texas at Austin fully funded, but I also received free tutoring, a faculty adviser, and a student mentor, plus invitations to myriad clubs and mixers. It was quite exciting—until I started meeting the other Latino scholarship recipients. Some were the children of migrant workers. A few had spent summers picking grapefruit themselves. Their skin was brown, and they had endured hardships because of it. I quickly realized that I had reaped the benefits of being a minority but none of the drawbacks. Guilt overwhelmed me. Should I give back the money I received? Transfer to a cheaper school? Or try to become that *H* emblazoned across my transcripts?

Mexifying myself was fun at first. I decorated my room with images of Frida Kahlo and the Virgen de Guadalupe. I taught English to Mexican kids and drank lots of margaritas. I changed my white-bread middle name (Ann) to my mother's maiden name (Elizondo) and made everyone use it. I even got a Colombian boyfriend (bad idea).

Then a Chicano politics class inspired me to work at the minority recruitment center at the office of admissions. Half of our student staff was Mexican; the other half, black. I became the volunteer coordinator, which meant I cajoled scores of students out of bed on Saturday mornings to help us call promising minority high school seniors and lure them to our school. We then sent buses to fetch them to Austin, where our volunteers showed them around campus and played host for the night. The afternoon of the first arrival, our boss called me to the podium to pair up the "mentors" with the "mentees." Not only did I butcher some of the black students' names, I couldn't remotely pronounce Echeverría or Guillermoprieto. The auditorium was soon in a mild uproar. "Who do you think you are, miss?" someone shouted.

For a biracial,* nothing is more humiliating than this: trying to be half of yourself while the other half keeps intervening—and getting caught. I tried to crack a joke about it. "A bad Mexican," I replied. But my voice trembled. Noticeably.

Just then, my colleague Rosa tapped my shoulder. I had an urgent phone call, she whispered. After excusing myself to the audience, I hurried offstage and into our office in the back as Rosa resumed the matching. There was, of course, no phone call. Rosa had simply tried to save some dignity—our organization's, and what remained of my own.

That was more than a decade ago. I've since made several attempts to study Spanish, enrolling in classes and stockpiling workbooks. But I dread using it. My Spanish sounds like a failure to me, as though everything I manage to say is an admission

---

* Technically, I am "biethnic" rather than "biracial," as Latinos are not a unique race. I use the latter term out of personal preference, as I have always felt a special connection to biracial communities.

of what more I cannot. What will Mexicans say when they hear it: "¿Tu mamá es mexicana? ¿Híjole, what happened to *you*?"

No. I'm not going to Mexico. I'm staying here in Brooklyn with my futon. And multiple roommates.

Today is my thirtieth birthday. I want to celebrate this landmark boldly, to commence something wholly new. I am so steeped in possibility, I step off at the wrong subway station on my way to work. I whirl around, but the doors roll shut in my face. I turn around with a sigh.

Plastered on the wall before me is a tourism advertisement. A woman lounges on a white sand beach surrounded by a cobalt sea. *I want to go to Mexico*, it reads.

I book a ticket as soon as I reach the office, before my verve fizzles.

CHAPTER TWO

MIRACLE CITY

Mexico City and Querétaro,
December 31, 2004–January 5, 2005

The final sun of 2004 is setting over Mexico City International Airport. Strangers wish one another—and me—a Próspero Año Nuevo, or Prosperous New Year. Arriving today is strategic: I want to spend the whole of 2005 here, ancestor seeking. My whole body quivers.

Everyone crowds around the conveyor belt to catch whatever spits out of the chute. I tend to fill my carry-ons with notebooks and laptop accessories, leaving underwear and toothbrushes to fate, and recognize the shortcomings of this system as the passenger clump thins and the luggage flow tapers. I catch the eyes of a Mexican man waiting on the opposite side of the conveyor belt with his arms folded across his chest. His face has weathered to near leather, as has his Astros baseball cap. We exchange half smiles.

Just then, a siren goes off. The conveyor belt halts with a jolt. No more baggage. Our eyes meet again and trade a thought: *shit.* We join the human swarm around an airline employee with a clipboard. She scribbles our names on a scrap of paper and tells us to return mañana. Even I know that mañana doesn't mean tomorrow but "sometime in the future, maybe." Moreover, I'm not staying here tonight but catching a bus to a city 125 miles away. I scan the baggage claim area for someone more official, but there are only other attendants with clipboards. Astros man approaches me with his palms raised skyward. "Ni modo," he says, then exits through the sliding glass doors.

Cultural anthropologists have written reams about the significance of this phrase, which loosely translates as "It can't be helped," or "There is nothing to be done." Somewhere along the past five centuries of religious and political oppression, they note, Mexicans accepted the fact that life was utterly beyond their control. Fires, floods, earthquakes, illnesses? Ni modo, that's God's doing; there's no changing that. Revolutions, tax hikes, peso devaluations? Ni modo, that's the government; can't do much about that either. Lost luggage? Ni modo, that's Continental Airlines. At least the plane landed safely, gracias a Dios!

Hoisting my laptop upon my back, I head through the sliding glass doors. Mobs of families crowd behind them. Spanish eyes, Mayan noses, Olmec faces. And then—off in the distance—a glimpse of salt-and-pepper hair tucked beneath an orange ski cap. Greg. We've known each other since Dollar Movie nights at Sunrise Mall in Corpus. A visual artist, he has spent much of the past decade in Mexico, painting, teaching, and traveling. In an e-mail a few months ago, he offered me his room in Querétaro, a state capital smack in Mexico's center, as he'll soon be leaving for an artistic residency in Spain. Querétaro has a good language school, he wrote, plus none of his roommates—three Mexican artists—speak English. I eagerly accepted.

Seeing him, a piece of my past, actualizes the present. We fall into each other's arms laughing, then head down to the bus station beneath the airport. We pull into Querétaro two hours before midnight. A historic city of 1.6 million, its horizon glimmers with floodlit churches, domes, and steeples. Greg's girlfriend Jésica—also a visual artist—picks us up at the station in a sports car, wearing a zebra-patterned jacket over a short red skirt. She welcomes me with a kiss to the cheek, and we jet off to my new home in the colonial heart of downtown. A wrought-iron door flings open to a New Year's Eve bash. Madonna's *American Life* album ricochets off walls painted hot pink and lime green. Tatami-style mats and pillows are situated around a low-to-the-ground table set for six and decorated with jars of Gerber daisies. Laughter erupts from the kitchen. We follow it. Half a dozen college-aged guys hover over a table, making Mexican sushi (seaweed and rice rolled with smoked salmon, cream cheese, and jalapeños). They greet us joyously, kisses all around. Greg introduces me as a writer studying Spanish.

"You come to Mexico to write about me? Corazón, I got stories!" a catlike creature says in halting English. He has spiky hair bleached white-blond and is clad entirely in black.

The others whoop in laughter. "You a learning Espanish? Can you say . . . pussy?"

They shout out a list of synonyms that is impressively long. The only one I catch is papaya.

"Papaya?" I ask. "¿Como la fruta?" Like the fruit?

"Sí, Esteffie," says the shortest of the bunch. "How long you no . . ." He mimics having sex.

So long, I lie. Even so, he is shocked.

"¡¿Cómo?!" he cries. "Tu papaya—it dry up, fall out!"

That does it: they are in hysterics, and I am too. Someone new walks in. Significantly older than the others—maybe even older than me—he has animated eyes and fuzzy facial hair. Greg introduces him as Fabián, one of my new roommates (and the only member of the party who actually lives here). After kissing my cheek, Fabián beckons us to the back of the house to show me my room. It has no furniture save a bed, but artwork adorns the walls, including urban photography and figurines sculpted out of chicken wire. The closet is crammed with canvases and clothes, but Fabián promises that our roommate Omar will clean it out when he returns from holiday.

"He to move out?" I ask.

Fabián's smile widens. "Sí. Into my room."

My suspicions are confirmed: they're gay. Every single one of them. My papaya grumbles in protest.

Mexican families and friends traditionally share a meal when the clock strikes midnight on New Year's Eve. Greg invites me to join him and Jésica. We rekiss every cheek in the house and then spill into the cobblestone street, which pulsates with families rattling noisemakers. Every few blocks is another plaza built around a fountain, statue, or gazebo decked for the holidays. A twenty-foot Christmas tree made of neon poinsettias blinks in one; in another, an ark's worth of statues visit baby Jesus. Mariachis stroll about, belting out corridos on fat bass guitars. Parishioners pack into seventeenth-century churches glowing with candles. Hidden from view, Jésica says, are the people scattering money throughout their houses and then sweeping it up for fortune in the New Year. Lonely hearts, Greg adds, wear red undies tonight for another kind of luck.

We enter a restaurant throbbing with revelers, no table sitting fewer than eight. Helium-filled balloons with curlicue streamers dangle in our faces. We order champagne and make rounds of toasts with diners at neighboring tables. Everyone welcomes me to Mexico. I can't stop grinning. Beside our plates are plastic bags of a dozen grapes. At midnight we eat them one by one, making new wishes for 2005, and I realize that mine have already come true.

When I awaken the following morning, my head still tingles from champagne. Greg is sprawled across the twin bed beside me. We spent the night at Jésica's, and judging by the onion-and-chile vapors drifting up the stairwell, breakfast is simmering down below. We dress quickly.

Jésica lives with her mother and older sister Lulú in a classic Mexican home built around a courtyard sealed by a high metal fence. Its three bedrooms, dining room, living room, and sewing room serve as a gallery for Jésica's artwork. Women are her primary muse: on one canvas, a long-haired damsel is engulfed in flames upon a cross. We join the family in the breakfast nook, which is encased by sliding glass doors that open onto the courtyard. Magnolia and hibiscus blossoms waft in with the morning breeze.

Everyone greets us with hugs and kisses and ushers us to the table, where mangoes, papayas, and guayabas fill a wooden bowl and home-baked biscochos, or sugar cookies, pile inside a bin. Freshly squeezed aguas frescas, or fruit water, trickle from pitchers. Jésica and her mother are making huevos rancheros in an iron skillet. They cover our plates with corn tortillas browned in oil, plop on fried eggs, and smother them with a ranchera sauce of tomatoes, onions, and chiles serranos spiked with garlic and cumin.

Lulú, who is many months pregnant, orders a quesadilla instead. "It's better for my bebé," she explains, patting her considerable belly. A boisterous woman with black hair and ivory skin, she bought this house after a decade of working as a manager for Kellogg's in Querétaro. She met her husband, a Canadian artist, at a wedding and married him three months into their online courtship. He still lives in Canada and she down here, but she hopes he'll join her after the birth of their son. "Can you believe it, we've never spent more than five weeks at a time together but are so in love!"

Jésica serves her a corn tortilla grilled with cheese and sits beside me. "What else can I bring you?" she asks, her eyes wide and earnest. "Melón? Tortillas?"

I request a story instead. Greg said she'd had some crazy Canadian adventures herself. What happened? All three women burst into laughter. "Only my Jésica," her mother says, dabbing her eyes with the edge of her napkin.

Jésica flew to Toronto on a tourist visa in 1995, soon after graduating from university. A friend worked there (illegally) as a nanny and helped her find a job for a couple with three daughters, ages two, four, and six. In exchange for cooking the family's meals, washing their clothes, and caring for the girls, they offered Jésica $700 a month plus room, board, and the chance to study English at a nearby night school. Although this violated her tourism-only visa, Jésica accepted.

"It sounded like a good deal," she says, stabbing into her huevos rancheros, "until those sweet little girls turned into rebels."

They kicked. They screamed. They bit. The four-year-old had a penchant for nudity, ripping off her clothes and tossing them out the window as soon as Jésica dressed her. She also enjoyed flooding the bathrooms by dumping whole rolls of paper into the toilets and flushing repeatedly. The six-year-old, meanwhile, occasionally disappeared. Once, Jésica had to enlist the police to help find her. "Never have I seen children behave like that."

Their parents weren't any better. No matter how many shopping lists Jésica compiled, they stocked the kitchen with little more than ham, potato chips, and beer. They left for work at dawn, rarely returned before the girls had been tucked into bed, and disagreed on nearly every aspect of child rearing. "The father said I was not allowed to spank the girls under any circumstance, but the mother gave me a spoon and urged me to hit them. I took up smoking and lost a lot of weight."

Jésica's tourist visa soon expired, but she decided to stay after securing an infinitely better job with a family who treated her as their own. When a friend from Querétaro named Adriana expressed interest in coming to Toronto, Jésica found her a job and drove to the airport to pick her up. An hour after her plane supposedly landed, she heard an announcement that Adriana's "party" was needed at the Immigration Office. Jésica knocked on the door and got whisked inside by officials. They had already determined that Adriana wished to work illegally in Canada and were deporting her back to Mexico. Now they wanted to investigate her "party."

Five hours of interrogation followed. Jésica stuck to her impromptu lie that she had only been vacationing there for three weeks and would be leaving the following week, but their unrelenting questions gradually wore her down. Before signing some incriminating paperwork, she demanded a bathroom break. Two policemen escorted her to the bathroom, but when she emerged, both stood a good fifty feet away, buying coffee and doughnuts.

"So I ran off," she says.

"No!" I exclaim.

"Oh yes!" her mother pipes in proudly. "Mija *ran*."

"Where to?"

"The parking lot. I got in my car and drove away."

"To freedom!" Lulú laughs.

We toast to her daring with our fruit water. This is the first of hundreds of immigration stories I will hear in Mexico. Its most unusual component is motive: adventure rather than desperation. Jésica's pluck will echo in all of them.

Word spreads that I arrived in Querétaro with no luggage, and Raúl soon materializes on my doorstep. A friend of my roommate Fabián, he is a twenty-two-year-old art student with that über-stylish, fresh-out-of-the-shower look that only gay men can muster: manicured nails, gel-spiked hair, sculpted eyebrows. I am touched when he offers to accompany me back to Mexico City to hunt for my luggage. I protest that it's too far away, that surely he must be busy, that I can go alone. But he is insistent.

"My dream is to make it with a pilot someday," he explains, flicking up the collar of his polo. "I like airports."

Truthfully I am grateful for the company, as Mexico City unnerves me. Known as "D. F."* by Chicanos and expats and plain-old "Mexico" by Mexicans, this city is a seductive disaster. A megalopolis of 22 million, it has stand-still traffic, baffling corruption, and lethal pollution (a day's worth of breath is equivalent to smoking two packs of cigarettes). It is also sinking—nearly thirty feet in the past century—and due to its prime positioning near the Pacific fault lines, occasionally tosses its residents out of bed and collapses buildings on top of them. Its many distinctions include "Kidnap Capital of the World." Last year, some two hundred people were abducted, held, and sometimes tortured for weeks while their families scrounged hefty ransoms, and thousands more endured "express kidnappings," in which they were forced at gunpoint to empty their accounts at ATM machines around the city. D. F. is a postapocalyptic place where—to paraphrase writer Carlos Monsiváis—people debate whether they are actually living the disaster to come or are among its ruins.

Raúl and I hop a bus to the airport and, three hours later, start knocking on office doors. The information kiosk at the international gate sends us upstairs. The people there send us downstairs. Notebooks are consulted; vintage computers are checked. Your bags are in Querétaro. They are in-flight back to Houston. No, espérame. Your bags are here; it's just unclear where. An hour passes, then another. A clerk leads me into the bowels of the airport, where hundreds of pieces of sad-looking luggage are lined up in single-file rows. None are mine. We return to the main office, where a clerk behind a desk makes a final call. Then he looks me dead in the eyes. "Forgive me, señorita. We have no idea where is your luggage."

There is a couch close by, piled with baggage. I collapse upon it. Having been a nomad for so many years, I've already whit-

---

* "D. F." is breezy shorthand for Mexico City's official name: Ciudad de México, Distrito Federal.

tled my shoes and clothes to the barest minimum. Now there is nothing. I sit a long while before glancing at the two pieces of luggage beside me. One is a purple carrying case for a yoga mat. How funny. Mine looks exactly like it. I glance at its tag. And that is my handwriting. As well as my address. My heart skips a beat. It *is* my yoga mat. And next to it is my potbellied backpack. I stare at it for a half-crazed second, almost afraid to touch it. But when I do, it doesn't disappear. I jump up and down. The clerk stares at me in wonder. I kiss his cheeks with gratitude, then heave my bags onto my shoulders and race out the door. Raúl awaits behind a barricade on the floor below. Though he is overjoyed by my story, he is not surprised in the least.

"This is Mexico." He beams. "We have miracles."

"Welcome to La Zona Rosa," Raúl says as we emerge from Metro Insurgentes a few hours later. He spreads out his arms as if to embrace it. "The gayest place on earth!"

Let me interject here that I didn't go to Mexico searching for the gay community. For starters, it's a terrible way to meet (straight) men, which would—at this junction in life—be kind of nice. But now that we're in their epicenter, I am intrigued. The status of gays and lesbians is a good barometer of the social progressiveness of a nation. And Raúl is an eager (and English-speaking) guide.

Originally a gallery district, La Zona Rosa has long attracted foreigners, artists, intellectuals, and—after a subway station opened here—prostitutes, beggars, and thieves. Its leafy streets are named after cities like Geneva, Dublin, London, and Warsaw and sprinkled with French-accented mansions built about a century ago. Its first gay bar was clandestinely christened in the late 1970s, and so many have followed that the neighborhood's name—the Pink Zone—has taken on a whole new meaning. On some streets, practically every other establishment is a hotel, bar, or restaurant with a rainbow flag unfurled above its doorway. Raúl stops at two connecting bars and lets me choose between the blue one called Gayta (which is packed with gay men) and the pink one called Pussy Bar (you guessed it). I vote for my genitalia and we order tequila drinks that are neon green. I start asking him about gay rights.

"We have none," he says flatly. "In all of D. F., I only can hold hands with my boyfriend here, in La Zona Rosa. One neighborhood in a whole city!"

That's partly because Mexico is fervently Roman Catholic and led by clergy who aggressively campaign against sex education, condoms, and alternative lifestyles. It also bristles with macho types—even at society's most distinguished levels. During the 2000 presidential campaign, Vicente Fox delighted in mispronouncing his opponent's last name, Labastida, as "Lavestida," or transvestite, and calling him a "mariquita," or sissy.*

Still, the gay-rights movement is making some strides, especially here in D. F. Its city council is currently considering a same-sex civil union law that would extend some marriage rights to gay couples,† and it has hosted massive gay pride parades for more than twenty-five years. In 1997, it sent Latin America's

---

* To his credit, in 2001 President Fox signed a constitutional amendment outlawing discrimination, including bias based on sexuality. Two years later, he required federal agencies to fund tolerance campaigns, making Mexico the second Latin American country to do so.

† The same-sex civil union law finally passed in November 2006. Although gay couples in D. F. still cannot marry or adopt, they now have the right to inherit pensions and property, join health and life insurance policies, and make medical decisions for each other. The border state of Coahuila passed similar legislation two months later.

first openly gay person (a lesbian, no less) to Congress,* and a year later repealed legislation that previously allowed police to arrest people for the "crime" of being homosexual.

A waiter daintily sets a plate of appetizers before us. His nails are pearly pink. As I gaze around the two bars, I realize that the clientele mirrors the gay communities I encountered in Russia and China almost exactly, from their clothing (fashionable and formfitting) to their hairstyles (slick and spiky) to their musical accompaniment (techno, pop, and Céline Dion). I mention this to Raúl.

"I don't know over there, but here we are the first generation of openly gay people in Mexico. We have no role models, so we learn how to be gay from TV." He pats his lips with a napkin and leans forward, grinning. "Now I tell you about La Casita!"

A veritable institution, La Casita is an old house with no marker save a rainbow flag. According to Raúl, you walk in, pay seventy pesos (about seven dollars), and, if so inspired, strip. They hand you a bag of tissues, condoms, and a number, and you go about your business.

"Which is . . . ?" I ask.

"To fuck."

My eyes widen.

"It is a maze down there. Rooms with beds and couches and TVs playing porn. No windows, and hardly any light. Every kind of man: rich, poor, young, old, and they have sex, right there in front of you! You can get lost down there. Some people even die there, I am sure of it. I think that is why they give you a number." He removes his designer glasses to rub his eyes.

"Did you meet anyone interesting?" I ask.

"No way! I was with my friend. We were too scared to leave

* Patria Jiménez, a forty-year-old lesbian activist, ran for Congress under the slogan "Sexo seguro, voto seguro, haz tuyo el futuro"—Safe sex, secure vote, make the future yours.

the sofa by the front door. The vibra [energy] is so dark, you cannot imagine. And the smell . . ."

"That's why I like being a woman," I say, taking a sip of neon green. "We don't do things like that."

"You think so? Well, you've never heard of the Supercito!"

This establishment is in Querétaro and caters to wives cheating on their husbands. The storefront resembles a supermarket, but if you know the secret password, you are granted passage into the bordello in back. "They hand their shopping list to the man behind the counter and when their hour is up, their groceries are ready to go!"

I refuse to believe this. Raúl swears it is true. By now we've drained our glasses. Time for the discos. We head into the street. Night has fallen. Music spills out of open doorways: techno, pop, rave, and something best described as mariachi ska. We dart into the one playing Selena.* A drag queen is onstage; we climb up to the platform beside her and let loose. The crowd thickens. I fully expect Raúl to ditch me for the first cute boy who catches his glance, but he dutifully dances by my side, even nudging other guys out of the way. Although we are technically competitors here, his sense of machismo—that is, his culturally conditioned instinct to protect female companions—overrides it. We dance for hours, then search for replenishment. I'm craving tacos from a stand, but Raúl talks me into wanting a slice of tres leches, a sponge cake made of three types of milk and smothered with whipped cream. The best one in town, he says, is served at this upscale diner called Vips. We walk in and are greeted by a hostess wearing a Wal-Mart logo on her name tag.

"Wal-Mart owns this place?" I ask.

"Yes, but it is very Mexican. See?" Raúl points at the hipsters stirring cups of coffee, then leads me to a booth. "And look at the menu: tres leches!"

The largest private employer in Mexico, Wal-Mart has

* Because she's from Corpus too.

opened 122 Supercenters, 78 Sam's Clubs, 228 Bodega food and merchandise stores, 44 Mi Bodegas, 2 Mi Bodega Expresses, 62 Superamas, 68 Suburbia apparel stores, and a whopping 315 Vips restaurants here since 1991. This is one reason I don't want to eat here; the other is that Vips lacks the charm of real Mexican restaurants. Their menus are laminated with full-color photos instead of being scribbled on a board. Their waitresses engage in suggestive-selling techniques like "Do you want a cafecito with that? How about some flan?" (In many Mexican restaurants, these items are automatically served with your meal.) And most significantly, diners here do not bid one another "Buen provecho"—Enjoy your meal—as they stroll past. They just drink their coffee around private booths and tables.

Yet Vips is so popular with late-night club-goers, it has become a Mexican institution in itself. We load up on sugar and caffeine and head back to the discos for another round, returning to our hostel just before 4 A.M. Raúl stirs me awake at noon. "Today, I take you to Palacio de Bellas Artes. It is the most beautiful building in the whole world. I am serious. And then we go to Museo Nacional de Arte. It is the world's best art museum. Really, I am not joking. But first we eat chilaquiles [fried tortilla strips slathered in salsa and cheese]. It is the best for la cruda [a hangover]."

And so we are off and running again. I keep thinking that at any moment, Raúl will need to part. He is a college student returning to campus after a long Christmas break. Surely he has classes to take, vases to sculpt. And he does. But he stays by my side. This is the flip side of ni modo. Life's injustices and disappointments might be accepted as God's (or Government's) will, but so are its pleasant surprises. When the universe tosses something fun in your lap, you are to disfrutar, or enjoy, it.

I lost this kind of spontaneity while living in New York. There, I had to make reservations with even my best friends weeks in advance. And if we set drink plans for six thirty, they likely had dinner arrangements with someone else at eight, and would be catching a show with another someone at ten. I began triple-booking as well, so that even when something extraordinary came up, I couldn't possibly flake on so many people to enjoy it.

I try to explain this to Raúl, but he doesn't understand. "Why you can't see your friends when you want? You just go to their house. They invite you in, you have a chela [beer], you talk to their mother. It is so easy and nice."

CHAPTER THREE

THE LAND OF NI MODO

Querétaro,
January–February 2005

Acclimating to my Mexican life requires some adjustment.

First is our house, which has a nickname: La Jotería. As the joke goes, you can find zapatos (shoes) in a zapatería; pan (bread) in a panadería; and jotos (fags) at our place. And it's true: young gay men flock in at all hours of the day and night, almost always unannounced and hardly ever alone. Since the majority live with their parents (most of whom don't know they are gay), our house is their oasis. Upon crossing our threshold, they beeline for the bathroom, where they dip into the communal jar of gel and spike their hair into tufts. Then they blast Dead Can Dance, flip through fashion magazines, hold their boyfriend's hand, tell stories. I love it: not only are they entertaining, but they are also teaching me a far more colorful vocabulary than I'm learning at the language school down the street.

But I worry sometimes about my roommate Omar. He takes classes at the Universidad Autónoma de Querétaro all morning, then dashes off to his full-time café job until closing (around 10 P.M.). He returns home exhausted, with hours of art class projects ahead of him. The only place to work is upon the living room table, which is inevitably swarming with people—who tend to get hungry. On many occasions, I watch Omar whip up caldos and crepes at midnight when he has an assignment due the next morning.

"I say to guests to go home so you to work?" I once ask in my shaky Spanish while carrying plates out to the living room.

He stares at me in horror, his spatula frozen in midair. "No, Fani.* They are our guests!"

And they are, night after night. One Monday, the doorbell starts buzzing around 6 P.M. My third (and last) roommate Karina spent the afternoon making guayaba water from scratch in a big silver pot, and is pouring me a glass when the first batch arrives. She doesn't actually know them, but no matter: guests are guests, no matter whose. She serves each one a tall glass, then prepares something for them to eat. Six hours and fourteen visitors later, the silver pot is empty and the kitchen sink is full.

"I like your water of the guayaba very much," I say as I tackle the dishes, glad to be alone in Karina's company. I must fight for it when others are around: our friends can't get enough of her juicy red lips and curvy brown hips. They flirt more with her than one another.

She beams. "Qué bien. I never did try it."

I turn on the faucet. Nothing happens. Water shortages are chronic in this city (and state and nation). We have a backup tank for emergencies, but it's empty too.

"¡Ni modo, Fani!" Karina says, laughing, hanging up the dish towel. She retires to her bedroom, pleased to be free from the night's final chores. An art restorer, she must rise early tomorrow to tend to some crumbling icons at a nearby church.

I stay in the kitchen, fiddling with the faucet. It takes half a dozen tries before I accept that it has run dry. I enter the bath-

* Fani is my nickname at La Jotería, pronounced "FAH-neeee."

room to prepare for bed. Showering won't be an option tonight, but I remember to discard my tissues into the trash can instead of the toilet. (Even when the water flows, few commodes can absorb paper in Mexico.) Then I head off to bed and dive beneath three layers of blankets. Our house is as cozy as a meat locker at night. After a week of conjugating verbs with blue fingers, I shelled out 280 pesos* (about $28) for a space heater last Tuesday. For three days, I reveled in warmth. Then I awoke to a toxic stench and discovered that the electric socket was smoking. I ripped out the heater's plug, which had scorched black. When I showed it to Omar and Fabián the following morning, they were equally surprised—but for an entirely different reason.

"Why you buy this?" they wanted to know.

I pretended to shiver.

"Why you change the room instead of yourself? Why you don't put on sweater? How much this cost you?"

I buried the heater in my closet. That night, they asked me to bring it out. Guests were over: they wanted a demonstration. I plugged it in, feeling like an imperialist. The house lights flickered off and on. They laughed at the heat that (blissfully) surged forth. "You buy this *here*? For *how* much?"

Back it went into the closet.

But while I've adjusted to the houseguests, water shortages, and cold spells, I am strangely resilient to a vital component of the Mexican household: the scrub brush. Every few days, Fabián engages in what I consider "spring cleaning." First he hauls out every piece of furniture into our courtyard. Next he comes back inside, gets on his hands and knees, and scrubs. Hard. Once the floors dry and the furniture has been replaced, he removes the many plants from the courtyard and washes down its pavement.

---

* In 2005, you could generally exchange one U.S. dollar for between 10.3 and 11.1 pesos. To simplify the math, I just knocked off a zero from every price tag, so that 50 pesos equated $5.

Then he embarks upon the kitchen, the bathroom, and the hallways. The whole process takes hours. Naturally, he asks me to pitch in.

I have lived in communal spaces for much of my adulthood. In college, I shared a three-story house with sixteen vegetarians; in Brooklyn, I never had fewer than two housemates. Never once has anyone reproached me for being a slob. But this is what I am known as here, for I cannot bring myself to clean something that gleams.

"Already pretty. Why to clean again, again, again?" I ask Fabián one afternoon.

He explains carefully, so that I understand every word. His country is chaos. Wages are slashed at random; jobs are lost without notice or severance pay. Crime is skyrocketing. Corruption is rampant. "Our home is the only thing we can control in our life. We like it LIM-PIA."

That means clean.

Fabián adds that he once lived with a woman from Switzerland who hated the orderliness of her own country. Her room, consequently, was a train wreck, because that was the one thing she could muck up.

This is a revelation. I walk the streets of Querétaro and realize it is a national phenomenon. On every corner, housekeepers, housewives, and store owners lather their sidewalks with gusto. Mercados reek of disinfectant. Back at home, Karina spends an entire evening scrubbing five pairs of tennis shoes with an old toothbrush, then delicately wrings out the laces. In Texas, the "dirty Mexican" is as much of a stereotype as the "white trash redneck." How did that happen?

No matter. If this is what it means to be Mexican, I'm game. The following day, I slip on sweatpants and spend the afternoon shining the already immaculate bathroom, hallway, and living room floors, appliances, and fixtures. Then I put away the cleaning supplies and (it shames me to admit) never touch them again. *I always clean up after myself in the kitchen; I even wash any extra plates in the sink. This house is so spotless, they'll never notice I don't do those other chores.*

But oh, they do.

Most of the acclimation process is a pleasure—especially where food is concerned. Following my roommates' example, I now eat a light desayuno in the morning (sweet bread, papaya, oatmeal), an even lighter cena a few hours before bed (soup, a quesadilla, one tamal), and a whopping almuerzo in between—the greatest of which is a "comida corrida." These four-course lunches include a soup, a plate of rice or pasta, a main dish (usually a meat with a side of vegetables and smear of refried beans), a dessert, freshly squeezed fruit water, and all the warm corn tortillas you can eat. Most businesses shut down between the hours of 2 P.M. and 4 P.M. so its workers can partake in this daily ritual (along with the requisite siesta).

Both Omar and Karina are aspiring chefs, so we often eat almuerzo at home. Chayotes rellenos, chilaquiles verdes, deep-fried flautas doused in cream. By my third week at La Jotería, I want to return the culinary gesture. But with what? Back in Brooklyn, I usually prepare Mexican food for dinner parties but have a feeling my tofu burritos will insult my roommates. Should I do Thai? Italian?

"Make us a typical American lunch," Fabián suggests.

The following afternoon, I make a grand production of boiling eggs and cutting tin cans as the three of them sit around the kitchen table expectantly. Because they are skipping their usual four-course meal for this, I go the extra mile, toasting bread and melting cheese. Then I cut four gourmet tuna fish sandwiches triangularly and arrange them on a platter garnished with carrot and celery sticks. Fabián, Omar, and Karina each take a bite and chew very slowly. They look at one another, then at me. Without a word, Omar leans over to the refrigerator and starts removing items: spicy mustard, horseradish, salsa, jalapeños, Thousand Island salad dressing, Parmesan cheese, packages of ham and bacon. They dip in butter knives and get to work. The innards of their sandwiches soon turn the color of the water can Omar uses to clean his paintbrushes.

I should have expected this. The Mexican palate, after all, is hardly subtle. They sprinkle chile powder into fruit cups and slather it over candy. They pump salsa roja or verde into their popcorn at movie concession stands. They eat peanuts in fiery flavors like enchilada sauce. Fabián calls this a form of machismo. "Even if we don't like something picoso [spicy], we pour it on anyway. Otherwise, what would we be? ¿Una niña [a little girl]?" In a wicked short story in Italo Calvino's *Under the Jaguar Sun*, two travelers speculate that Mexicans' penchant for pica dates back to the ritual cannibalism of the Aztecs. They must have needed heavy spices to camouflage the flavor of flesh.

Then again, Mexicans seem to do everything in extremes. If a radio or TV is turned on, it is blasted. If there is a party, it will last until dawn (and, to quote Nobel Prize–winning writer Octavio Paz, "friends will get drunk together, trade confidences, weep over the same troubles, discover that they are brothers, and sometimes, to prove it, kill each other"). Politicians here are more scandalously corrupt; killers are more coldblooded and ruthless. And Mexican newspapers are surely among the world's goriest, with full-color sections devoted to the most hideous of yesterday's deaths and dismemberments.

But while I understand that a tuna fish sandwich might be a little bland for my friends, it makes me sad to see what they have done to it. "It's not tuna fish anymore," I say.

"Sí, Fani, it is," Omar says reassuringly. "We just made it better."

Mexicans are pros at this as well, which Raúl is quick to point out. Last time he visited, he played highly danceable music that turned out to be techno mixed with mariachi riffs. Mexican DJs do the same with hip-hop, rap, and R & B, he said, "and it's the greatest music in the world, I swear." He then offered to take me out for "the best hamburger you ever try anywhere, I mean it." I admit to being skeptical—until he drove us to a purple shack where a family fried burgers at a grill. Between two slices of bread, they piled on a hamburger patty, three kinds of cheese, ham, bacon, avocado, jalapeño, onion, garlic, and squirts of potent sauces. Though it ignited my tongue on contact, I had to admit that I'd never tasted better.

Raúl smiled proudly. "This is what we Mexicans do: we take what exists and we make it our own. Like when the Aztecs mixed their blood with the Spanish. They created a whole new mestizo race, taking the best elements of each. That is why we are stronger. Better. More complete."

Two months into my life in Mexico, I start making linguistic sense. This is partly due to the language school where I study six hours a day, but mainly to Fabián. After years of teaching art to small children, he has acquired a monkish patience. He will wait as long as it takes for me to nail down a subject, select a verb, conjugate it, hunt down its object, flip the sentence around so it makes sense in Spanish, and spit it out, at which point his whole face lights up—"¡Qué bien, Fani!"—and inspires me to assemble another.

Like now. It is Wednesday, and he, Karina, and I are in our usual spot, slouched across the pillows atop the mats in the living room. They are teaching me a new word: flojo.

"It's what we're doing here," Fabián explains, stretching out his arms. "Lying around, doing nothing. We're being flojos."

It is nice to know there is a word for it. Back in New York, I was working seventy-hour weeks, gulping down meals while running to the subway or pounding away at a computer. Being floja is a luxurious change of pace: at last, I am breathing instead of panting. Some of my new friends breathe so deeply, they are on the verge of becoming yogis. Fabián, for one, seems to do little outside his shifts at a café and cleaning stints. I once asked why he never paints anymore, and he explained that he created so much art in college, he needed to rest. Yet he graduated several years ago.

"This is the part of our culture that keeps us down, our flojera," Fabián adds. "I sometimes wonder how we would be if the Spanish didn't conquer us. They were *really* flojo. Maybe we would be harder workers if the French had come instead. Or the British. Or even the Portuguese."

Karina lifts her head ever so slightly in agreement. "Look at our ancestors—the Mayans, the Aztecs. They were all hard workers. That was our original culture. But then the Spaniards came and turned us into Catholic flojos."

This idea will resurface in conversations throughout my travels in Mexico. Nearly every societal ill, from corruption to gender discrimination to racism, is said to have sprung forth the moment Spanish explorer Hernán Cortés set foot on this land in 1519 and started Conquesting.

"We . . . you . . . Mexicans are not *all* flojos," I say. For years I have spoken about Mexicans in the first person, but now that I am actually here I am shifting to the second, as I am clearly perceived to be—and, admittedly, am—as much of an outsider as any other foreigner. "You should see Mexicans in Brooklyn. They work two or three jobs at once. They do not walk down the street. They run!"

This prompts Fabián to sit up. "Of course they do. They're in the United States. They *have* to be that way if they want to survive. They aguantar."

Aguantar means to endure. According to Fabián, this is another national trait. Once a Mexican has overcome his flojera, he can pull off amazing feats, like march fifteen miles in chanclas or—in the case of undocumented laborers—work fourteen-hour shifts six days a week thousands of miles from home.

"But do you think they *like* to aguantar?" he continues. "Ay, no. You told me that you work so hard in New York, you break out in hives. Who wants that? It is much better to lay here like this, nice and tranquilo."

We resume dead-man poses atop the pillows.

After a time, the doorbell rings. Raúl saunters in with an entourage. They just had an idea, he announces, to hold a group art exhibition. We gather around the dining table to brainstorm.

"It must be big . . . and profound . . . and distinctly Mexican!" Raúl enthuses.

"But nothing with the Virgen de Guadalupe* on it," Fabián grumbles.

I suggest they do something around the topic of homosexuality. This incites an animated discussion about whether their role as gay artists is to educate homophobes or not. I quickly get lost as they debate—too many voices, not enough pantomime—but sit at the table for hours anyway. With Karina's punk-rock hair and Omar's red parachute pants, they look straight off the

---

* As the story goes, La Virgen appeared to a campesino named Juan Diego Cuauhtlatoatzin on a hilltop near Mexico City in 1531, and recruited his help in convincing a local bishop to build her a shrine. When Juan approached the bishop, they were both astonished to see that the Virgen's image was emblazoned on his cloak. La Virgen has since become the symbol not only of Mexico's faith but also of the nation itself—and she still makes public appearances now and then, according to believers. Novelist Carlos Fuentes once said, "One may no longer consider himself a Christian, but you cannot truly be considered a Mexican unless you believe in the Virgen de Guadalupe."

set of a vintage Pat Benatar music video, and emit as much energy. Raúl says he'll buy wine for the opening and serve platters of cubed cheese. I offer to write their artwork's captions in English so gringo tourists can read them. Deadlines are dispensed; follow-up meetings are scheduled. Everyone leaves invigorated.

The next morning over desayuno (pecan yogurt over granola), I chatter about the night before, but Fabián is curiously reticent. He changes the topic. A week slips by, and I bring it up again. Has he chosen a subject for his piece? No. Has anyone? Don't know. More time elapses. When I inquire a third time, he levels with me. There will be no group art exhibition. Many reasons are cited: It is impractical. They will never scrape together enough money or resources. Nobody has the time.

"The Aztecs, they used to be a very collective-minded people. They worked together in harmony; they worshipped many gods. But then the Spanish came. They made them worship one God, they killed their sense of collectivity, they made them individuals. So collectives don't work in Mexico anymore. We are too individualistic."

I call Raúl and he confirms it: no exhibition. I ask if it is because of the Spanish, and he says no, it is because of the crabs.

"An old woman was selling baskets of crabs on the beach in Veracruz. A little boy ran up to buy some and noticed that one basket was covered by a lid and the other was not. He asked what was the difference.

"'Pues, these under the lid are American crabs,' she explained. 'These others are Mexican.'

"'Why don't the Mexican crabs need a lid?' he asked.

"'Because every time a Mexican tries to break away, his compañeros pull him back in.'"

Class is over, and I am ravenous. My ongoing project is to find the ultimate comida corrida in Querétaro. It's a challenge, as nearly every restaurant is a contender. I wander downtown on sidewalks so narrow, you must turn sideways to pass someone, until I notice a café whose back wall features a mural of a lady skeleton wearing a fancy plumed hat: La Calavera de la Catrina.* Mexicans are quite fond of skeletons, eating skull-shaped sweets on the Day of the Dead and adorning their homes (and themselves) with skeletal artwork. Comedian Héctor Suárez says this is the Mexican way of befriending death so it won't have anything to do with him. Writer Octavio Paz contends: "The reason death cannot frighten us is that life has cured us of fear."

Not a soul sits inside the café, but that's because it is one thirty. Comida corrida crowds don't arrive until two. The waitress brings me a bowl of sopa azteca, tortilla soup with avocado and cheese, and a basket of warm corn tortillas wrapped in embroidered cloth. After a time, two guys my age glide in. They bow their heads in my direction—shorthand for buen provecho—and park at a nearby table. The one facing me has dark almond eyes and Che Guevara hair. I try not to stare but fail. He catches my glance at least four times. And grins. When his friend finally leaves, he saunters past my table and asks what I am reading. I show him the cover of my child's comic book version of *Don Quixote de la Mancha*.† He declares it a favorite.

* An iconic figure in Mexican art, Catrina symbolizes how even the rich are susceptible to death. The satirical illustrator and lithographer José Guadalupe Posada (1851–1913) is generally credited as her creator.

† Mexicans are mildly obsessed with *Don Quixote*. Readings, festivals, and theatrical productions of this seventeenth-century classic abound, as do artistic renditions of Quixote and his loyal sidekick, Sancho. Guanajuato even has a (fabulous) museum devoted entirely to Quixote iconography from all over the world.

I invite him to sit and elaborate. Everything he says escapes me, but that's okay: I'm already fantasizing about us strolling off afterward, hand in hand. But when he pauses for an extended moment, I realize it is my turn to contribute. So I crack a joke about how if nothing else, at least the Spanish gave Mexico this great book.

"What do you mean? The Spanish gave us everything."

"Of course they did! I was just referring to . . . you know, the Conquest . . . ," I say, then start to laugh.

He doesn't. "So am I. The Aztecs, they were terrible. Murderers, who committed sodomy! They stole from and raped and enslaved every tribe around. That is why so many Indians joined the Spanish. They wanted to help defeat them."

"But the Spanish were intruders. Colonists. Imperialists! They destroyed the ancient traditions and religions, and those who refused to convert were killed."

"At least the Spanish let people choose. The Aztecs just sacrificed them. They cut out their hearts and offered them to their idols. Their altars were pools of blood!"

My entire liberal arts education is crumbling down. "At least they only killed a few at a time! The Spanish gave everyone smallpox. They wiped out whole tribes at once."

"Where do you think Mexico would be now, if it weren't for the Conquest?" he demands, rising from his chair. "I'm glad the Spanish came. I would have jumped into the ocean to greet them!" With that, he leaves.

My thoughts are racing too fast to contemplate the perks of colonialism. I just want to run home and tell Fabián that I found something to blame on the Conquest too: it quashed my would-be love affair.

I am telling my roommates a story and realize I don't know the Spanish word for "Jewish." "You know. It is the religion of the people of Israel."

"Muslim?" they guess.

I grab a dictionary and flip through its pages. Judío.

"Oh," Fabián says. "I know about them. They are the ones who didn't get killed on September eleventh."

"Perdón?"

"They knew the planes would crash into the towers, so they didn't come into work that day. They own everything in your country, right?"

My stomach in knots, I conduct an impromptu history lesson, starting with the Holocaust and concluding with the Middle East's latest conflicts. Fabián feels the need to explain himself afterward. "Our biggest problem in this country isn't just that we are flojos," he says. "We are also uneducated."

"Because of the Conquest?"

"Because of our government. They don't want us to be too educated and start making demands, so they limit our educational opportunities."

He proceeds to describe Mexico's school system, which is troublesome. While 98 percent of children enroll in primaria (first level), only about 65 percent stay for secundaria (second level), and 24 percent continue on to preparatoria (high school). (By comparison, U.S. enrollment is 92, 89, and 83 percent, respectively.) Although Mexicans have a high literacy rate—91.6 percent—they read just over two books a year. A quick browse through any bookstore shows a big reason why: novels generally cost between 120 and 200 pesos. Nearly half the nation, meanwhile, subsists on less than 40 pesos a day. This explains why I am living in a house full of college-educated artists who have fewer than a dozen books between them. They literally cannot afford them. Libraries don't seem to pick up the nation's literary slack, either: the ones I frequent, at least, have few and dated offerings. In 2004, Mexico City tried to promote literacy (and curb crime) by lending out 1.5 million books on the honor system at subway stations around the city, but had to stop because so few riders returned them.

The Internet could be Mexico's intellectual saving grace. In downtown Querétaro, Internet cafés anchor practically every corner, and the main public library offers unlimited access to hundreds of wired computers for fifty pesos a year. But when I point this out, Fabián says, "Yes, there might be Internet cafés everywhere, but we only use them for porn or chatting. Stupid things. Not information."

I can't argue with this. I use those library computers nearly every day and have noticed that the majority of users are indeed instant messaging their friends (as is the case in Internet cafés throughout the globe). Porn is more of an issue—specifically, what constitutes porn (or anything salacious enough to be thwarted by the library's Internet filter). One afternoon, the teenage boy next to me watched a cartoon video of dark-skinned men in loincloths chasing a blond-haired, blue-eyed woman not wearing a stitch. When they finally caught her, they gang-raped her, tied her to a stake, and roasted her over a fire while she screamed. Meanwhile, the library's filters kept blocking my searches for a story I was writing, including the words "condom," "abortion," "sexually transmitted diseases," and "SIDA" (the Spanish acronym for AIDS). I also couldn't access the *New York Times.*

Moreover, many Mexicans lack the resources to travel internationally, and countries like the United States routinely deny them visas out of fear they will emigrate. Although Mexico is ethnically diverse, with twelve million indigenous people, fifty-six distinct ethnic and language groups, and more than a hundred dialects, it is nationally quite homogenous. Fewer than 2 percent of its population was born elsewhere, the bulk (one million) being U.S. citizens. So the average person's exposure to world culture is generally limited to TV, movies, and tourists.

The ramifications of this are stark, which I realize the night we watch the film *Innocent Voices* about child soldiers in El Salvador's civil war in the 1980s. To be sure, the average American would be hard-pressed to offer details about this conflict too (despite the fact that our government helped fund it), but I thought my roommates would know more, given the war's relative proximity and the fact that it was waged during their lifetime. I was also under the (false) impression that Mexico's education system stressed U.S. involvement in Latin American affairs, considering how they lost half their territory to the United States after their own war ended in 1848. But since my roommates know little about the conflict—and they seem genuinely interested—I share some background on Reagan's policies in Central America and mention Bush's meddling in Cuba today.

"Whatever happened to him?" Fabián asks.

"To Reagan? He died eight or nine months ago."

"No, not him. To Bush. Did he win that election?"

It takes a moment to respond to this, for more than three months have passed since Bush's 2004 reelection. I was trekking around Central Asia during President Clinton's scandals, and even rural sheepherders pumped me for details. I've never met a college-educated person anywhere who couldn't name the U.S. president*—especially Bush, whose actions are so notorious.

"See? I *told* you I am uninformed," Fabián says, almost triumphant.

"But Bush's policies affect us all, the state of the world, life as we know it!"

Omar speaks for the first time this evening, in his quietly impacting way. "Sí, Fani. What you say is true. We know that it is true. But we can either live tranquilo, or we can worry about things we cannot change. Which do you think we'll prefer?"

Something in Omar's eyes gives me pause. This isn't just

---

* And, for the record, I haven't since—and certainly no one else in Mexico.

another case of ni modo. No, it is deeper than that. This is a fatigue, a self-resignation, an acceptance that life is not only beyond his control but out of control. And I've seen it before, in the eyes of my post–Tiananmen Square friends in Beijing. I don't mean to compare these two nations; Mexico, after all, calls itself a democracy. Yet the decade before Omar was born, federal troops massacred hundreds* of student protesters and workers at Tlatelolco in Mexico City in the days leading up to the 1968 summer Olympics. In the so-called Dirty War that followed, the military kidnapped, tortured, raped, and exterminated unknown hundreds of more "subversives."

This look haunted me for years after leaving China, and here it is again. I didn't expect to find it here.

* The exact death toll of October 2, 1968, remains a disputed mystery. While the government has always claimed that only 30 died, *The Guardian* calculated 325 deaths and thousands more injured, imprisoned, or both. Statistics from the June 4, 1989, massacre near Tiananmen Square in Beijing are also unknown. The *New York Times* has estimated between 400 and 800 slain, and as many as 40,000 arrested.

CHAPTER FOUR

¡MUCHA LUCHA!

Querétaro,
March 2005

Of all the days that compose a week, Mexican Sunday is the best. Lounging in bed as the church bells ring, strolling through the plaza, hunting for bargains in the tianguis (flea markets), eating until your buttons burst. It's midafternoon, and we've already done all but the latter. Omar claims to know the perfect spot and leads us down Calle Madero to an open-air mercado where a family of four tends to a family of eight under a tarp. We join them on plastic stools set around a table lined with clay pots full of guisos: chorizo (crumbled pork sausage with chile), picadillo (ground beef and potatoes), chicharrón (deep-fried pork rind slathered with salsa verde), red chile chicken, black chile beef, mushrooms sautéed with onions.

"¿Qué quieres?" the father asks me kindly.

It costs nine pesos for a taco (a tortilla stuffed with your choice of guisos); ten for a quesadilla (same as a taco, but grilled with cheese) or a sope (an extra-thick tortilla covered with guisos and sprinkled with cheese, like a pizza). I order a mushroom quesadilla. Two sisters break off lumps from a mountain of masa and pat and twirl them into round tortillas, which they lay onto the grill and cover with cheese. The mother then scoops them into her bare palm and ladles in the guisos, immune to the heat. "¿Quieres salsita? ¿Quesito? ¿Aguacatito?" she asks.

We say yes to everything. The cheese is white and crumbly; the avocado is thick and chunky. She serves them on plastic plates covered with Saran Wrap so that she need only discard the wrapping when we are finished, rather than the whole plate. The dining family bids us "Buen provecho" as we feast. So many textures and flavors! I order a second, then a third. More people gather. "¡Amigo!" they call out to the father, waiving their pesos in the air. The family is soon cooking for seventeen, but they easily manage. The sisters sneak bits of fresh tortilla into their mouths; the mother wipes the sweat off her brow and smiles.

We roll off the stools and continue on to the fruit stands. "Guayaba, guanábana, plátano, jícama, pera, manzana, naranja," Karina pronounces the name of each, then waits for me to repeat. She is wearing movie star sunglasses and recently streaked the tips of her spiky hair purple and yellow; Omar and Fabián wear ivy caps and scarves. Passersby stare at their arty flamboyance and my foreignness.

A barefoot woman with oystery eyes approaches. A shawl covers her head and shoulders; her hair hangs in loose plaits. She holds up a plastic bag of prickly pear cactus and offers a new word: "¿Nopales?"

Karina smiles, says thanks but no, then whispers, "She comes from the mountains, where the nopales grow. She picks them herself and scrapes off the needles."

We reach the licuado stand: one woman, two blenders, crates of fruit. Fabián and Omar order smoothies with granola and honey; Karina and I choose agua de jamaica, red hibiscus water that tastes tangy and sweet. The woman pours our drinks into plastic sandwich bags and hands them over with straws.

That's when I see it: a row of black-and-white posters featuring two masked men in tights, capes, and booties, plastered on the side of a building. I point excitedly.

"¿Lucha libre?" Professional wrestling? Fabián wrinkles his nose. "You go to this in your country?"

"No. There is . . . is . . . naco." This is my latest slang word. It means hick, more or less.

They laugh. "And who do you think goes to lucha libre here?"

"No nacos." I search for the right word. "¡Chidos [cool people]!"

Fabián sees where this is headed and tries to talk me out of it. "No, Fani. Lucha libre audiences are grosera. They will grab your butt! They will pee into their cups and throw it!"

This makes me want to go even more.

"This would be a good experience for Fani; we should take her," Karina says, staring pointedly at Omar. Begrudgingly, he agrees. Shaking his head, Fabián concedes defeat.

Located on the far side of town, La Arena Querétaro is roughly the size of a high school gym. The walls are painted blue; the chairs are chipped yellow. Perhaps a hundred spectators have gathered, mostly families and old men. Children fill the wrestling ring, flipping, rolling, screaming with glee. A man in a sweatshirt that says CANADA climbs in beside them. Cupping his hands, he shouts that the match is about to begin, could you please get your children? Mothers obediently do so as the theme song from *Ghostbusters* blasts through the speakers. Two pudgy men jog down a stairwell: one wearing white tights, boots, and briefs with a red-and-white mask; the other clad in black. They leap into the ring and start swinging. The crowd rises to their feet.

"¡Mierdero!" they cry out. Full of shit!

"¡Mamón!" Crybaby!

"¡Culero!" Asshole!

A nearby father takes it up a notch. "¡Pinche princesita!" Stupid little princess!

At that, the luchador known as the rudo, or bad guy, climbs out of the ring and storms over. "Who you calling a princess?" he growls.

"You!" the father's small son pipes up, jumping up and down.

The rudo raises a fist threateningly, but the técnico (good guy) intervenes. Poking him hard in the back, he takes a swing when the rudo turns around.

"¡Mátalo!" screams an old lady. Kill him!

"¡Quiero ver sangre!" hollers another. I want to see blood!

They scuffle back into the ring. The rudo grabs the técnico's hand, wraps it around his back, throws him facedown on the mat—WAP!—and plops on top of him—FUMP! The técnico flounders as the rudo raises his arms in victory. Almost nobody applauds, for this is Mexico. Fans root for the nice guy, who inevitably gets clobbered.

In marches the referee. The crowd erupts in jeers. Referees are like judges or policemen, not to be trusted. "¡Ven-di-do! ¡Ven-di-do!" everyone chants. You've been paid off! You've been paid off!

The rudo is declared the winner; he salsas around in triumph. The técnico waves apologetically and shuffles off. We cheer for him anyway: who can't relate? Then the theme song to *Rocky* surges forth as two more masked men rumble toward the ring. Arms and torsos and legs start flying.

"Can we go now?" Fabián whines.

"¿Ya, Fani?" Omar asks. Had enough yet?

I glance over. They have shrunk into their seats, as if fearful of being seen. Fortunately, Karina is enjoying the show too, and machismo mandates that you can't leave women alone—especially in a joint like this.

Commotion erupts. A dozen luchadores appear in a flurry

of capes and colors. They dive into the ring, brandishing leather whips. For a few delicious moments, it is pandemonium. They smack one another on the back and butt. They bounce off the ropes and slap their slick chests together. They pin one another down. Two referees climb into the ring to restore order and are promptly punted out. Karina and I jump to our feet, cheering, and soon Omar and Fabián do too. Three luchadores climb to the top rope and leap into the ring, simultaneously tackling three opponents. A group of técnicos gang up on a rudo and knock him silly. Sweat pours. Faces bleed. The referees push their way back into the ring. Someone falls; an arm is lifted. Victors are declared. And then the house lights flood the auditorium as ranchera music jangles forth. Families maneuver through the aisles, clenching the wrists of children, who beg to play in the ring again.

The following Friday afternoon, I notice that Auditorio General Arteaga, the city's premier downtown auditorium, has a line wrapped clear around the block. I ask the man at the tail end what they're waiting for, and he says the magic words: tickets to lucha libre. When I wrote to my sister to brag that I'd been to a match, she reminded me how our great-uncle Benito—now deceased—used to be a fan. "Remember how he would scream at the TV set, wearing his Fruit of the Loom undershirts?"

So lucha libre is no longer just a kitschy Mexican sport to me. It is an *ancestral* kitschy Mexican sport. And the man in line assures me that this match will be a good one. "They come from D. F.," he says, eyebrows raised. This, I presume, means they'll whoop some ass.

The ticket office is a slit in a wall; only the tips of the vendor's fingers are visible. I slide in some pesos and—on a whim—ask if any luchadores are around. The fingers point to a compact man standing off in the distance. "That's Atómico."

Up close, Atómico looks more like a roadie than a wrestler. Mustachioed and ponytailed, he wears paisley sweatpants with a fanny pack strapped across his gut. When I ask to chat, he grunts agreeably, unlocks a gate with a ring of sixty keys, and leads me through the auditorium, occasionally poking his head into gyms full of beefcakes. Three follow us into a room where candles burn around an altar to the Virgen de Guadalupe. The iron door snaps closed and we sit down.

First things first: luchadores never reveal their identities. To anyone. So I can either have their birth name or their moniker—not both. I ask for the latter, and they introduce themselves as Atómico, Astroman, Dance Boy, and Dragón de Oriente II (his identical twin being Dragón de Oriente I). Only Dance Boy will fight tonight. Dressed in a silver tracksuit, he has a bowl-shaped haircut and ankle-deep dimples. I ask his age and am shocked to hear fourteen.

Dragón delves into the history of lucha libre, which he dates back to the ancient Aztecs and Mayans. They wore the masks of jaguars and other powerful animals when charging into battle as a way of channeling their strength, he says, just as modern luchadores do today. Their masks pay homage to this past—which is why every luchador fears having it ripped off: they will lose face, literally and figuratively. According to tradition, they must then fight without one for five years. Hence, the longer they keep their mask, the more renowned they become as a fighter.*

"We'd much rather play to shave our heads than to rip off

---

* History's most revered luchador was El Santo. According to legend, he won every match of his thirty-five-year career, some 5,000 in all. He died of a heart attack in 1984; as per his request, he got buried in his silver lamé mask. Many of his fifty-plus films are classics: check out *Santo vs. the Mummies of Guanajuato.*

our masks," Astroman says. Then he ticks off other things luchadores should stray from: eye poking, biting, choking, punching with fists, or anything involving the genitals.

"But none of it is real, right? You don't actually . . ."

Atómico swipes up a metal folding chair and holds it above my head. "Is this real?"

Before I can reply, he smashes it over his own head. The noise is terrific, and his point is made. (Dragón later whispers the formula: lucha libre is 80 percent realidad, 20 percent espectáculo—for the show.)

"So you are a bunch of machos then?"

"No, no," they protest. "We are a bunch of mandilones."

Seeing that I don't understand, Atómico ties a towel around his waist and prances around, pretending to scramble eggs. An apron-wearing wife-pleaser. I decide I want to date one. "And that is why you're so popular?"

"Everybody likes to see a good fight, whether it is between cocks or dogs or us," Dragón reasons.

"We give people the strength to stand up for themselves," Atómico adds. "When they are having problems with their bosses or the police, they can think about us and how we might handle things."

Indeed, luchadores are a rallying icon in this nation. After hundreds of thousands of people lost their homes in Mexico City's 1985 earthquake (and subsequent governmental negligence), politician Marco Rascón created a luchador called Super Barrio to save the day. When families faced eviction from squatting in their collapsed apartment buildings, a masked crusader showed up with television crews and blocked the bulldozers. Luchador Ecologista Universal, meanwhile, has led public opposition against nuclear power plants.

"The reality is that most Mexicans are like técnicos: we play by the rules and we lose," says Astroman. "And our bosses are rudos: they fight dirty and win."

Everyone shakes their head sullenly.

"Lucha libre is changing now," Atómico says, breaking the silence. "The wrestlers tonight, they are with AAA [Asistencia Asesoría y Administración], which is modeled off [the U.S.] WWE.* They are much more popular than luchadores like us, who fight the traditional way."

Someone knocks on the door. Showtime approaches; Dance Boy must go. Everyone rises. Atómico invites me to observe his class next week. "I teach real lucha libre, not like what you'll see tonight."

I agree to drop in Monday, then hurry out the door. There is just enough time to eat before the show.

By the time I arrive, Auditorio General Arteaga is slammed-packed with several thousand fans. Children hold homemade signs that say PARKA: QUERÉTARO SUPPORTS YOU 1,000 PERCENT! Women hold signs that say LATIN LOVER, WE LOVE YOU! Men drink Tecate. Vendors weave through the aisles, hawking everything from luchador masks to fried nopales dunked in salsa.

Beneath the stage lights, a hulking red devil and a minotaur with a steroidal six-pack are escorted to the ring by busty blondes wearing wedding veils over bikinis. Perhaps this is a way of establishing their heterosexuality: as soon as the brides depart, the minotaur pins the devil into a position that can only be described as Kama Sutric and proceeds to ride him—hard. The devil ingeniously escapes and scales the ring's highest rope in a

* WWE stands for World Wrestling Entertainment. It was called the WWF—or World Wrestling Federation—until 2002, when the original WWF (World Wildlife Federation) won its trademark battle and forced the wrestling organization to change its name.

single bound. The minotaur is staggering about, searching for him, when the devil leaps out from behind, knocks him to the ground in a headlock, spits in his face, returns the hanky-panky, then lifts him high above his head and tosses him onto a nearby table, which collapses into a heap of splinters. And that's just round one.

The differences between this and the previous lucha libre match are striking. For starters, only a few of these wrestlers wear traditional face masks, opting instead for full-body costumes like Ninjas and Grim Reapers, or almost nothing at all. (The popular Latin Lover spends much of his match stripping from a suit and tie to a white Speedo covered with kisses, much to the ladies' delight.) Dragón's formula of 80 percent realidad/20 percent espectáculo has been reversed as well. Rather than tell a story of good vs. evil, these luchadores simply put on a campy macho pageant. With the spitting, simulated sex acts, and chair-and-table throwing, it is almost indistinguishable from the WWE. And the result is strangely boring. As the night drags on, the highlight is a midget dressed as Casper the Friendly Ghost who soars through the air, pummeling his opponents.

It still might be fun to date one, though. When the match is over and Queen's "We Are the Champions" has been sung, I follow the hordes of little kids and middle-aged women out to the parking lot, where the buses await. The luchadores trickle out one by one. Each gets mobbed, but they handle it graciously, posing for every digital camera and kissing every cheek. Finally the one I want appears: Intocable. (He has the best hair.) Every female in the parking lot joins in the bum-rush, and I (somehow) get crushed up against him. I want to tell him he's beautiful, but then I read his black T-shirt—CHINGA TU MADRE (Fuck Your Mother)—and realize he already knows it.

The following Monday, I walk through the unlit halls of the auditorium to the gymnasium, turn left at the weight room, duck beneath a tarp, and nearly run into a wrestling ring. It is a wooden construction with a thin layer of foam covered by a mat and tarp. Dangling above are spotlights long ago burnt; behind are punching bags and an exercise area. The air whiffs of underarms and tamales.

Dance Boy waves hello as he leads the warm-up. There are fourteen students ranging in age from three to thirty-five. Four are professional; three are women. Lucha libre is the last thing you'd guess they have in common—until they start exercising. The first stretches are basic (butterflies, toe touches, the splits) but then they play leapfrog. The game quickly evolves from hopping over partners who are squatting to diving over partners bent at the waist and then tucking into a head roll. The three-year-old tries everything, and when he can't quite make it, the others somersault his body through the air.

Once Atómico arrives, they enter the ring. They turn head rolls across the mat—fast—to the cardinal directions, each just seconds behind the other; then they practice flipping over their own shoulders onto their backs. Combination moves are next: turning a roll, running to a corner, jumping onto the second rope (which is higher than most of their waists), flinging themselves backward, turning midair, and landing in another head roll. Then they break into pairs: one group lays flat on their backs while the other group leaps off the second rope, swings out their feet, and lands smack on their own back, with a leg on either side of their partner's head. At any moment wrists could snap, knees could pop, shoulders could dislocate. Yet they throw themselves with abandon. WHAP. SMASH. SPLAT. The noise is alarming—and addicting. This is old-school Mexican wrestling: capoeira with dashes of acrobatics, tae kwon do, yoga, and theatrics thrown in. I am especially impressed with Atómico, whose missile-shaped body glides through the air with something like grace, the star soloist in this muscular ballet.

After class ends, I follow one of the women and her two sons to the basketball court. "My thirteen-year-old has been training with me since he was three, the same age as the little one is now," she says as they race off to play. "They both want to grow up to be luchadores like me."

Although her skin is porcelain white, her moniker is Lady Black. At thirty-five, she has been fighting professionally for more than a decade. Heavily made up with eyeliner and rouge, she wears her hair in a chin-length bob and curls her bangs into a crisp, inverted C.

Her parents were lucha libre aficionados who regularly took the kids to matches. When women started appearing in the ring in the late 1970s, she fantasized about battling them someday. She now competes in up to eight matches a month in cities across the country, but that doesn't mean she can quit her day job. "Only luchadores with AAA can live off their salaries. For me, it would be impossible." So she works part-time as a civil servant. Her colleagues didn't know she was a luchadora until an opponent ripped off her mask last August.

"That was such a hard night. I had a beautiful mask: black and gold with a crown. Atómico designed it for me," she says. "But since my identity was no longer a secret, I could tell people."

Now everyone attends her matches—save her husband. He grew jealous of her training long hours with sweaty men and didn't like her kissing the fans after matches. They've since divorced. Lucha libre has taken other tolls. She recently broke her shoulder, and her knees perpetually ache. She prefers combating men than other women. "Of course they still hit us, but gently. Women are brutal."

I ask how the sport has changed over the years, and she shakes her head. "Now it is all about show, like that lucha on Friday night. That was puro Americano—not Mexican at all. But you saw how the audience loved it. There is hardly any puro Mexicano lucha libre left. That is why I take my kids to Atómico, so they can learn the traditions."

She suggests that I talk to Bulldog Quintero, the oldest luchador in Querétaro (and, she thinks, all of Mexico). "He will tell you everything."

While my Spanish now allows for face-to-face conversation (where pantomime is utilized), it is nearly hopeless over the phone—and Bulldog is hard of hearing. We shout at each other for quite some time before I grasp that he's inviting me over at two this afternoon. His directions lead me to a gated community of cottages connected by a catwalk on the verge of collapse. A mountain of a woman in a polka-dotted dress welcomes me into a modest but spotless home and sits me in the living room while she pours refrescos. Hanging above the couches are crucifixes and family portraits, along with a blown-up photograph that combines the two: Bulldog gripping someone in a headlock, their faces cut up and bloody.

Bulldog's wife lumbers over and hands me a glass of Coca-Cola. Normally when I travel to foreign countries, people serve me Coca-Cola because I am from the United States and they assume I must like it. In Mexico, they serve Coca-Cola because *they* like it. A lot. At 522 cups per person per year, they drink more of it than anyone in the world, U.S. citizens included. Though I'm actually not a fan, Mexican Coke tastes noticeably better than American Coke because it is sweetened with sugarcane instead of high-fructose corn syrup. We clink our glasses and drain them.

Bulldog enters a few minutes later wearing a Hawaiian shirt halfway buttoned over a tank top. Greeting me in a sandpapery voice, he extends a hand. It is rougher than tiger tongue, each finger three times the width of my own. His smile is nearly toothless; his hair is white and carpet thick. Born to a family of seven in a rancho in Nuevo León, he began training as a boxer at age eighteen. "Ever since I was little, I liked a little action. If I'd lived back in Roman times, I would have been a gladiator. Sí, even against those animals! It's true. My first lucha was in Tamaulipas. It was a full, full ring—¡Híjole!—on March twenty-third, but I forget the year."

During his career, he combated the greats: El Santo, Aníbal, Dr. Juan, Super Ratón, Pantera. "Santo was a real gentleman, not like those luchadores today who throw trash cans and Dios knows what else. I fought him once. Of course he won, the whole town showed up to root for him! The only difference between us is he had more publicity. But look at us now—Santo is dead and I'm still fighting!"

He trains three times a week and travels extensively for matches. This month alone, he'll be hitting Monterrey, Laredo, Reynosa, and Matamoros. Fortunately, his job at the nearby gasoline station has flexible working hours. He does the graveyard shift, from 9 P.M. to 6 A.M.

I ask if he performs any rituals before a fight.

"I always pray, because injuries can happen any time. Gracias a Dios, I've never had a serious one. Just once, someone hit me in the mouth with their head and knocked out my front teeth. Not so bad. See, I have a mouthpiece right here. . . ."

As he reaches over to pull it out of a drawer, something plops out of the folds of his neck. A tumor, half the size of a baseball. I can't fathom how I missed it—or, more important, how other luchadores manage to.

"Mira," Bulldog says, holding up a row of yellowing teeth. "It's real ugly, no? Come on, I show you what else I got."

We walk into his bedroom, where spit-polished trophies gleam from every surface. He removes a plastic bag from a drawer and hands me its contents one by one: placards, programs, posters, photos, and certificates spanning a forty-plus-year career. I ask how many matches he's fought. His eyes scrunch with contemplation.

"Five hundred?" I prod.

"Oh, no, mija. More than that."

"One thousand?"

He stares at me with wide eyes. "That's a lot of fights, no?"

I sort through the photos. His hair is wild in all of them, save the one where a masked man is shaving it. He favors black boots and briefs with red tights emblazoned with lightning bolts. Pulling out my camera, I ask to shoot a new one. He grows almost giddy, buttoning up his shirt and running his fingers through his hair. He poses in a fighter's stance before his trophies, deliberately losing—as do many Mexicans—his smile seconds before I snap the photo. Then he sits on his bed and thumbs through the photos. Some make him laugh; others give him pause.

"Lucha libre is something you must have inside you, and you have to train a lot to bring it out," he says. "Sometimes, I look at the luchadores in the ring today and get sad, because they don't have it. They think this is a show instead of a battle. But ni modo: times are changing, and I'm an old man. I just know that I will fight until I die, and I will die when I can no longer fight."

CHAPTER FIVE

THE COYOTE'S WIFE

A Pueblo Twenty Miles Outside Querétaro,
March 2005

Dreams come to me more vividly in Mexico, and one repeatedly: me, in a car, in the desert. Driving. I come upon those border crossers. Though I pound the brakes and swerve, I hit them head-on—a collision of flesh and metal. But while I fling out of the car, they land gracefully inside. We stare at one another wildly before they wave and drive away in the direction from which I've come, while I limp toward the yellow sun, following signs that say MEXICO.

We need new chairs, Fabián announces. These plastic ones are a disaster.

It is a flojo Sunday afternoon. We're lounging in the living room, digesting the chilaquiles and chocolate smoothies Omar whipped up in honor of his cousin César, who is visiting us from D. F. (Six feet tall, he has a muscular build, flawless skin, and amber eyes—but alas, he is gay as well.) César appears to be dozing but lifts his head and makes the offer we're hoping to hear: "I've got my car, ya vámonos!"

Road trip! The five of us pile in and crank up the radio. The strongest station plays 1970s rock. We sing along to Steely Dan as we exit the city. Roadside stands soon appear: ramshackle huts beneath flapping tarps. César stops at one stacked with jars of cajeta (a caramel-like spread made of goat milk) and rompope (Mexican eggnog, heavy on the rum). Both come in flavors like vanilla, pecan, wine, and cappuccino. I buy a picnic-size basket of strawberries for sixty pesos and want to devour them right away, but Fabián says no, there might be "animalitos." We must disinfect the berries at home first, with that little bottle Omar squirts on lettuce.

Now pueblos are zipping by, each famous for a different craft: guitars, leather shoes, puppets, and finally—furniture. We pull over. Fresh pine wood and sawdust saturate the air. Shop after shop sells armoires, dressers, bed frames, and trunks with forged iron hardware finishings, some with carvings of calla lilies or Aztec suns. Each piece is rustic and handsome and so outrageously affordable, I must stop looking before submitting to temptation. I sit at a table and an old man joins me: the owner of the store. His cocker spaniel sniffs my toes as I ask about business. He lets out a low whistle. "No more tourists since September eleventh. They used to drive down from San Antonio, but no, not anymore."

When he learns I am from the United States, he confides that his only son lives there.

"Really, where?" I ask brightly.

"In Tampa. He crossed the border como mojado seven years ago."

Como mojado. Like a wetback. In South Texas, this is the Spanish equivalent of "nigger," so it jolts me to hear it.

"He's got it real good now," he continues. "He's married, has a family."

I ask an unintentionally cruel question: "Ever visit?"

"Oh, no, mija, we can't do that, unless we want to be mojados too. And I'm too old for that," he says, smoothing back his slick white hair. "My wife wants to go real bad though, because our son, he has leukemia and is very sick. Can't come home to visit us, and we can't get a visa to go see him."

My face falls. He tries to prop it back up. "Did you hear what happened when the Migra [the Border Patrol] caught the mojados?"

I shake my head.

"The Migra, they catch some mojados trying to cross the border, and ask where they are going. The mojados, they know a few words of English, so they say they are coming to the United States. But the Migra, they don't understand. They ask them to repeat themselves again and again. 'We come here, we come here,' the mojados say, but the Migra still doesn't get it. So finally the mojados, they say it in Spanish: 'Ir aquí, ir aquí.'

"'You're Iraqui?!' the Migra shouts. 'You're coming with us!'"

This is equally sad, but we laugh until our eyes leak. Fabián joins us. I've told him about my border-crossing visions, and as we head back to the car, he says that if I want to understand immigration in Mexico, teachers are the best source. "They know *everything* that happens in the community because los niños [children] never shut up. I'll find one for you."

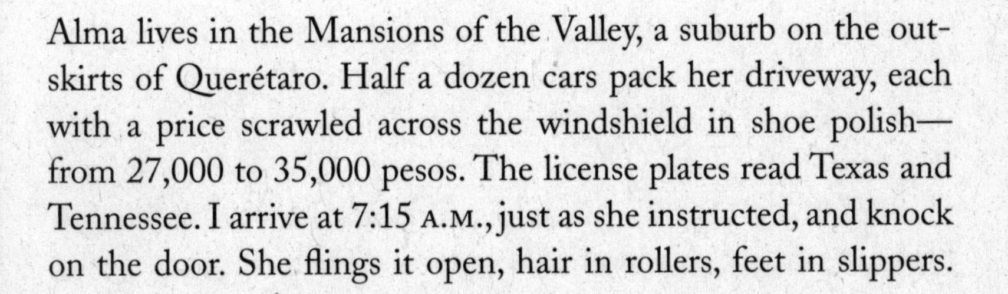

Alma lives in the Mansions of the Valley, a suburb on the outskirts of Querétaro. Half a dozen cars pack her driveway, each with a price scrawled across the windshield in shoe polish—from 27,000 to 35,000 pesos. The license plates read Texas and Tennessee. I arrive at 7:15 A.M., just as she instructed, and knock on the door. She flings it open, hair in rollers, feet in slippers.

Grabbing me by the elbow, she hustles me inside. She is a robust woman with a booming voice. Nodding at the living room, she charges up the stairs. I sit upon the L-shaped couch, taking in the synthetic floral displays and cages of parakeets. Alma's four-year-old daughter soon appears, dressed in a school uniform and with a Barbie backpack. "Mamá says you're from Los Estados Unidos where Tío Esteban and Tío Tomás live," she says, joining me on the couch.

Mexicans have many terms for the United States. Los Estados Unidos is the most literal, while El Norte—or The North—is the most common. I try to answer the little girl's questions about her uncles' new homeland.

"Ya vámonos, we're late!" Alma yells. We scramble into her car and roar down the street, merging into morning traffic. At every stoplight, she applies another layer of makeup in the rearview mirror, from which dangles a stuffed pig wearing a pink boa. After we've dropped off her daughter at school, Alma glances at me. "So you're interested in immigration? Tell me what you want to know; I've got stories."

No doubt, she does. Alma teaches kindergarten in rural Huimilpan, a municipality in the state of Querétaro. Of her forty students, thirty-six have fathers living as undocumented workers in the United States. Of the four fathers who remain, two moonlight as "guides" who smuggle migrants across the border.

"See that pueblo?" She points her finger. "Puras mujeres, all women. As soon as the boys turn fourteen, they go to El Norte. They come home once a year to impregnate their wives and then they take off again."

We drive a bit farther. "But see that one? Nobody there goes. They've all found a way to make a living here. Those pueblos are just two kilometers apart; I don't understand it. If one man goes, the rest follow."

I ask about her own relatives in El Norte. Her brothers live in San Antonio and Nashville. Those were their cars parked in her driveway: they buy them there and sell them here at marked-up rates. Alma wants to join them, but her ex-husband won't let her take their daughter across the border. "Hombres," she grunts. Men.

We are in the countryside now and turn onto a road with so many potholes, it appears to have been carpet-bombed. On either side of it, campesinos plow alfalfa fields with burros. Alma swerves around the yapping dogs and waves at everyone we pass. We pull into her pueblo of employment—which, when the men are home, has a thousand residents—and drive by vacant lots piled high with cinder blocks. "When the men return on vacation, they build new houses brick by brick. American style—never Mexican," she says. By this, she means a pointed roof (useless in this climate, as it never snows) and a redbrick finish, with no traditional inner courtyard or colorful facade.

We park by the kindergarten, a cinder block structure with a mural of Mickey and Minnie Mouse. Children in gingham aprons tear around the playground, their backpacks neatly hung upon an outdoor rack: Pokémon, Rugrats, Spider-Man, the Incredibles. Inside await the mothers, each with a baby wrapped in a shawl tied across her chest. In the pueblos, teachers are responsible for educating the entire community and must periodically hold workshops on some skill or craft. Alma teaches embroidery. She rolls out yarn, charging by the centimeter. The mothers call her La Maestra, or The Teacher, with grave respect.

The classroom has neither heating nor air-conditioning but is well stocked with art supplies and books. Beans sprout in plastic Coca-Cola bottles lined with cotton. After tending to the mothers, Alma rings a cowbell, and the children file in. I had hoped to monitor her class but cause too much distraction: the children can't stop gawking at me. Alma sends me off with a thirty-something father just now dropping off his child.

"My name is Ángel," he says, smiling, pointing to his baseball cap. ÁNGEL is spray painted graffiti-style across the front. His eyes are bloodshot and he smells faintly of beer, but he has a good excuse for partying so early in the morning: he will be crossing the desert to El Norte for his dozenth time at the end of the week. As we walk through the playground, I ask what his journeys are like.

"Well, we always cross through Laredo. It is much better to cross there than anyplace else. Tijuana is the worst. I don't like Reynosa either. I once got mugged there. He took my earring and my ring and my necklace and even my shirt because it had the Virgen de Guadalupe on it. I don't like Reynosa para nada!"

The excursion takes four days. He packs two of everything: pants, shirts, socks, plus food—corn, tortillas, frijoles, cookies. Whatever is light. And two liters of water. Pools of water can be found in the mountains, but they are usually dirty. "It is beautiful though, and peaceful. We always walk during the night, but it gets cold in the winter. In the mornings our water has ice in it. There are lots of snakes and spiders, but they hardly ever bite you. Sometimes we catch a rabbit or armadillo and eat it. I once saw a man beneath a tree and thought he was sleeping, but he was dead. I think he was drunk. A lot of people get drunk before they cross. That is a really *bad* idea."

Sometimes they stumble across people who have been ditched by their guide, as many as fifty or a hundred. They invite them along. The Migra patrol the sky and highway, but Ángel says you can avoid them by walking at night. "A couple of times I've run into the Migra, but they just ask if we're Mexican and if we have papers. When we say no, they put us in their van, which is all nice and air-conditioned, and give us cookies and water and drive us back to the border. I don't mind. They are just doing their job. And they tell us maybe we'll have better luck next time. Because they know that we are just doing our job too. I like your Migra much better than ours!"

We reach the foot of a mountain. A cinder block construction stands at the top, crested by a cross. Ángel says that the men of the community make pilgrimages here to pray before their journey. As we climb its footpath, he points out the different kinds of cacti. "Mira, how pretty their flowers are! But don't sniff. Those thorns will get sucked up your nose, and then what will we do? The prickly pear fruit are good to eat. They'll wipe those pimples clean off your face."

I ask what type of work he does in El Norte.

"All sorts, but usually trash or construction in Louisiana or Alabama. I work with lots of black people. They are so lazy! They only want to work eight hours a day, and if they are just a little bit sick, they don't come in. And they always want to take a vacation!"

He shakes his head in disgust while mine undergoes whiplash. Did he just say that?

"Not like us Mexicans. We work thirteen hours a day, fourteen hours a day. We come in even if we're sick. The bosses like us a lot. They say we work like burros. And we do! Like Mexican burros though. Not like American burros. Your burros live like kings! They don't do anything, they are just pinche burros, but they live better than me."

As if on cue, a burro brays in the distance. I can't help but laugh, and Ángel does too. "You see? They agree."

I ask about his work week.

"We go in six days a week and on Sundays we rest. Sometimes we go fishing, but we don't have a license, so it is risky. I drive but I don't have a license, so that is risky too. My whole life in El Norte is illegal! Sundays are fun because we are together and we make food and eat and drink and fish. But it is also the hardest day, because we think about our families here. But I have built a house with my money. My girls have beds now. My wife has clothes now. I don't ever want my daughters to go to Los Estados Unidos. That is why I go, so they don't have to."

We have summited. I gravitate toward the cinder block construction, which consists of three walls and a roof. Inside is the community altar. Candles and flowers carpet the floor and hundreds of photos hang from the green felt tacked upon the walls: family portraits, graduations, quinceañeras, weddings, baptisms. Mingled in are rosaries and crucifixes. Tiny metal votive offerings. A bowling trophy. Braids of human hair. I drop coins into the lockbox and step aside as Ángel kneels before the altar and bows his head. After a reflective moment, he grins up at me. "You should come back May third. We throw a big fiesta up here! The priest climbs up and gives Mass and a band plays and we have a barbecue and make chorizo and mole and eat and drink and dance all night. Everybody goes. It's worth crossing the desert for!"

We start down the steep mountain. "It's easier if you do like this," he demonstrates, trotting down the rocks like a deer. Sensing my apprehension, he takes my hand and assists me.

"I guess I wouldn't last too long out there in the desert," I say.

He smiles kindly. "Crossing the border is always hard for women. Only men should do it."

For years this was the case, but lately sociologists have been documenting an upsurge of Mexican migrant women. Princeton scholar Douglas Massey cites several reasons, including the tightened security at the U.S. border, which has made it much more difficult, dangerous, and costly to cross. Rather than being deterred from entering, migrants who've already made it are staying in El Norte for longer periods of time (if not permanently) to amortize the expense. And their wives are joining them.

Ángel drops me off at the kindergarten. Since class is still in session, I set off exploring. A smattering of businesses line the main street: a tortilla factory, two convenience stores, a meat market, an Internet café. Entire buildings are painted like soda ads. Some are cherry red with Coca-Cola's signature logo and swish; others are blue and stamped PEPSI. Throughout rural Mexico, these companies will paint your home or business for free if you pose as their billboard. I will later visit impoverished villages in Guanajuato and Michoacán where virtually every standing structure is a Coca-Cola ad because the residents couldn't otherwise afford paint.

I turn down a residential street paved with stones and dog and horse feces. A bearded man stands behind a table decked with a blender and bowl of fresh fruit. I order a smoothie. He tosses chunks of papaya, guayaba, and strawberries into the blender and adds milk and honey. Noticing his Tommy Hilfiger T-shirt, I ask if he's ever worked in El Norte. He laughs. "Fifteen times, at least. I started crossing when I was fourteen years old and will be leaving here again in a week or two."

"For how long?"

"I don't know. A year or two."

He usually goes with friends, he says. They know the way, but beginners can hire local guides. In migrant parlance, guides are called "coyotes" and the people they escort are "pollos," or chickens. This sums their relationship: nearly a third of coyotes harm their clients in some way, robbing or raping them or abandoning them in the desert. Journalist Cecilia Ballí recently chronicled their latest scam: kidnapping clients and holding them for ransom—or allowing another coyote to do the same and then splitting the profits afterward.

"If you come back later this month or anytime until November, these streets will be empty," he says. "Only women and children will be left."

He has five kids himself—and half a day at a construction site in Dallas pays more than two weeks of blending smoothies here. I thank him for the drink and continue along the street. Nearby is a building marked Centro de Salud. I enter. A young man in a lab coat and glasses sits behind a desk. He beckons me over. His name is Adolfo, and he oversees the health and nutrition of five surrounding communities. (Emergencies are dispatched to the city of Querétaro.) When I reveal my interest in immigration, he shakes his head. "At least eighty-five percent of the men from here go. It has its advantages. They can make good money. But money isn't all kids need. They are basically being abandoned, albeit out of necessity. Talk to the boys here. They all want to go to El Norte and return with a truck. That is their only ambition. It is the only thing they dream of."

In addition to depleting populations, immigration contaminates communities with diseases, especially sexually transmitted ones. "We don't have any cases of AIDS* yet, and I do mean *yet*, but I've seen everything else. The men go to El Norte and sleep with prostitutes because they're lonely, and don't use protection because they don't know better and then bring the diseases home to their wives. I hand out everything for free here: condoms, injections, diaphragms, everything. Totally free. And I make the women take it home. But they never use it."

"Why?"

"Machismo. Their husbands won't approve. Or else they are religious and think the Church won't approve. A lot of women believe that contraception will give them cancer, and I can't convince them otherwise. There isn't much we can do with the older generation, but we are trying to educate the little ones."

Then there is alcoholism, which steals more lives than anything else.

"I didn't notice any cantinas here," I say.

"Who needs one? The street is the biggest cantina around! The men buy it at the store and drink it at home. Of course, alcoholism existed before immigration, but not drugs. They get hooked on them in El Norte because they have to work such long hours. They come back addicts, but they can't always find

---

* Mexico's AIDS rate is nearly half as low as the United States', with a 0.3 percent HIV infection rate for people ages fifteen to forty-nine (as opposed to 0.6 percent). Yet the percentage of Mexican HIV carriers who previously lived in the United States was as high as 79 percent before Mexico stopped releasing such figures in 1992. See Marc Lacey, "Mexican Migrants Carry HIV Home," *New York Times*, July 17, 2007.

the drugs here, so they go through withdrawals. And that leads to domestic violence. This is huge here, men coming home after months away and then beating their wives. Of course, domestic violence is a problem throughout the world. The difference here is that the women don't think there is anything wrong with it."

He is going somewhere profound with this but stops, as if realizing he has already said too much. This happens often in Mexico: just as I seem to be nearing the core of an issue, my informant silences. I cannot determine if this is due to a cultural notion that they shouldn't bash their motherland in front of outsiders (particularly those scribbling in notepads), or if they lack the heart to go deeper. Whatever the case, Adolfo switches gears. "But overall, the people here are great. They live very happily. The majority of men who leave come right back home, or at least try to. They just stay long enough in El Norte so they can build a new house, and then they return."

Someone knocks on the door. A mother and child appear. Patients. I stand up to shake Adolfo's hand and quietly ask his age.

"Twenty-four," he says with a grin, then laughs at my reaction. "You thought I was older, right? It's the desk. Medical students are required to do their residencies out in pueblos like this. Otherwise, these people wouldn't get any health care."

Back at the kindergarten, the children are eating deep-fried tacos and gorditas. I brought a peanut butter sandwich from home, but Alma insists that I share her lunch. From a woven bag, she lifts out a Crock-Pot of scrambled eggs and hot dogs in salsa verde, canisters of refried beans and fideo soup, corn tortillas wrapped in embroidered cloth, and two bottles of Coca-Cola. While we eat, I ask the nearest table of children what they want to be when they grow up. As their eyes widen with wonder, Alma rises to take a more formal poll.

"Who wants to be a doctor someday?" she calls out.

"Me! Me! I want to be a doctor!" the kids cry.

"And who wants to be a teacher?"

Everyone changes their mind. "Me! Me!"

Alma calls out a few more professions, then asks, "So none of you want to go to El Norte?"

"I DO, I DO!" they scream, jumping up and down.

"But if you go to El Norte, you won't be a doctor or a teacher or a taxi driver. You won't be anything. You'll just be a mojado."

Too late: they are brimming with plans. One kid says he wants to go to Los Estados Unidos to buy a truck so he can drive it home and be a chauffeur. Another wants to go so he can build Mamá a house because Papá never will. Alma looks at me and shrugs. My stomach shrivels.

It is half past noon: mamá time. Two enter the room, grab brooms, and start sweeping; others gather around Alma's desk to buy more lengths of yarn. One unsheathes her project—a hacienda in a field of maguey—from a pillowcase and says she knotted the last thread this morning. After congratulating her, I ask to snap a photo. She obediently holds up her artwork—directly in front of her face.

"Stephanie, this señora's husband escorts people to El Norte," Alma says pointedly, her hand atop the shoulder of a heavyset woman.

A coyote! The very word conjures a smarmy man with six gold chains and ample chest hair, but considering that he works out of his hometown, this coyote probably runs a clean business. His clients' families can hold him accountable, after all. And his wife seems perfectly pleasant (aside from the YOU SHOULD HEAR THE NAMES THE VOICES IN MY HEAD ARE CALLING YOU black T-shirt she is wearing). She embroiders sunflowers as we speak; our eyes never meet.

"Sí, my husband is a coyote. Pues, he just takes people across. No, he doesn't have any papers. How long? He's been crossing the desert since he was fourteen and now he's thirty-one. He knows the way. He takes five or ten or fifteen people each time. ¿La Migra? Pues, he got caught last month. They locked him up on a Saturday and by Tuesday he was free. He's coming back home this weekend. He charges one thousand dollars apiece. We are building a house with the money. Three bedrooms. How do I feel when he's not here? Alone. No, immigration has had no impact on our community. Everything is good. No, I can't tell you where he crosses the border. It's his secret. Me? I'm twenty-eight. Where? We met at a store. ¿Mande? I live with my in-laws. They are dying."

I thank her and circulate the room, striking up conversations with mothers in T-shirts featuring the Care Bears or city names like Palm Springs. They know—or divulge—little of their husbands' lives in El Norte. Texas is confused with California; their husbands share apartments with seven (or was it eleven?) others. They are unaware of how much money their husbands earn, but can say to the last centavo what they have personally received in the past week, month, and year. (It is no small amount: Mexicans will send home about U.S. $20 billion in remittances in 2005.)

The women answer my questions in as few words as possible, a sharp contrast to Ángel and the smoothie maker. Whether this is due to the inherent differences between Mexican men and women, or the fact that the former are more accustomed to speaking with foreigners, I do not know. But they seem uncomfortable, so I soon stop talking and simply sit at the table with them, admiring their embroidery.

After a time, two women in their early twenties walk in with toddlers perched on their hips. Both wear figure-flattering jeans and bangs teased high with hair spray. One zeroes in on me and asks who I am. When I mention my interest in immigration, her eyes flicker.

"I don't like what is happening here at all. As soon as boys turn thirteen, fourteen years old, they leave. My son is only five and he's already saying he wants to go. Men don't have any ambition to do anything here," she says. Her own husband left soon after they married at age eighteen. They've since had three children—one every other year of their marriage—and he hasn't helped raise any of them, opting to wire money in his place.

Has she ever thought of joining him?

"Sí, pero who would take care of the babies?"

"We want to go to El Norte too, but we need to watch the kids," her friend pipes in. "The only women who go aren't married. For us—it's too late for that!"

At that, the women in the room laugh, some demurely covering their mouths. I open the package of cookies I've brought and plunk one down before each of them. They smile in acceptance. The mood lightens as they continue embroidering landscapes of villas and beaches.

Alma helps her last customer and announces that we must go. I pack our leftovers from lunch and bid the women well. As we walk out the door, one of the young mothers shouts: "If you want company next time you go back to your country, give us a call!"

"We'll be waiting for you right here at the kindergarten," her friend adds.

Again, the mothers laugh. This time, no one covers her mouth.

CHAPTER SIX

MALALECHE, SPOILED MILK

Querétaro,
March 2005

Black Levi's and cowboy boots.

Fabián and I see them standing upright in the distance in the garden of Calle Guerrero. A crowd has gathered. We join them. There is no torso above the jeans. The mannequin consists solely of legs, and his boots are walking upon the plaster faces of hollow-eyed women.

"¿Qué es eso?" people whisper. What does it mean?

The faces are set inside a strangely shaped platform. Fabián stares at it intently, trying to extract meaning from the shape. At the exact moment he announces it is the Mexican state of Chihuahua, I determine it is a statement about violence against women. And then we know the subject of the art installation: the killings in Ciudad Juárez.

Some might argue that globalization took root in Mexico when the Spanish came half a millennium ago, but it unquestionably burgeoned on January 1, 1994, the day the North American Free Trade Agreement (NAFTA) kicked in. This agreement created a trading bloc between Canada, the United States, and

Mexico that eliminated duties on the majority of tariffs on products traded among the three nations. Then–Mexican president Carlos Salinas declared it would put his country on the fast track to economic development and "create jobs instead of migrants." According to the Carnegie Endowment for International Peace, Mexico has actually lost more than two million agricultural jobs since its implementation. It has, however, gained about 700,000 jobs in export manufacturing,* particularly in the maquiladoras (foreign-owned factories) that have been cropping up in border towns and other cities since the 1960s. Young, impoverished women constitute the bulk of this workforce, laboring hard sweaty hours on deafening factory floors for about fifty pesos a day that help support families in villages far away.

In Ciudad Juárez, the border town/metropolis neighboring El Paso, Texas, some four hundred women have been slaughtered since 1993, about a quarter of whom work in these maquiladoras. Kidnappers usually seize them on their way to or from work, often in broad daylight. They rape, murder, and occasionally torture them before tossing their bodies into deserts or ditches—some within walking distance of the maquiladoras, which are a stone's throw from the United States.

Freak theories abound. They are butchered for their organs. They are filmed for snuff pornography. They are ritually sacrificed by satanic worshippers. But most likely, these women are murdered because they can be—a gruesome sport with no consequences. People speculate about possible culprits: narco-

---

* Scores of developing nations in Asia and Latin America have joined the global race to build export-oriented economies in recent years. According to Mexican economist Carlos Salas, this competition has led to a decline in workers' wages, benefits, labor conditions, and ability to organize, as the success of export industries all but mandates the lowest possible overhead. See Carlos Salas, "The Decline of the Decent Job," *NACLA Report on the Americas*, July/August 2005, 23.

traffickers, wealthy businessmen, foreigners, corrupt police. Yet, shockingly few arrests have been made.

Fabián and I roam the streets, sensing there might be more art installations. Sure enough, in Plaza Constitución, there is a long row of body bags, each wearing a tag that says CIUDAD JUÁREZ. In Jardín Zenea, police tape cordons off the mannequin of a young woman sprawled across the pavement, naked save for a soiled G-string. Battered and bloodied, she has a whistle dangling from her neck and a set of keys spilling from her hand. (This refers to the former governor of Chihuahua who—after implying that the victims were "women of the night"—advised city residents to start wearing whistles and carrying their car keys for protection. Of course, none of the victims actually own a car.)

We cross Avenida Corregidora to Calle Cinco de Mayo. The entire cobbled street is paved with small, coffin-shaped concrete boxes spaced inches apart. Kleenex pops through the cross-shaped holes of each. There appears to be one for every documented victim, and they stop at the foot of Plaza de Armas, where university students hold an unrelated protest.

One major public square remains: Plaza de la Corregidora. We retrace our steps along the trail of implied tears, make a right, and see the final installation: a blue and white coffin with a propped-open lid. We approach it cautiously. I anticipate another ravaged mannequin inside, but no. There is only a mirror, cracked in half. We stare at our own wide-eyed reflections.

Fabián returns home from the café that night grinning triumphantly. Plunking down a piece of paper, he announces that he just served cappuccinos to the artists of the installation. This is their phone number. I cover his face with kisses and give them a ring.

We meet at the Italian Coffee Company* the following afternoon. Laura is swathed in denim and has pixielike hair and freckles; Piedad is Rubenesque and wears a black leather jacket; Anaíd has long, fuchsia-tipped hair, a pierced nose and lip, and bangle bracelets. Together, they are called Malaleche, or Spoiled Milk.

Laura explains that they founded their artist collective two years ago and work exclusively on the theme of death,† which they have experienced in visceral ways—especially Piedad. When she was fifteen, her father—an undocumented worker—died in El Norte and got shipped home weeks later in a cardboard box sealed with masking tape. This so upset her mother, Piedad had to open it and identify him.

Malaleche's first exhibit examined the brutal murder of a Querétaro woman the year before. They are now confronting their nation's infamous serial killings. "We wanted to raise consciousness about this feminicidio [female genocide], so we made this exhibit as a form of protest," says Piedad. "And because it affects women who are abducted from the street, we brought our art directly into the street."

Which was no easy feat. Last fall, the collective drew up a proposal and presented it to the municipality of Querétaro. They were swiftly granted permission (which, they imagined, meant their proposal had not been read). They requested to hold the exhibition during the week of November 25, in honor of the United Nations' International Day for the Elimination of Violence against Women. This date was declined, however, as the city planned to set up its Christmas decorations that week. When Malaleche filed a new request for the week of March 8 (in honor of International

---

* The Italian Coffee Company is a popular coffeehouse chain, like Starbucks but not as viral. In big cities, there is usually one in the main plaza and in upscale neighborhoods and shopping centers.

† Octavio Paz once declared that the most notable trait of the Mexican character is their "willingness to contemplate horror."

Women's Day), they were informed that the city's calendar had been filled for the entire upcoming year. This, they interpreted, meant that their proposal had now been read. So they enlisted the help of Nadia Sierra Campos, a local activist who works for both the left-leaning political party known as the PRD* and a feminist group called Milenio Feminista. After some string pulling and weight throwing, Nadia procured their permit.

I ask if they consider this attempted censorship.

"Not really," Anaíd replies. "Our government thinks that art is just art, without any political meaning. They censor more overt things, like protests and demonstrations. Art is only censored when it offends the Catholic Church."

"Like that time someone painted the Virgen de Guadalupe as a puta [whore]!" Laura interjects.

They laugh. "Oye, that really caused a scandal. . . ."

"What's been the public reaction to this exhibition?"

"We thought those Catholic viejitas [little old ladies] would tear it down in the middle of the night, but that hasn't happened. Yet," says Anaíd.

"Someone laid a rose inside the coffin—we don't know who—and put another one beside the woman in the plaza," says Piedad. "But by the next morning, both were gone."

Just then, Piedad's cell phone rings. They are late to the next interview. After a quick round of kisses, they dash off. I set a hundred-peso note on the table and walk across the street to Jardín Zenea, where the mangled woman lies with keys tumbling out of her hand. A father and daughter stand beside her. "Who hurt the woman, Papá?" she asks, twirling her ponytail around her index finger.

---

*The Partido de la Revolución Democrática (PRD) is one of the three major political forces in Mexico. It was founded in 1989 by Cuauhtémoc Cárdenas, who is widely believed to have won the fraudulent 1988 presidential election. The PRD tends to attract students, intellectuals, workers, and the poor.

"I don't know, mija," he replies. "But if I did, I'd kill him myself. No one here ever will."

Four days later, two men pass me on Calle Guerrero, struggling with something heavy. The state of Chihuahua, festooned with plaster faces. It takes a moment to register it as a piece from Malaleche's art installation. Isn't their exhibit supposed to last until the end of the week? I stare at the men, now turning a corner. They don't look like artists—or even city employees. Where are they taking it? I call Piedad on my cell. No one answers. I continue on to Jardín Guerrero, where the piece previously stood. It is empty. A security guard leans against the side of a building, perhaps forty feet away. If those men were stealing the exhibit, he would have stopped it. Right?

Feeling queasy, I hurry on to the other plazas. Half of the installations are missing. I am about to check on the coffins of Kleenex when I notice a large dump truck illegally parked on Avenida Corregidora. Piedad and Laura stand beside it. I trot over.

"They are taking it down," Piedad mumbles.

"Four days early," Laura adds.

Some workers appear with armloads of coffins and toss them into the back of the truck. Chips break off. We wince.

"Cuidado," Piedad says softly. Watch it.

Laura sighs and shakes her head. I anticipate her "ni modo" before she even says it. After a time, I place my hands on their shoulders and invite them out for drinks. Piedad promises to call, then does a week later. We meet at a café—minus Anaíd—and they tell the story.

Four full days before the exhibit was scheduled to close, the municipality called to say they needed to shut it down, effective immediately. The official reason was bureaucratic and vague; Malaleche suspects political motivations. Perhaps the government of Querétaro (which is run by the conservative PAN* party) feared drumming up bad publicity for the former governor of Chihuahua, who has major political ambitions. Or else the city wanted to remove the exhibit well in advance of Semana Santa (Easter), when tourists flock in.

"They think our exhibition hurts Querétaro's image of being a clean, safe, family place. But in reality, exhibits like ours impress foreigners. It makes Querétaro seem progressive and artistic," Piedad says.

Laura confides their more sinister experiences during the exhibition. Late one night, a man called her cell and sneered: "What you did was trash, and you are going to suffer the consequences." Laura thought little of it. Her number was written on one of the exhibit's explanatory boards; it must have been a prank. When he called back, however, she changed her number. Then he called *again.*

"I hung up and changed the number right away," she says. He hasn't called back on the new one, yet.

Theft was another problem. The day before the exhibit closed, someone stole the Levi's jeans and cowboy boots trampling across the faces in Jardín Guerrero. "They used professional cutters," says Piedad. "A security guard stands right by there, twenty-four hours a day. I don't know how he didn't see it."

Even worse was how the city dismantled their work. Malaleche spent more than six months on the project, feeling at times they were maquiladora workers themselves, repeating the same task over and over again as they sculpted each new piece.

---

* Founded in 1939, the Partido Acción Nacional (PAN) tends to attract business owners, the religious, and the elite. President Vicente Fox ran and won with the PAN in 2000.

They received a state art grant of 40,000 pesos and invested it in materials.

"All that time and money, and they sent a dump truck to collect it," Piedad says. "What they normally send for picking up trash."

What took Malaleche six hours to install, the city tore down in one. They estimate that 80 percent of the artwork got scratched or chipped in the process. They had the exhibit appraised at 300,000 pesos prior to installing it, and it sustained about 145,000 pesos in damages.

"What are you going to do?" I ask.

They smile for the first time that afternoon. "Publicize."

In the weeks and months ahead, Malaleche will send press releases to magazines and periodicals throughout Mexico and be interviewed on radio and TV. The municipal government of Querétaro will eventually offer them 65,000 pesos to shut up. (And though it is only a fraction of their project's value, they will accept.) Meanwhile, invitations to show the exhibition elsewhere will pour in—both in Mexico and abroad.

Right now, however, they mourn the loss of their art and don't know how to proceed. They feel fairly certain that Querétaro will never grant them permission to show in their hometown again. Just ninety pesos remain in their collective savings account (which is the same amount of our coffee bill). They wonder if it is even feasible to start something new with such scant money and resources.

Meanwhile, that same week in Ciudad Juárez, a seventeen-year-old student disappears. She is later found raped and strangled on a quiet city street, her partially clothed body discarded like the art that once represented her.

CHAPTER SEVEN

MEXICAN ROAD TRIP

Querétaro, Guadalajara, and Aguascalientes,
March 2005

Fabián is late for work, but only I am concerned. We're catching up at the kitchen table over mugs of hot chocolate stirred with cinnamon sticks. Fabián has become my faux-pas checker, Spanish-to-Spanish-I-can-understand translator, and confidant here in Mexico, but we haven't spent much time together lately. Now that my Spanish is intelligible, I am usually chasing stories by day and transcribing notes half the night. He calls me loca (crazy) for exerting such energy.

"You can work when you return to New York," he says. "Why don't you relax, live your life here?"

I try to explain that my work and my life are the same beast, but he shakes his head. Even if this were possible, he doesn't see how I could enjoy it.

"Speaking of work, it is five fifteen. Go to the café, ya!" I say.

He is out the door at half past five and returns within the hour, his face wooden. "Fabián, what's wrong?" I gasp.

He has been fired. It was a clean break: the owner asked for his apron and then sent him out the door. Fabián managed that café; his responsibilities included training employees and recording inventory. But the owner offered no explanation or opportunity to improve. Fabián will receive no severance pay.

Having been fired twice myself, I start describing what the ordeal was like for me, from the emotions endured to the strategies devised for finding something new. He doesn't want to hear it. "Ni modo," he says firmly.

In the weeks that follow, Fabián spends his days either sunning in the courtyard or listening to music. He is clearly content, but I cannot shake my notion that joblessness is a crisis to conquer rather than a freedom to enjoy. So I tell him about the worker-for-hire signs I notice in storefront windows. I offer to help write a résumé, to design a letterhead on my laptop. He graciously declines, which troubles me even more.

He in turn finds my work ethic bewildering. "Why work so hard, Fani, when it can be lost so easily? All that matters are your friends, your family, your peace of mind. The only thing worth striving for is tranquilidad."

It takes time to realize that Fabián has such scant respect for work because it has accorded him—and everyone he knows—so little. Nearly all of our friends are losing their jobs these days, in ways downright humiliating. Someone's sister is fired for resisting her bosses' sexual advances; a friend, because the boss is bringing aboard a nephew far less qualified. Maybe this is why Fabián routinely showed up to the café hours late or skipped out altogether. Why invest in something that yields so few returns?

Still, I can't shake my desire to help, and one night hatch a plan. I want to explore the impact of immigration in other states and could use a native speaker's assistance. I ask Fabián if he will accompany me for a week or two if I cover our expenses and pay him a stipend. He refuses the stipend but accepts the invitation, then reminds me that Omar's cousin César recently lost his job in D. F.—and has a car to boot. We give him a call. Not only does he want to tag along, but he can also leave as early as Saturday. Now I am really excited. This will be like that film *Y Tu Mamá También*—except my companions already know they are gay. I withdraw five thousand pesos* and we agree to travel until the last one is spent.

⁂

"Nine-dee-nine bot-tals of bir on thee . . . cómo? Wahl? Oye, so many beer?" César asks. A former engineer transitioning into the business world, he practices English with cassette tapes while trapped in D. F. traffic. He is pleased to add this new song to his repertoire.

We are 150 miles outside Querétaro, heading west toward Guadalajara, the capital of Jalisco. The radio slipped out of range an hour ago, so we're teaching one another road songs. Fabián contributes his childhood favorite:

> Un elefante se columpiaba sobre la tela de una
> araña.
> Como veía que resistía fué a llamar a otro elefante.
> Dos elefantes se columpiaban. . . .
>
> An elephant was swinging on a spider's web.
> When he saw how well it could hold him, he
> ran off to call another elephant.
> Two elephants were swinging. . . .

---

* This was my monthly budget during the year I traveled 45,000 miles across the United States, documenting its history for a Web site for kids (www.ustrek.org) in 2001. I (naively) thought it would last for ages in Mexico.

As we sing, I flip through an atlas. I originally wanted to tour the major migrant-sending states in central Mexico (Puebla, Michoacán, Jalisco, Zacatecas, and Guanajuato) but need to revise our itinerary, as road tripping here costs a fortune. Every twenty-five miles or so, we pass a toll booth that charges a hundred pesos, and gas is seven and a half pesos a liter. I've spent nearly a thousand pesos and we haven't even been anywhere yet.

Our spirits are high, however. Fabián regales us with stories about his grandfather, a famous matador from the Yucatán. "Every morning before a fight, he would drink a vial of bull's blood for strength and squirt lime juice in his eyes so he could see more clearly," he says.

I, in turn, tell them how my great-great-grandparents joined the mass exodus of a pueblo called Cruillas in the 1850s and walked hundreds of miles to El Norte to work on the King Ranch of South Texas (which, in its heyday, was the largest ranch the world had ever known). "They were America's first cowboys, only they called themselves Kineños [King's Men]."

Before I can share the exhaustive details, Fabián grabs the atlas and turns to the index. To my surprise, he finds a pueblo called Cruillas in the northern state of Tamaulipas, neighboring South Texas. "Is this the one?" he asks.

I stare at it in wonderment. According to Texas legend, Cruillas ceased to exist the day American rancher Richard King invited all one hundred of its citizens to join him. Certainly my own family never returned to Mexico. Two generations spent their entire lives on that ranch, and a cousin and aunt still work there today. But if the pueblo remains, perhaps a distant relative does too. "Can we go there?"

"Querida, we can do whatever you want!" César laughs.

I gaze out the window at the magueys dotting the landscape like lazy desert octopi, their aquamarine leaves swirling in the wind. The soil is red as brick; the mountains amber and green. And the road leads to lands of ancestors and dreams.

By morning, our plans have changed. Again. The night before, we pulled into Guadalajara—Mexico's second most populous municipality—and spent three hours hunting for a cheap place to sleep where César didn't fear for his car. We wound up at a four-hundred-peso/night flophouse where a gaggle of men drank in a nearby hallway until two in the morning, when I stormed out in my boxer shorts and screamed at them. Over breakfast, we surmise that even if we eat only tuna and crackers, our money will run out in four or five days. Cruillas, therefore, is beyond reach, and we probably shouldn't venture outside this state, Jalisco. We decide to visit San Martín de Bolaños, a pueblo that has been so rocked by immigration, a Mexican scholar I recently met online is writing her dissertation about it.* I call the contacts she passed on, and they agree to host our visit.

But first we must find our way out of this rambling city.

As we navigate the streets, César's cell phone starts buzzing every few minutes. He is soon conducting multiple text-messaging sessions while reading a map and swerving through traffic. Before I can suggest pulling over, we veer off the road, crash into a median, ride its rim, and land with a sickening THUNK many meters away. César continues driving, albeit slowly. No one says

---

* Here's the gist: so many people have migrated to the same "sister city" in the Los Angeles area, they have formed a Hometown Association in which they pool together paychecks to build roads, schools, and hospitals back in Mexico. The research of Miriam Cárdenas Torres (a professor at the Universidad de Guadalajara) focuses on San Martín's popular Web site, upon which local residents can anonymously post frustrations about local corruption. Members of the Hometown Association in the United States then call the culprits, demanding an explanation. Because they pump so much money into the community, their calls are generally heeded.

a word. Maybe if no one acknowledges our accident, it didn't happen.

A bicyclist appears beside us and sticks his head in César's window. "No manches, guey, your car is fucked up!" he says gleefully. He tells us what we appear to have broken, and the list is alarmingly long.

I look out the window. People are gathering on the sidewalk, pointing at our trail of car parts. César pulls over and collapses his head atop the steering wheel. Fabián and I run out and swipe up hubcaps, bolts, and other shiny metal things. We return to the car and stare at César. No one knows what to say or do.

César's insurance will cover the damages, but the car will take three days to repair. César announces that he will return home as soon as it is fixed. This sparks a fight, but we cannot change his mind. Feeling responsible for César but wanting to continue the journey, I offer to pay for his food and lodging while Fabián and I visit San Martín de Bolaños. Our hosts there say a five-hour bus leaves for the pueblo at 6:30 A.M. daily. The following dawn, Fabián and I roll out of bed and trudge to the station a few blocks from our hotel. A ticket seller informs us that our bus departs from the station on the other side of town. We leap into a taxi and arrive with five minutes to spare. One company says that no bus in this station goes to San Martín de Bolaños. Another says there is a bus, but it doesn't leave until 4:30 P.M. A third tells us to return to the previous station, and the fourth questions the existence of the pueblo altogether.

"I keep telling you Mexico isn't like Los Estados Unidos," Fabián says, a bit smugly. "You can't just go anywhere you please."

"Yes we can," I say through gritted teeth.

We return to the motel. While Fabián and César sleep, I remember reading about an immigration advocacy organization in the neighboring state of Aguascalientes. I call, and they agree to meet with us tomorrow. After lunch, Fabián and I return to the bus station and pull into the state's capital—also called Aguascalientes—three and a half hours later. After checking into a posada, we hit the streets.

Aguascalientes literally means "hot waters," and its 650,000 inhabitants are affectionately known as hidrocálidos, or "hot thermal people." They are out completing the day's errands, their arms full of groceries and children. They smile as we pass, bidding us a pleasant evening as we stroll across plazas dotted with colonial mansions, eighteenth-century churches, and neoclassical theaters. At the far edge of downtown stands a circular building painted pink and slapped with advertisements for Corona beer. "¡Plaza de Toros!" Fabián exclaims. A bullfighting ring. We enter.

In the arena, a dozen boys line up by height, each holding out a pink or red cape for the instructor's inspection. Fabián and I slide in with the parents in the amphitheater to watch the boys strut across the ring, twirling their capes. The older ones have perfect posture—gallant and proud—and the little ones puff their chests in imitation. The instructor rolls out a wheelbarrow-type contraption fitted with a bull's head. The tallest boy grabs a pair of pointy purple sticks and charges as his peers clap and sing. The bull rolls out to greet him, only to be impaled on either side of the head. Everyone cheers. Then the second-tallest boy sprints forth, his parents shouting encouragements from above: "To the left, Enrique, to the left! That's it, stick him good!"

The old man seated before us proffers a bag of tamarind lollipops. Wormlike scars burrow from the tip of his nose to the bottom of his chin and across his lips. He catches my stare and grins. "Un toro," he says, tracing his scars with his fingertips. "Un toro magnífico." A bull. A magnificent bull.

He fumbles through a bag, extracts a matador cap, and plops it on my head. His name is Raúl Rodríguez, he says, but fans once called him Las Canitas. From 1967 to 1981, he slayed five hundred bulls across Latin America. "The bulls, they understand everything. They listen to what you say," he confides, leaning close. "So I would talk to them. I would say, 'Come here, beautiful bull, I am going to feed my family with you.' And they would smell their death and cry. Bulls always cry."

"Did they ever strike back?"

"Three times. Once right here, in my mouth and in my nose. I spent eight days in the hospital and another week resting, but then I went back into the arena. I didn't want anyone calling me a maricón [fag]!"

Fabián and I exchange glances. "Why did you quit?"

"I wanted to be famous . . . but it never happened. I could never find the good patrons in Mexico City. That is how you make your money. So I became a chef. Thirty years. I like to work with raw meat."

I hand back his cap, and he holds it close. "It was hard, because where I really wanted to be was out there, in the arena. Many of my compañeros, they died of sadness, of alcohol, after their careers ended. When a matador leaves the ring, he never feels that high again."

The sun melts over the horizon. No one turns on the stadium lights; it is simply time to go. The students roll up their capes and the instructor wheels away the bull-barrow. Las Canitas urges us to visit. "I will show you my photos, my traje de luces [suit of lights]. I will introduce you to my compañero Miguel Espinosa. ¡Híjole! Is he a legend."

I jot down his phone number and chirp about the possibility of interviewing these old matadors all the way back to our posada. When I solicit Fabián's help, however, he refuses. "You don't know anything about bullfighting. You haven't even been to a fight. That would be like interviewing Van Gogh without ever visiting an art museum. It is disrespectful."

He is right, of course. My preparation plan consists of a fast session with Wikipedia. I apologize, and he snaps off the bedroom light. Fabián is clearly unhappy with how our trip is unfolding. But while I am perceptive enough to notice, I lack the wisdom to heal it.

Early the next morning, we visit the immigration advocacy group Consejo Estatal de Población de Aguascalientes (COESPO). The office walls feature entries to a children's art contest about the dangers of border crossing. Vultures circle over skulls and crossbones in the desert; giant white Border Patrol agents apprehend tiny brown people. A man cradles a dying friend in his arms, his openmouthed wail taking up half the page.

A secretary serves us coffee and cookies before leading us into the office of Víctor Guerra, the state coordinator. A pensive man with an owlish face, he speaks with quiet intensity. He has arranged for us to meet a number of people today, but first he wants to give us the lowdown. About 16 percent of Aguascalientes's citizens work in the United States. They send home roughly one million U.S. dollars a day. That's the good news; the rest is mostly bleak. "They leave here dressed in traditional pants, long-sleeve shirts, and sombreros, and they come back like cholos, with their jeans halfway down to their ankles. They bring home the culture of gangs and of drug addiction, especially those who go to Los Angeles. It is understandable why they adapt to the local culture in the United States: if they don't join a gang, they'll be attacked. But it really clashes with our culture here in Aguascalientes. The younger ones generally only return a couple of times to visit their family and then they just stay in El Norte. Their families here disintegrate."

The secretary pokes her head in. Our first interview subject has arrived. Víctor shifts topics: ever heard of the Braceros?

We're about to meet one. In lumbers a bear of a man who is eighty if a day, with a white-tipped cane and a baseball cap that reads TEXAS JUMBO JET, INC. "José Montañez Aguilar," he says, bowing with a flourish. "A sus órdenes." At your service.

Between 1942 and 1964, some 4.6 million Mexicans like José traveled to the United States to fill in the nation's manual labor shortages created by World War II. Forbidden from joining unions, these "Braceros" toiled up to twelve hours a day in the fields and on the railroad, often enduring sunstroke, squalid living conditions, diseases, and NO MEXICANS signs in local pool halls and beer joints. Even Lee G. Williams, the U.S. Department of Labor officer in charge of the program, called it "legalized slavery."

One facet of the Bracero program remains unresolved to this day: pensions. The United States withheld about 10 percent of every paycheck and deposited the money into a Mexican bank, but the Mexican government has never released the funds. (Víctor believes it is worth about $500 million today, but most of the paperwork disappeared in Mexico City's 1985 earthquake.) COESPO leads the fight for these pensions in Aguascalientes.

I ask José why he became a Bracero. He rasps in a voice gone gravelly from decades of unfiltered cigarettes, "There were ten of us kids. We had nothing to eat, no clothes to wear. My parents didn't want me to go to El Norte, but I had to do something. We didn't even have chonies [underwear]!"

He was seventeen when he stuffed his few possessions into a sack. His father gave him his .38 pistol, which he pawned for two hundred pesos. He slipped one hundred to his mother and saved the other hundred for the road. At the labor office in Irapuato, he stripped naked for inspection. An agent issued his documents and train ticket and warned him not to lose them.

"My parents came to see me off and they cried so hard. My mother, she said, 'My son, my child, don't leave us, don't go to

El Norte!' She brought me a plate of capirotada* because it was Friday and she always made capirotada on Friday. She brought all of it for me and handed it to me through the window of the train."

That first ride was somber. The men sang corridos as the climate grew cold. By the time they reached Montana, three had frozen to death. José caught a south-bound train to Ventura, California, to pick limes and Santa Paula to pick grapefruit. "Then we went to Texas in a train car full of cattle skulls and bones. Some of the men in there would kill you for a bottle of wine."

Despite the hardships, José enjoyed El Norte. Americans, for the most part, treated him with kindness and respect. He just wishes his government would release his pension so he could distribute it among his eight children and thirty-six grandchildren.

Víctor escorts José out of the room and returns to divulge another project of his organization: repatriating the bodies of migrants who die in the United States. "We bring back ten to twelve a year, one every month or so," he says. "But those are just the ones who die on the job, from falling off a roof or getting trapped in a machine. The majority die crossing the desert, and their bodies are never found."

And those rates are rising. Heightened security measures like fences and beefed-up Border Patrol have channeled migrants away from traditional crossing points (such as border towns like San Diego and El Paso) and into the desert, where they face fewer Migra but brutal climates. Those who don't make it get

---

* Capirotada is made by boiling cane sugar, cinnamon sticks, and anise down to a thick molasses and baking it between layers of old bread and Muenster cheese and topping with peanuts and candied sprinkles. Spicy sweet, it strongly evokes home.

mummified by the sun and buried by the sand.* We're about to meet the mother of such a victim, Víctor says. He exits the room and returns with a woman so slight, the chair nearly swallows her. Sienna-skinned with an elfin haircut and a birthmark smeared across her jaw, she fixates on her palms as she speaks.

"My name is María Guerrero de Alvarado. I am fifty-two years old. I come from a rancho in Zacatecas. We were nine kids. We did the sowing and the seeding and the picking of prickly pear cactus for our father. All I wanted was to leave the pueblo and progress, to live a little better than at the rancho. So I married at fifteen, thinking it would change my life. And it did, but for the worse."

Her husband squandered their paychecks on gambling and beer. Their second of ten children, Ramiro, tried to flee his shadow but could find nothing more lucrative than a part-time job at a bakery. And he had a wife and small children to feed. So last November 27, he and some friends hired a coyote and set off for El Norte.

"He got drunk the night before crossing to calm his nerves. By the time they reached the desert, he was hallucinating. He thought everything was the Migra: the trees, the rocks, the shadows. And he ran from them. For three days. Then the group stopped to rest a few hours. When they awoke, Ramiro had disappeared. They couldn't find him anywhere. The coyote finally said, 'You can either wait for your friend or you can come with me.' So they left."

María has since sought help from the Secretaría de Relaciones Exteriores, placed an ad on TV Azteca, reported him

---

* According to Princeton sociologist Douglas Massey, the number of migrant deaths has risen to around 460 per year, while the probability of apprehension by the Border Patrol has fallen from a historical average of around 33 percent to today's 10 percent. See Douglas Massey, "Foolish Fences," *The Washington Post*, November 29, 2005.

missing at the consulates along the border. No news has surfaced. Those friends never called again.

She is crying now, into a wad of tissues. I want to hold her hand, but the table is too wide for my reach. I look to Fabián for help. His face is chalk white.

"I have always looked out for my children," María continues, her voice somehow untrembling. "I cleaned clothes and ironed; I lived the cheapest way possible so that they would have something. But now mijo's wife is living with her parents. Every time I visit, their children run up and ask if I have heard from their papá. I don't know what to say. My daughter-in-law has no plans but to wait. Like me."

My Spanish has run dry. I can only say gracias. Fabián adds some comforting words and escorts her out the door. There is no time to process: in walks another mother of a disappeared. She hasn't heard from her son since he called to report being too fat to fit inside the trunk of his coyote's car. ("I'm going to demand my money back," he declared before hanging up.) Next is a wife whose husband got imprisoned in Texas for reasons that escape her. She can't call him for lack of funds (and a phone); letters aren't received in either direction. She now raises their daughters alone.

Everyone we interview is dressed in their Sunday best. They accept my business cards with reverence. Mine? To keep? María leaves it behind, as though afraid of it. They break down one by one: the Bracero, when describing leaving his parents; the wives and mothers, when reminiscing of their losses. Immigration encapsulates the whole of human experience. Dreams, ambitions, envy. Struggle, sacrifice, risk. Culture clash and assimilation. Survival. Triumph. Death. And everyone in this nation has tasted this, because they *all* have someone in El Norte. A child, a husband, a cousin, an aunt. In a single phone call, they can learn that these loved ones will never return. That they vanished in the desert. That they got arrested, no one knows why. Days turn into months turn into years with no news.

El Norte is like a black hole. An abyss that sucks people away. Families don't know where their loved ones work, what they do, who they live with, who they cross with. They don't know the name of their new hometown, which state it is in, or even what side of the country. It is all just El Norte, and they went there as pollos, entrusting their lives to a coyote they met in a cantina. They send home paychecks, and when they return—*if* they return—they have changed irrevocably.

You'd think everyone would hate Los Estados Unidos, given this. But they can't, because El Norte is in Mexico too. Wal-Marts and Sam's Clubs. Domino's and Starbucks. Coca-Cola. Los Estados Unidos is in their airwaves, their silver screens, their grocery stores. It is inside their children's cereal bowls. Its ambassadors walk their streets, lounge on their beaches, buy their traditional courtyard houses, plop on their sombreros, and get piss drunk and laugh.

Mexicans realize that immigration is a two-way invasion. And they wonder why no one in El Norte seems to. Maybe because they are too busy building fences to keep the Mexicans away.

Before we leave, a happy story, Víctor promises. Every year, his organization secures a hundred temporary visas for locals to work at catfish canneries in rural Mississippi. Our last interviewee is preparing to return for her third eight-month stint. He brings in María Luisa, a forty-something woman sprinkled with moles and wearing a blue fringed sweater over khakis and Reeboks. She exudes inner confidence, reaching over to firmly shake our hands and establish eye contact. Clad in a navy school uniform, her teenage daughter Bernice carries a diorama of ancient Egypt. They settle into the seats across from us and share a bite of life.

The first daughter in thirteen kids, María Luisa quit school after primaria to cook for her family. Then she married and divorced (twice), bore five children, and opened an embroidery business. She is the first in her family to go to El Norte. "Four of my brothers and two of my sons signed up to work in Mississippi, but I was the only one chosen. I was so proud!"

Her first trip was in February 2003. Entrusting Bernice to her older sons, María Luisa boarded a twenty-four-hour bus from Monterrey to Mississippi. They stopped at a diner along the way but—unable to read the English menu—she could order only Coca-Cola. Upon arriving at the cannery, María Luisa noticed that the owners, supervisors, and managers were white; the majority of the workers were black; and the underlings were Mexican. "The blacks didn't want us there and would insult us in English. I used to want to study English, but then I thought maybe it wasn't a good idea, because then I would understand what they were saying, and I didn't want to fight them," she says. "But after a while, they noticed that I brought salads in my Tupperware for lunch. They seemed to like salads, so the next day I brought enough for everyone. That is how I made friends with them. Last time we arrived, they greeted us with hugs and kisses."

Mexicans earn $200 a week at the cannery. María Luisa believes that the blacks earn twice that amount but contends that the Mexicans work much harder. "When I first arrived last March, four blacks were assigned to clean the machines. After a while, the manager fired two of them and put two Mexicans in their place. By May, they had fired the other two blacks and just the two Mexicans remained. Two of us could do the work of four of them."

I don't know what to make of this. Harvard economist George J. Borjas has found that low-skilled immigrants like María Luisa depress the wages of poorly educated Americans by up to 7.4 percent (if they don't swipe their jobs altogether), and the Congressional Black Caucus Foundation contends that

African-American males are the hardest hit. Yet the thought of someone exploiting María Luisa's work ethic is upsetting too. *Fast Food Nation* author Eric Schlosser has documented convictions in six different cases of "involuntary servitude" among migrant farmworkers in Florida since 1996. In one case, hundreds were forced to toil without pay by labor contractors who threatened to slice off their tongues if they tried to escape.

I ask María Luisa why she thinks Mexicans and African-Americans approach work so differently.

"I don't know. Necessity? We are in a strange country and we know that if we don't work hard, we won't eat. On the assembly line, the bosses stand us Mexican, black, Mexican, black, to keep us from talking to one another, and so that the blacks will see how hard we work. Sometimes the black women get into fights. They yell really loud. Once, two started fighting with their knives. The manager threw them out."

The Mexicans live together in an apartment complex ten minutes from the cannery. In the women's section, each apartment is equipped with one refrigerator and four bunk beds for eight people. "It's not so bad. Sometimes the men have up to eleven!"

On Saturday mornings, a shuttle runs them into town for grocery shopping. There is little else to do—not even a movie theater. The men tend to drink; the women take turns riding the communal bicycle. "When I first arrive, I call home once a week, but by the end I'm calling nearly every day because I miss my children so much. My roommates and I try to keep one another's spirits up. We say: 'Just two months left, just seven weeks left, just six days left.' Then we return home for four whole months with our families."

María Luisa is rebuilding her house with her paychecks. She used to have a dirt floor, "but now it is real." She plans to continue working until Bernice graduates from university. "When I first went to El Norte, I told her to use the money to fix her teeth, but she wants to study instead. She likes computers and astronomy."

I glance over at Bernice and smile. She returns it, shyly. Her teeth are streaked yellow and brown and protrude at different lengths. I ask María Luisa if the cannery provides health insurance.

"They pay for accidents," she says brightly. "Once, a Mexican chopped off his fingers while cutting fish on the assembly line. They gave him three days of rest and then he came back to work. Now he just uses his other hand."

When Fabián and I retire to the posada that night, we are physically exhausted and emotionally spent. Yet I retain that inexplicable high that journalists get after landing a poignant interview, however tragic. Fabián notices and is repulsed. "I can't understand this psychology of journalists. You pretend to care for the people you interview, but what you really want is their story!"

I realized the danger of this years ago. It is partially what drove me to leave daily journalism and work for advocacy groups. So Fabián's words aren't what steal my breath. It is his tone. He is genuinely angry with me.

"What gives you the right to come here, to write about us, analyze us?"

I try to explain that writing about Mexico is a way of exploring myself, a deeper part of myself. But it sounds ridiculous. "Finding oneself" is a bourgeois concept, especially to someone who mainly strives to be tranquilo.

"You think you are Mexican, but you are not. You know things from books, but you know nothing about our psyche. And when I try to explain it to you, you don't even listen!"

My insides are caving in. "How can you say that, Fabián? I am trying, I am trying so hard. . . ."

"No you're not. The simplest things you don't do. Like at home. You said you would help with our chores but you don't. You think you are too good to hold a mop!"

"No, no. It's not that," I gasp, realizing that I had indeed turned my roommates into my housekeepers. "Sometimes I just get . . . I get . . ." I try to think of the word floja but am too upset. Besides, he probably wouldn't believe me, given my manic approach to every other type of work.

"And you are so . . . so . . . fría!"

He has just negated the moral framework under which I work. I admit to having been professionally "cold" when I was a reporter, but now . . .

"I am not . . . am not . . ."

"Yes you are. ¡FRÍ-A! Those people today, they opened their hearts to you. They *cried* in front of you. And you just took notes and listened!"

"Fabián, this is what writers do, we tell people's stories so that others will know . . . so that others will understand. . . ."

"They need to not be in this situation in the first place!"

But they are, and I come from the nation that helped land them there. I have told Fabián about my race-based scholarships, how I essentially financed my college education by claiming a Mexican bloodline. He probably sees me doing the same thing now, collecting these stories to use for my own profit. And it is true: America not only allows but rewards such absurdity.

Fabián paces between our beds, his face flush from argument. But I have lost the ability to defend myself. My Spanish flows neither in nor out. All I can think about is how much I hate Fabián for turning into my conscience, for telling me every ugly thing I dreaded to hear.

CHAPTER EIGHT

BLOOD OBLIGATIONS

Querétaro,
April 2005

Back in Guadalajara, the mechanics repair César's car in record time and he picks us up the following afternoon in Aguascalientes. We drive home in silence. Our car might be fixed but our friendships feel broken. Guilt is eating me alive.

After retreating to my bedroom, I take stock of my situation. It is April now. I'm flying out to the States in ten days to replenish my dwindling bank account with some speaking and teaching gigs. I was hoping to return to La Jotería afterward, but given what has transpired, that no longer seems a good idea. Besides, Omar has been hinting that he'd like his old room back. I decide to explore other parts of the nation upon my return. Like the South. Oaxaca. The Yucatán. Campeche.

My last days in Querétaro are bittersweet. Raúl takes me to nearby Tequisquiapan, where we climb to the top of a mountain and gaze across the fertile valley. Of all my friends, Raúl best understands my reasons for coming here to Mexico. Who wouldn't want to "be more Mexican"? In his eyes, it is the greatest way to be. But he says to be patient, that Mexico is so complicado it confuses him too, that I will confront even more complexities when I travel south, where a whole other world exists. Then he takes my hand and helps me climb down the side of the mountain. Along the way, we sing the elephant song. His personal record is 206 elephants swinging on a spiderweb, sung on a family road trip when he was seven. As we try to beat it, I wonder if such childhood memories aren't what connect you most to a culture. Does learning these songs as an adult count for anything? I ask Raúl, and he shakes his head. "If you keep thinking so hard, your brain will explode, and then what will we do?"

"Race you down the mountain!" I laugh, then dart ahead. We run to the bottom and through the town, winding up at a taco stand on a street corner. Two women roll out blue corn tortillas with melted cheese and our choice of guisos. We sit on stools and they pour us Negra Modelos served michelada-style, mixed with a concoction of chile and lime juice plus a ring of salt on the rim. Even beer is spicy in Mexico and tastes just short of glorious.

Karina asks me to save my final night for her. We arrange to meet at home at 6 P.M., but I end up spending the whole day there, packing. With no one else around, it is uncommonly quiet. I pass an hour atop the pillows in the living room writing farewell letters to my roommates. Fabián's is hardest. We have been avoiding each other since our trip. The heart of our problem seems to be this: I am essentially homeless, while his whole life revolves around home. That is why he considers this house to be so sacred—and why I was so utterly disrespectful in neglecting to help clean it. It was akin to making Fabián "lose face" in the Asian sense, and it seems to have colored his interpretation of many of my actions. I want to write a letter of hopeful amends, but the longer I stare at the blank page, the fewer the words that fill it. I finally settle for banality, thanking him for his hospitality and wishing him success in the future.

By six thirty, it is apparent that Karina is throwing me a surprise party. Guests trickle in with presents hidden behind their backs, swearing they are staying only a minute before sprinting off into her bedroom. Then her sister drops off two colossal pasteles on silver platters. One is like a sandwich with multiple layers of breads, spreads, meats, and cheeses; the other, a quadruple-layer chocolate pastry. No one has ever prepared so much food in my honor before. I follow Karina into the kitchen and ask when she found time to make them. She smiles and says she spent the whole day at her sister's.

"But you had to go to work today!" I object, hoping she didn't take the day off to do this.

Something sweeps over her face—fleetingly, but perceptibly. "Karina. Why didn't you go to work today?"

"No reason," she says brightly. "Just a holiday."

I follow her out to the dining area, where she proceeds to set the table. I help, then trap her in a corner on the way back to the kitchen. She finally admits to getting fired from her art restoration job yesterday. "It's okay, Fani, I can ask for more hours at the café," she tries to soothe me. "Ni modo."

My stomach sharply contracts, then expands with guilt. This party will cost money that should not be spent. Karina holds my hands in hers. "This is our last night together, Fani," she pleads. "We can't be sad. Look at all of our friends."

Raúl makes his grand entrance then, decked out in a glittery shirt that says PORN STAR. He is followed by Omar, César, and a half dozen others—a blur of hair gel, cologne, and laughter. The whole Jotería is here now, minus Fabián. (He later breezes in, clasps a note in my hand, and leaves. In it, he reminds me that people are loved for who they are, not for what they do or have done. Don't work so hard, in other words: be tranquilo. I want to thank him for this, but he never returns.)

We drink the night away at the table. Madonna serenades the first round of toasts, but then Raúl proposes a more Mexican send-off. Pablo Jiménez soon croons old ballads. Karina carries out the pasteles and hands me a knife. Everyone demands a speech, but emotions are strangling me. I can say only that I love them, that they're all my jotitos (little faggots). Then I cut myself a slice of pastelito and eat until I am almost gagging. So many uncertainties, so many regrets. But ni modo. Tonight is my party and it is my blood obligation to disfrutar it.

CHAPTER NINE

MOTHERLANDS

The King Ranch of South Texas and Cruillas, Mexico, June 2005

Mexico follows me back to the States. Undocumented workers are everywhere—pouring cement, busing tables, mowing yards, blowing leaves—and finally I can talk to them. They are full of suggestions on where I should travel next in Mexico: their home villages. They scribble the names and addresses of their families and urge me to visit.

Where I really want to go is my own ancestral village, that pueblo Fabián found in the atlas called Cruillas. According to Texas history books, an American riverboat captain named Richard King ventured there in 1854, looking for cattle. After buying every single one, he purportedly looked around and, "seeing the sadness in the faces of the ranch folk" realized that "the people living there were left with nothing to do." So he "offered to move the entire village, one hundred people in all," to come work with him. They packed up their burros and their chickens, their pots and their blankets, and marched like an "old Spanish entrada" several hundred miles north to a plot of land called Santa Gertrudis, the future King Ranch. Books like Mona Sizer's *The King*

Ranch Story conclude: "The village of Cruillas disappeared on that very day and its name was forgotten for generations."

If this is true, why does the village remain in the atlas? Did some residents stay—or return? And could I be related to one of them? An online search leads me to a society of Latino genealogists tracing their ancestry as far back as written records allow. I write to one named Irma Garza Cantú Jones, who has spent the past decade researching and publishing the baptismal and marriage records of Cruillas from 1767 onward. Among the 25,000 names in her database, she discovers that my great-great-grandfather, Juan de Dios Silva, was indeed born in Cruillas in 1823. Moreover, she is certain that her own relatives—who were not Kineños, or employees of the King Ranch—lived in Cruillas after 1854. "And we have very fertile ancestors!" she writes.

Irma passes along the number of a distant Kineña relative of mine named Lupita Quintanilla, who still lives on the ranch. I call her while visiting my parents in Corpus Christi.

"You're a Silva?" Lupita exclaims. "Come on over, mija, I'd love to talk to you."

When I was growing up, most of my mother's family lived in a row of yellow brick houses on the Laureles Division of the King Ranch.* They drove big trucks, ate red meat, and wore cowboy hats with cowboy boots and gleaming silver belt buckles. Mom completely transformed when we visited them, trading her IBM power suits for jeans and her Louis Vuitton purse for a Miller

---

*The King Ranch commences about half an hour south of Corpus Christi and stretches six counties toward Brownsville, some 825,000 acres in all. If it declared itself a nation and joined the U.N., it would be larger than twenty-three other members.

Lite. Then she'd head over to the poker game at the women's picnic table, where Spanish laughter erupted continuously. Mom laughed much harder in Spanish than she did in English, and she seemed funnier too, forever cracking jokes.

"What's so funny?" I'd demand, climbing onto the bench.

"We're just remembering when we were little," she would say in English, then shoo me away. The only thing Mom ever told *me* about her childhood was that she spent her summers picking cotton under the blistering sun for fifteen cents a pound. Why did they laugh so hard about that?

Exiled from the poker table, I'd wander over to Dad. He wasn't hard to spot: a blue-eyed, red-bearded musician sipping Dr Pepper amid a pack of brown-skinned, beer-drinking cowboys. His Spanish vocabulary consists solely of "tacos" and "salsa," but that's never kept him from bonding with anyone. Before marrying Mom, he spent fifteen years drumming around the world with a U.S. Navy jazz band, including a two-year stint in Japan. He is well seasoned in the art of the nonverbal* and has a happy, easy laugh.

Eventually I'd grow tired of hearing the men's military stories and would run off with my primos. We'd sneak over to the cattle pens and dare one another to jump the fence and dart across. Or we'd take turns knocking on the abandoned shed that Bloody Mary supposedly inhabited. Thoroughly spooked, we'd then crowd around one of our cowboy uncles—usually Tío Juan—and beg for another story about roundup. He always swore that during a full moon, you could hear a phantom chuck wagon creak across the range.

---

* My dad once played tour guide to my mother's cousin Tomás, who is from Monterrey, Mexico, and doesn't speak a lick of English. Dad took him to an athletic club and pointed out two women playing table tennis. "Ping-Pong," he enunciated for Tomás, whose eyes lit up. From then on, whenever a pretty woman walked past, Tomás would elbow my father and whisper "Ping-Pong! Ping-Pong!"

"Who drives it?" I'd ask, shivering in the heat.

"Pues, one of the old-timer cooks. He'd only be about a hundred and thirty now, not too old for a ghost," he'd say, then laugh as we squealed.

If anyone knew about ghosts on the King Ranch, it was Tío Juan. From the time he was tall enough to saddle a horse, he'd braved fires, floods, cacti, droughts, and rattlesnakes on that land as he branded, castrated, inoculated, fed, and bred the cattle. In return, he received substandard wages but free housing, medical care, and basic schooling for his kids. The ranch encouraged Tío Juan to teach the tenets of ranching to his sons as soon as they were capable; his retired parents—who taught *him* the trade—could keep their ranch houses until their final breaths. That was how the King Ranch maintained family lineages of employees for well over a century. Debt mounted though, and the ranch modernized and corporatized in the late 1980s to cut expenses, including the cradle-to-grave benefits. After discovering that three helicopters could round up as many cows in three hours as fifteen cowboys could in a week, they invested in some, causing the Kineños to scramble for ways to justify their employment. Those who couldn't got fired. Within a decade, nearly my entire family had moved off the ranch and taken jobs at places like Wal-Mart. Their homes have since been turned into hunting lodges. Nowadays, we can only enter the ranch with a tour group or as a resident's guest (and our generations of family buried in the cemetery don't count).

I last visited the King Ranch about five years prior, with my friend Paul Stekler. A documentary filmmaker, he'd heard its many legends—like how someone once parked their '32 Chevrolet behind some brush and couldn't find it for twelve years—and wanted to see it for himself. I knew that gaining entry would be a challenge, but when we approached the main gate branded with the famous running W logo, nobody appeared to be standing guard.

"Gun it!" I shouted, and we roared on through in his convertible.

I tried to find my Abuelita's old house in the Laureles Division, but the King Ranch is bigger than the state of Rhode Island. Disoriented by the endless cactus and mesquite, we headed toward the coast instead, using an atlas as a guide. Twenty minutes into our adventure, a monster truck appeared behind us and flashed its lights. It was the ranch's equivalent of a sheriff. He wasn't happy. Paul braced his hands atop the steering wheel, expecting to be shot, while I started babbling about how my Abuelita was buried here and I had only wanted to visit her.

"Then why did you charge through that gate like you owned the place, instead of asking permission?" he asked sternly. "María was standing right inside there."

There was hope: "You mean, Tía María?"

As luck would have it, the last of my many ranch aunts was working the front gate that day. This didn't mean we could stay, but it saved us from getting charged with trespassing. The sheriff led us out the nearest gate and locked it behind us. We drove away feeling like fugitives.

Today, however, I arrive at one of the ranch's many side gates and am greeted by a genuine Kineña. With an ebullient smile that masks a decade of her eight, Lupita unlocks the gate and waves me through. I follow her golf cart to her ranch house, which includes a sewing room ("I've got twenty-twenty vision, honey, oh yes. You didn't get your blindness from the Silvas!") and a cabinet full of dolls from every country she's visited with "la church." As the first Mexican woman to rope cattle on this open range, Lupita is something of a historical treasure.

"When I was little, I was always sneaking out with the boys to milk the cows," she says, pouring me a glass of Coca-Cola. "I started working for the ranch in 1943, in my late twenties. Mr.

Kleberg* put me on the payroll himself. I had my own horse, saddle, chaps, everything. I even handled a gun."

She walks over to the deep freezer and fumbles through its contents. "One day we branded six hundred calves. I was bien cruda [hungover] that morning, because we had a big pachanga the night before. My brother had just gotten home from the service and I didn't go to bed the whole night and the guys teased me, 'You going to make it, Lupita?' but I did, honey, I never went to sleep, oh no, even though it was a long, hard day. We worked seven days a week back then, sunup to sundown, and that's with no time off. I knew how to work, let me tell you."

A box of cookies has been unearthed, along with some caramel candies. She serves them frosty on a saucer. "Ever hear about Trina Cuellar? A beautiful lady, but oh, was she crazy—so crazy, they had to lock her up! There was a hole in her roof and she'd go up there and sing songs from way back. Mothers used to tell their kids, 'If you don't behave, Trina La Loca is coming to get you!' That would put them in their place right quick."

I steer the conversation to our family's journey from Cruillas, and she pulls an album from a shelf. A yellowing photo depicts Juan de Dios Silva leaning on a cane beside a woman in a hair bun. "You're their sixth generation, mija. But they didn't come up with Captain King, oh no. They came later, in 1879, when my daddy was seven. They walked all the way here from Cruillas."

That settles it. Cruillas couldn't have just "disappeared" after King bought its cattle, as so many Texas historians contend.

---

* Soon after Richard King died in 1885, his lawyer married his youngest daughter, Alice. Their son, Bob Kleberg, grew up to be the president and CEO of the King Ranch for half a century. Some say he was the inspiration for Rock Hudson's character in the 1956 film *Giant*, which was based on a novel by Edna Ferber. (She asked Kleberg for permission to live on the ranch while writing it, but he refused.)

My great-great-grandparents had to be sharing quarters with *someone* during those missing years between 1854 and their own departure in 1879. And I want to know whom.

When I first started traveling at age twenty-one, Dad was all for it. He spent much of his early adulthood chasing wanderlust, and even today—at age sixty-nine—considers anyplace under five hundred miles away "just a Sunday drive." Lately, he's been trying to convince my mom to drive to Alaska with him—from South Texas. "It will be a good little trip!" he says.

Mom supported my travels too, if not my destinations. "Why can't you go to London or Rome?" she asked as I tried on down coats for Russia.

"Why do you always go to depressing places?" she implored when I got my shots for China.

Mom didn't relate to my fascination with the developing world because she had lived it growing up. Born in a one-bedroom bungalow with no air-conditioning and six people to share it with, she was raised on beans, rice, and Catholicism. Suffering was what you did at home; traveling should be glamorous. This perception changed when she visited me in Beijing, however, and experienced its chaotic bliss. We are now avid travel partners. When I invite her to join me in Cruillas, she eagerly accepts. (Dad, meanwhile, says he'd rather visit his own family in Kansas.)

Days before our departure, turmoil ruptures in Nuevo Laredo, a border town a couple of hundred miles northeast of Cruillas. Locked in a power struggle over drug-smuggling routes, rival gangs turn the city into a battlefield, shooting one another—and whoever gets in the way—in the middle of the street. Their latest victim is the town's new police chief, assassinated within six hours of taking his oath of office. Dad solemnly shows me a newspaper editorial announcing that the U.S. State Department has issued an advisory against traveling to Mexico. I rather enjoy visiting places the State Department explicitly discourages, but how can I take such a risk with my mother? Gripping the paper, I enter her bathroom, where she is applying mascara before a mirror. She scans the headline, then reaches for a lipstick. "I just want you to find what you're looking for," she replies.

Mom just said ni modo!

At the bus depot in San Fernando, Tamaulipas,* Mom and I descend into heat so infernal, it desiccates our lips on contact. We walk down the street until we spy some bleary-eyed taxi drivers cooking on a curb. They rise when they see us. Mom tells them our destination, and they huddle together, speaking in low voices without moving their lips. The one in the blue baseball cap steps forward. "Ochocientos," he says boldly. Eight hundred pesos to be rented for the day.

"Quinientos," I barter. Five hundred.

They confer. Voices rise, then fall. One swats the sweltering air with his cowboy hat. "Seiscientos." Six hundred.

I look at Mom, who nods. "Ya vámonos." Let's do it.

We step into an '89 Ford Crown Victoria that could fit a family of eight. The driver—a russet-skinned man in a button-down shirt named Óscar López—fires up the engine. Something beneath lets out a high-pitched screech. We move a foot, and

---

* Tamaulipas is the Mexican state that borders the southern tip of Texas. The city of San Fernando is roughly halfway between the border town Matamoros (which neighbors Brownsville, Texas) and Ciudad Victoria, the state's capital. Cruillas is about twenty-five miles southwest of San Fernando.

another something rattles like a gourd full of beans. Undeterred, Óscar pulls out from the curb and rolls toward the highway at his maximum speed of thirty-five miles per hour.

"We're sure putting a lot of faith in this man," Mom murmurs, crossing herself. It's true: we have about one thousand dollars tucked inside our money belts, along with our passports and credit cards. I scan Óscar's dashboard for something reassuring and find it in the puppy-dog stickers plastered over his speedometer.

Cruillas is so often described as a "lost village" in the "dusty mountains of Tamaulipas" that I am expecting to see an extension of the South Texas desert—the land that inspired Civil War general Phil Sheridan to declare that if he owned both, he would rent out Texas and live in hell. Yet as we float down the highway in our boat-size taxi, the landscape turns more into a desert jungle thick with mesquite, yucca, maguey, and nopal. The earth is surprisingly green and dotted with wildflowers; dark mountains rise in the distance. An occasional cow pokes her head through the barbed wire to nibble at grasses growing through cinder blocks. Cicadas scream from the treetops.

After a long, sweaty while, we reach the turnoff to Cruillas. Óscar has to slow to fifteen miles per hour to avoid the holes that pock the road. Then eleven. Then four. "Muy fea," he comments, using the full expanse of his arms to navigate the steering wheel. It's very ugly.

We are passing by a dead cow doused in lime and sautéeing in the sun when a noise explodes beneath the car, like a water sprinkler turning on full blast. We look at Óscar in alarm. He confirms our fear: "Las llantas." The tires.

"You have a spare, right?" Mom asks.

"Sí, pero it's flat too."

We increase our speed to cover as much distance as possible before the tire gives out. I am trying to remember the last time we saw a passing car, when suddenly the incline we are on gives way to nothing. After a brief airborne moment, we crash and skid into a gravel pit. Mom flings an arm in front of me protectively as Óscar slams the brakes and I scream. Another car part groans as the Crown Victoria crawls out of the pit.

"When you make a trip like this, you are taking a risk," Óscar says solemnly. "You'll only make it con un favor de Dios [with God's blessing]." He makes the sign of the cross and kisses his fingertips. Mom and I follow suit.

As it turns out, Crown Victorias can last fifteen kilometers on just three tires. Óscar deposits us at the plaza in Cruillas and heads off in search of a new tire. Mom and I share a flash of panic: what if he doesn't return? Ni modo, we're home now! We pull out our cameras. The plaza features a gazebo and concrete benches beneath rosebushes and shade trees. It is surrounded by single-story, pastel-colored buildings and a whitewashed church. Fabián would appreciate its tidiness—even the dirt appears swept—but there isn't a soul in sight. It is too oppressively hot. After snapping some photos, we start looking for kin. Our first stop is the nearby Presidente Municipal building, where three women sit around a water tank, fanning themselves. When we explain that we are researching the mass exodus of their town in 1854, they stare at us blankly. They've never heard of the King Ranch or even Richard King, for that matter.

"But today is our town's anniversary," one offers as compensation. Indeed, Cruillas was founded with sixteen families and three soldiers by Spanish settler José de Escandón on another undoubtedly scorching June 16, some 240 years prior. Their descendants are planning a big baile, or dance, to celebrate later this month.

One woman calls out our query to an elderly man passing by, and he invites us home to talk with his wife. "She's the town money exchanger. She's been here forever," he quips.

Señora García sits in an unlit room with every shade pulled down and the ceiling fan blowing full blast. She has the same wild red hair that pops up in our family every generation or two, which gives me hope we share some blood. She doesn't know of any Silvas in the area, however, not even from way back. She is certain that both her parents and grandparents were from Cruillas and assumes that her great-grandparents were too. She's never heard of the town evacuating to a Texas ranch, but "if people from here did leave back then, pues, they still do today. All of our boys go to Texas, como mojados, right after secundaria. They take the bus up to Matamoros and hire coyotes who take you wherever you want to go."

We continue walking down the row of office buildings surrounding the plaza, receiving similar responses at each. The last office seems promising initially: La Asociación Ganadera Local, the Local Cattle Association. Two middle-aged cowboys with paunchy stomachs and a pretty woman in platform shoes sit around a fan whirling from a desk topped by an electric typewriter and stack of notebooks. But they've never heard of the King Ranch either, or any mass exodus. "How would I?" one asks. "Do I look one hundred and fifty years old to you?"

They do, however, suggest we speak with Cruillas's oldest living resident, just a few blocks away. We turn right at the POLLO RICO [delicious chicken] sign and find a family sitting on dilapidated chairs in their courtyard. Wire coops full of chickens cluck in the back.

"We're looking for Lupe Garza Maya," we announce.

An ancient man in an undershirt smoothes back his sheet-white hair, stands, and bows, extending a sun-spotted hand. "A sus órdenes." At your service. His family drags over chairs for us to sit upon as the eighty-four-year-old recites two generations' worth of stories. (Sadly, nearly all are lost on us, as his absence of teeth makes his Spanish difficult to decipher). But he's never heard of an old Spanish-style entrada that cleared out the whole town either, and certainly not to some ranch in Texas. "Why, we've been here, mija, all along. And you can stay here too: we've got a cot right in back for you and your mamá, anytime you want."

Though disappointed by these responses, we are not entirely surprised. We spent the past two days interviewing historians and archivists in Ciudad Victoria, and only one had ever heard of this Texas legend: Dr. Octavio Herrera, a scholar who has published extensively about the history of the border.

"Of course I know of Richard King," he said as he welcomed us into his office at the University of Tamaulipas. "He was the biggest cattle thief in history—a real hijo de la tostada" [loose translation: son of a biscuit].

A comment like that could get you hung where we're from. King is an icon in South Texas, the very father of cattle ranching in the United States. Apparently not in Mexico.

"King basically went around telling Mexicans, 'I'm the Patrón, I'm the Godfather. Come work for me and I'll be your benefactor. I'll feed you and care for you until you are old. You just have to do what I say.' And what he said was, 'Go out and steal cattle from other Mexicans,'" Dr. Herrera said. "And many did. They were hungry and they wanted to work, so they were easily manipulated. He would also take land by burning people out. He was like Al Capone. But newspapers all over the United States claimed that the Mexicans were the criminals. King always had a grand image; nobody cared what he did to Mexicans because they were the lowest people on the caste—lower even than slaves."

He leaned back in his chair and chuckled. "Not that I have a vendetta against King. If it hadn't been him, it would have been some other gringo. The circumstances were just ripe for it to happen, after Mexico lost so much land in the Treaty of Guadalupe Hidalgo."

Over half of its land, in fact. After winning the Mexican War in 1848, the United States bought all or bits of present-day California, New Mexico, Arizona, Nevada, Colorado, Utah, and Wyoming from Mexico for $15 million. This inspired the old Chicano saying: Nosotros no cruzamos la frontera; la frontera nos cruzó a nosotros. We didn't cross the border; the border crossed us.

Plenty of individuals lost land as well. After the Texas-Mexico border was drawn along the Río Grande,* Tejanos who owned property had to prove it. A (non-Spanish-speaking) U.S. government commission traveled across the state, collecting some hundred original land titles. The documents got filed in a trunk and stored on a ship—which sunk in November 1850, taking the titles with it. (Lawsuits are still fought over this today.) The subsequent seventy years were pandemonium in South Texas, with cowboys from both sides of the border stealing cattle and killing one another for it. The Texas Rangers were sent in to settle matters and slaughtered so many hundreds of Mexicans in the process, the *San Antonio Express* noted in 1915: "The finding of dead bodies of Mexicans . . . has reached a point where it creates little or no interest."

While this history fascinated me, we came to learn the origins of the first Kineños. Did King take the whole village of Cruillas or not?

"Impossible," he snapped. "Of course, King might have taken *some* people—Mexicans were the best vaqueros [cowboys], and he knew it—but there is no way he took *everyone*."

He hypothesized about the mechanics of the journey, estimating that it would have taken about a week for them to ride on horseback from the village to the border and north into the ranch. They would have packed plenty of carne seca (dried meat) and tortillas, and drunk water from pools in the hills. As a nomadic people, they would have endured just fine.

"In other words," he said, lowering his spectacles to peer at

* The 1,885-mile-long Río Grande is called the Río Bravo in Mexico.

me, "it would have been just like it is today. Those Mexicans who cross the border are the hardest workers around, and everyone knows it. That's why they get hired. Yet they aren't welcomed at all—on land that once was theirs."

Back at the plaza in Cruillas, Óscar has a smile on his face. "I found us a tire *and* directions to the cemetery." We pile in and he drives us down a dirt road toward some horses grazing in mesquite along a low stone fence. A graveyard stretches the length of a city block behind it. We wade through the shrubbery to the gate, and after agreeing to shout if we find a Silva inscribed on a tombstone, we split up.

There is little order to the cemetery, the plots seemingly dug wherever families felt inspired. Tombs are engraved with doves and angels; the ribbons of faded floral displays undulate in the wind. Some of the older markers are difficult to read, their etchings worn smooth by rain. But I examine each one carefully. I want to find something here: a marker that will legitimize my connection to this nation, this culture, this people, this place. I want ancestors to anchor me.

I make out families named Pérez and García, Garza and De León. None are named Silva.

Half an hour later, we regroup in the cemetery's center.

"Nothing," Mom says, her lips stretched thin with disappointment.

"Nada," Óscar concurs.

It is 3:30 P.M. We have a long bus ride back to our hotel in Ciudad Victoria, and Mom doesn't like traveling after dusk. But I am not ready to depart. "Let's go back to the plaza."

The epicenter of Cruillas's social scene appears to be the small blue store adjacent to the whitewashed church. It has a blanket awning over plastic chairs that were crammed with people sipping sodas a few hours ago, although they have since dispersed. I walk inside. From behind a curtain appears a barefoot woman wearing a Betty Boop T-shirt that says ROCKSTAR HOT BABE. She introduces herself as Marjila de León García, the owner. I ask about business, and she shrugs. "It's one of about ten in town. In Cruillas, you either get a job in a store, the school, a ranch, a municipal office, or else you go to El Norte."

Her own husband crossed the border to work in Houston four years ago but got caught by the Migra. "They put him in jail until he told them, 'I have to come across the border, otherwise my family will die.' Then they let him go," she says. "It's true, too. We have no clothes; there is no place to buy anything. Our men cross the river and either die or disappear. Hardly any return."

Out of nowhere, a black cloud darts across the sky. It begins to pour. Bidding Marjila adiós, I hurry out of the store toward the taxi where Mom and Óscar await, clearly ready to go. We can't leave yet. The chances of returning seem so slim. But what would we do if we stayed? There is no place to eat; the church is bolted shut. And the sky is hemorrhaging rain. Reluctantly, I duck into the Crown Victoria and Óscar pulls away from the curb. As we exit Cruillas, the hot road steaming from the cool rain, Óscar confides that he too wants to work in El Norte. He has four kids and his taxi fares barely feed them.

"How will you get there?" Mom asks.

"Como mojado," he says simply. Like a wetback.

This word has acquired an almost biblical connotation for me. "To cross over, to be a wetback is itself a baptism into a new life," author Rubén Martínez once noted. "The river anoints the pilgrim, and the pilgrim enters the Promised Land."

"Do you know anyone in El Norte?" I ask.

"Half of Tamaulipas!"

As we drive back to San Fernando, I contemplate the second half of my Mexican ancestry. About forty years after Mom's maternal (Silva) family entered the United States on horseback, her paternal (Elizondo) family came by rowboat. They had been living in a village called Hidalgo in the state of Nuevo León, where my great-grandfather worked at an old barite mine. Every day, one of his five sons brought him a hot lunch from home. He was crossing the tracks to retrieve tacos from my future Abuelo one afternoon when a runaway cart struck and killed him. (Witnessing this left Abuelo with a permanent stutter.) My great-grandmother gathered their sons and headed to El Norte. According to family lore, it cost too much to cross the Río Grande legally by bridge, so they waited for nightfall and caught a rowboat. Then they traveled north to Corpus, where family awaited. Eventually she remarried and bore two more children.

The Great Depression detonated soon afterward. Undocumented workers became a scapegoat for the nation's massive unemployment. Abuelo used to tell a story about returning home from school one day to find the whole neighborhood being loaded onto trucks to be shipped back across the border. Between 350,000 and 600,000 Mexicans were repatriated from 1929 to 1937, including many U.S. citizens. Abuelo ran back to school to tell his teacher.* She hurried home with him, gathered the neighborhood children into her arms, and boldly lied to the authorities that every last one had been enrolled in her school for the requisite five years. Because of her, their families could stay. Abuelo grew up to marry a young woman from the King

* This teacher was the venerated Rose Dunne-Shaw. A feisty Irish-Catholic, she worked with Mexican-American children for some fifty years as a teacher, social worker, and principal. A historical marker was recently erected on the south side of the Nueces County courthouse in Corpus Christi, commemorating the land where her Cheston L. Heath Grammar School once stood.

Ranch, merging the Elizondos with the Silvas and sprouting our family roots in Los Estados Unidos.

In the end, it doesn't really matter whether or not Richard King led a Spanish-style entrada from Cruillas to his big ranch in Texas. Because the entrada is happening *now.* Some 6.2 million "unauthorized" Mexicans already live in the United States, and hundreds of thousands more slip in each year. My ancestors were simply among the first arrivals. Over the years, they learned a new language, absorbed a new culture, and composed a new story—shedding their old ones in the process. As did the immigrants before them. As will those who succeed them.

All of which leaves me here in their former homeland, trying to establish a connection in their wake. Seeking solace in the fact that at least we've seen the same sunset. That our boots have collected the same dust.

CHAPTER TEN

WHO KILLED OCTAVIO ACUÑA?

Mexico City and Querétaro,
June 2005

Mom must go now, but neither of us wants her to.

During the past two weeks, we crisscrossed central Mexico. In Zacatecas, we donned hard hats and descended into a mine to sense what my great-grandfather's abbreviated life was like. In Real de Catorce in San Luis Potosí, we gazed at thousands of exvotos* lining the church walls where St. Francis of Assisi once staged a miraculous appearance (as saints here are wont to do). In Monterrey, we visited family and traded stories around the kitchen table. For the first time, Mom did not need to translate for me. I could share in her Spanish laughter.

And here we are in D. F., where she'll catch a flight home.

* Exvotos are devotional paintings that express deep gratitude to Christ, La Virgen, or any number of saints for a particular deed—the curing of an illness, the securing of a job, the return of a mojado. Generally commissioned from artists who work in the local mercado, exvotos are created on small, rectangular sheets of copper or tin and hung in churches for all to admire. In Real de Catorce, the Templo de la Purísima Concepción boasts a spectacular collection.

We rise early her last morning for another glimpse of the Zócalo,* the capital's colossal public square. Eons ago, the Aztecs built their grand Templo Mayor pyramid here, marking the heart of their empire's capital. After the Conquest, the Spanish erected modern-day Mexico City right on top of it, smothering Templo Mayor for hundreds of years until construction workers stumbled upon it in the early 1900s. Archaeologists are still excavating it today but can only dig so deep, as the Catedral Metropolitana† and the Zócalo block the way.

Mom and I are weaving through the crowds toward the pyramid when we hear the pounding of tribal drums and the shaking of dried bones. We follow it to a circle of barefoot men and women in full Aztec regalia, dancing with abandon around bowls smoking with incense. We crouch down before them. Breathing in the blue incense. Watching the Templo Mayor burst out of the pavement. Meditating history.

Hours later, I collapse into a chair in our hotel lobby. With my mother gone, the road feels as open as a canyon—and equally capable of swallowing me whole. From this point on, there are no plans. Except, perhaps, finding a cheaper place to pass the night. After a few phone calls, I slip on my backpack and catch a cab to a grotty hostel on the outskirts of La Zona Rosa. The guy at the front desk charges fifty pesos more than we agreed upon over the phone. We argue ferociously until I give in. After storing my laptop in a locker and my backpack beneath a

---

* While many Mexican cities have zócalos, only the one in the capital is officially capitalized.

† The Catedral Metropolitana was also built upon the ruins of the Aztec empire with the stones of toppled temples. The oldest cathedral in the Americas, its construction began in 1573 and took two and a half centuries to complete. It's been sinking ever since, and its structure is badly cracked.

bunk bed, I take to the streets to dream up an itinerary. The sky promptly blackens and it begins to pour. I dart into a café for cover. It is empty save for a schoolboy sitting upon a stool before a 1950s-style bar. I join him and order cinnamon tea from a barista wearing a vintage pink dress with a frilly apron over thigh-high black boots. Her colleague has spiky hair with gold highlights and rainbow-colored rings clasped around his wrists. I state the obvious—I'm new to town—and he whips out a copy of *Ser Gay,* a weekly gay magazine.

"Oh, mija, are you queer? Everything you need to know is right here!"

I say no, but he flips through it anyway. "Mira, we've got gay discos, gay bars, gay cafés, gay restaurants, gay encuentros. You can also get felt up during rush hour on the Metro: just raise your hands in the air and see what happens, wooh!"

We all laugh as he pours my tea and introduces himself as Alberto. When I mention I'm a writer, he leans over the counter and winks sassily. "I first did it with my cousin. In Mexico, if it isn't your cousin, it's your teacher."

This was true of the crew at La Jotería. I conducted an informal poll there, and nearly everyone said they'd first slept with their cousin. "We have big families," one explained, "and they're always around and someone is inevitably cute." None had mentioned a teacher, but one had recently ended a three-year affair with a priest who was a quarter century his senior.

I ask Alberto when he came out of the closet.

"I've known I'm gay since forever, but my parents didn't find out until I was sixteen. My dad saw me kissing my boyfriend in his car, and when I got home, he yelled: 'I don't want any putos in my house!' and kicked me out. I went to my mom's and told her what happened and she did the same thing. I was out on the street without a sock to my name and had to learn how to cook, how to clean, how to do everything."

Life has improved since he moved to La Zona Rosa a few

years ago. "At least here, people accept you. But you still have to be careful. Last Saturday after the disco, I took a walk around the block for some fresh air and some men in a car grabbed me and threw me into the backseat. They took turns raping me, and then they stole my cell phone, my money, my jewelry, everything. I couldn't sit for two whole days. I was so lucky. They usually kill people after that."

I choke on my tea. He didn't say lucky, did he? Oh yes. Mexicans can say ni modo even to violence. If you were robbed, at least you weren't raped. If you were raped, at least you weren't killed. And if you were killed, pues, at least they only came after you and not your whole family. What is most disturbing about Alberto's story is how calmly it is told, and with such distance. I ask if he has experienced other hate crimes, and he says no, gracias a Dios, although the police can be troublesome. A few months ago, one accused him of being a prostitute. ("I think because I was wearing tight white pants and a black-and-white striped shirt.") Although Alberto insisted he was not, the officer tossed him into the back of his patrol car and started driving toward the station.

"He asked how we could resolve this situation, meaning, what kind of bribe would I offer. He wanted a thousand pesos but settled for a hundred and my cell phone. Then he drove me home."

I must look horrified, because Alberto swiftly changes the subject. Mexico is such a wonderful country. We have everything here: fruit, vegetables, petrol, minerals, the mountains, the ocean, the jungle. Things you can't find anyplace else. Isn't that right? I nod, and he smiles. Then he grabs a butter knife and makes more sandwiches that only he, his colleague, and the schoolboy will eat. (During the three hours I spend here, no other customers arrive.) When I finally inquire about the price of my long-drained tea, the schoolboy says he paid for it. I vehemently protest, but Alberto refuses my pesos. I stuff them into the tip jar instead and kiss them all good-bye.

Back at the hostel, backpackers are drinking Indio beer in the lounge. I sit with Miguel, who works the nightshift at the front desk. Dressed entirely in black with skull rings on his fingers and steel spikes through his lower lip, he is what Mexicans call a darketo, or dark person. We strike up a conversation, and a blond-haired, blue-eyed man from Poland joins us. When Miguel is called to work, the Pole and I switch to Russian, which sounds inexplicably comforting to my ears. We clink beers and trade stories half the night. At one point, we accompany Miguel on a beer run to a nearby OXXO mart. The Pole invites me to a late supper, but while I am tempted—he is handsome; I am hungry—I say no, as I'm painfully sleepy. Maybe tomorrow. He grins before strolling away.

As Miguel and I walk back to the hostel, he says he's glad I didn't join him. "That chavo is creepy."

I laugh, tell him he's jealous.

"Who wouldn't be, over a chava as pretty as you?" he replies.

It is so good to be back in Mexico, where even men with spikes in their lips always say what you want them to.

The following morning in La Zona Rosa, nearly every standing structure bears a rainbow flag. Hordes of people mill about, carrying homemade signs on sticks. I ask someone what's the occasion. "Mija, it's Gay Pride Day!" he cries, adding that their annual parade is about to depart from El Ángel.* I walk over to Paseo de la Reforma, the city's grand avenue. Thousands gather

---

* Erected in 1910, the Monumento a la Independencia is a victory column topped by a seven-ton angel that celebrates Mexico's freedom from colonial rule. It is the launching pad of many marches and rallies in the capital.

on either side of it. Queens with fairy wings. Skeletons with armloads of roses. Aztec warriors in plumed headdresses and tight denim shorts. Transvestites wear wedding veils over negligees, their Mayan noses surgically sculpted into Michael Jackson beaks. Scantily clad dancers cram the floats, mobile discotheques pulsating club music. At each stop, they toss out condoms and Frisbees that say LIVING, narrowly missing the bicycle vendors peddling mango and cucumber spears alongside them.

We are nearing a soundstage when the emcee (a queen, of course) announces the dedications for this year's parade, the city's twenty-seventh. After reading some names, she requests a moment of silence in honor of Octavio Acuña, an activist whom she says was assassinated in Querétaro just four days ago.

Querétaro? I grab a passerby. "Sí, didn't you hear? It's in the paper," he says. He is too pumped to elaborate though, shaking a can of Silly String and spraying it all over me. I try to text-message Raúl for details, but the crowd won't wait: I am being physically transported down Paseo de la Reforma and onto Calle Cinco de Mayo. Scores of tourists peer upon us from hotel balconies. One couple is especially attractive. The whole crowd notices. "¡BESO! ¡BESO!" they chant. The couple obliges, taking each other into their arms and kissing. Everyone cheers and a new chant begins: "¡SEXO! ¡SEXO!"

At last, we reach the Zócalo, where a Snow White vixen entertains thousands from a rock-concert-style stage. I have just secured a good spot when the sky tears open and rain pelts upon us. I pop open an umbrella. Strangers slip beneath it. Vendors appear out of nowhere, hawking garbage bags to use as ponchos. It is too late for the drag queens: their hair hangs in ruins and makeup runs in torrents. One removes her eight-inch platforms and splashes about in fishnets ripped up to her kneecaps. Clothes shed. A man slips past in a luchador mask, tennis shoes, and nothing else.

Just then, a float pulls up by the Catedral Metropolitana.

Everyone aboard has stripped to their underwear. Shakira's "Ojos Así" bursts forth, and a well-endowed man proceeds to belly dance, emitting so much energy, everyone swarms the trailer to join him. A dancer unfurls a giant Mexican flag and twirls it around as we start another chant: "¡MÉXICO! ¡MÉXICO!" Thunder claps, and it rains even harder. We dance in frantic surrender.

Five songs later, I squish off to the Metro and exit at Insurgentes. It is raining so hard, no one dares leave the station. I squat beside a chavo wearing a rainbow button. He removes a makeup kit from his backpack, extracts a mirror, and meticulously reconstructs the fallen spikes in his hair. Then he pulls out a compact and powders his nose with a puff. Nearby, a little girl watches him with big round eyes. Her father shakes his head and grimaces.

Back at the hostel, two of my roommates—a grad student from San Francisco and an activist from Chicago—are standing by the lockers. The activist has just discovered that his padlock has been cut, although nothing appears to be missing. I glance at my locker. It has no padlock at all. I fling it open. My computer bag is still inside. My laptop is not. Gravity sucks me to the ground as I realize the magnitude of this loss: interviews, contacts, stories, e-mails. The grad student runs off for the receptionist, who proceeds to search the room.

"My computer isn't fucking here, someone fucking stole it!" I scream. "Call the police!"

"That is not the best—" she starts.

"CALL THEM!"

She dashes off as my roommates and I huddle together, piecing the clues. The grad student spent the whole day here working on her own laptop, leaving only for a half-hour lunch break—during which the Polish guy remained alone. I eliminate him in my own mind, however. We spoke Russian; he invited me to dinner. There's no way he stole my computer. No, the thief is Alejandro, that clerk I fought my first day here. He is the closest thing I have to an enemy, and I tell the receptionist so when she returns to announce that the police are on their way. Her face flushes. "I don't think—" she begins, but I am belligerent. CALL HIM! Taking a deep breath, she rings Alejandro and hands over the receiver. He is understandably upset. "I didn't steal your pinche computer! Go ask your gringo roommates where it is."

But I don't. American grad students and activists are wholly to be trusted.

The police arrive. Four of them. My roommates and I start talking at once.

"Tranquilo, tranquilo, we need to write this down," the head officer says. "Anyone got a pen?"

I lend him mine. He pats his breast and back pockets, presumably for paper. I grab a notebook, but before I rip out a page, his colleague spots a stack of flyers for an upcoming rave atop a table, and hands him one. He asks for my passport and carefully prints its number along the border of the flyer, which is covered with pictures of drug paraphernalia and fluorescent smiley faces. My roommates hand over their passports as well. Then the officer sets down the flyer and folds his arms across his chest. "You might not know this, and we don't want to frighten you, but the crime rate is rather high here in Mexico. We know this because we are the police. We work very hard to make Mexico a safe place for everyone. But we can only be responsible for what happens on the street. We cannot control what happens inside buildings like this."

The three of us nod. The four of them bow, then take their leave. With my pen. Without the flyer.

Miguel arrives next. I tell him my suspicion, and he says no way: Alejandro is practically his brother. He thinks the Pole did it, but I defend him. Biting his spikes, he walks off.

Over the course of the night, my roommates convince me that the Pole really was the thief. Although he paid for the past two nights, he didn't sleep here either night. He's also paid for tonight, but none of his stuff is here. Moreover, the receptionist says he left in a hurry with his backpack while the grad student was at lunch this afternoon. Guilt smothers me: why did I so quickly accuse Alejandro?

We retire around midnight, exhausted from the drama. An hour later, our bedroom door creaks open, and someone sneaks in. A fresh arrival. Slipping off her heavy pack, she climbs into the bunk bed above me. And gasps.

"Um, hello?" she calls out in a thick French accent. "Something is in my bed."

The activist flicks on the lights. Rubbing our eyes, we gather around as she unwraps a plastic bag. My laptop is inside it. Gravity strikes me down again, but my roommates pull me up into a hug. We dance around as the French girl blinks from bed, confused. I am so relieved that—as with my luggage, six months ago—I don't question how this happened. It is just Mexico.

But once I resettle beneath the covers, my laptop cradled in my arms, it occurs to me how perceptive the staff has been about this entire situation. Alejandro suspected the thief was a roommate; Miguel didn't trust the Pole from the start. The receptionist had a hunch that my computer was still in the room, and she knew that involving the police would be futile. Why did I have so little faith in their (Mexican) instincts, trusting only those of my (American) roommates?

The following morning, I call Raúl. He actually sought counseling from Octavio Acuña before coming out to his own family. "This is so terrible you cannot imagine," he says, sounding almost frightened. "People are saying the police did it."

I catch the next bus to Querétaro and text-message everyone I know. Nadia Sierra Campos, the activist who helped Malaleche secure their art permit, agrees to meet me at the Italian Coffee Company that evening. A bookish young woman in a business suit and glasses, she says that she hasn't slept since Octavio's slaying. Her bloodshot eyes concur.

"You need to understand that Querétaro is a very conservative town," she says, stirring her iced mocha as if in a trance. "Men have to be men and women have to be women. Gays and lesbians have started standing up for their rights over the past few years, but now society is fighting back."

At twenty-eight, Octavio was the community's most outspoken activist, rallying local groups and denouncing discriminatory laws. Two years ago, he opened a condonería, or condom shop, that not only sold sex toys but distributed pamphlets about HIV and STDs as well. A clinical psychologist, he facilitated support groups for gays and lesbians inside the store, and met privately with individuals struggling with their sexual identity. He also hung a rainbow flag on a wall visible from the street—a rare sight in a city plastered with SOMOS CATÓLICOS (We Are Catholic) stickers. Soon after its opening, the condonería fell target to prank calls, homophobic graffiti, vandalism, even a break-in. "There is another condonería in town owned by a gay man. He installed video cameras everywhere, but Octavio never did. He knew the risk he was taking, but he did it anyway."

In September 2004, Octavio took a late-night stroll through Jardín Guerrero with his partner of seven years, Martín, and wound up on a park bench around 1:30 A.M.* They neither held hands nor kissed; they simply sat. Two policemen approached and said, "This is a family park. It isn't for people like you, who conduct immoral acts." Deeply insulted, Octavio wrote down their names—which

* Martín supplied the facts in these next two paragraphs during our interview in July 2006.

angered the officers. They said they would return in ten minutes, and if the couple had not left, they would haul them off to the police station. At Martín's insistence, the couple went home.

Harassment at the condonería intensified. The phone rang repeatedly with prank calls that grew increasingly threatening. Octavio filed a complaint about the officers' behavior with the State Commission on Human Rights. They did nothing. He wrote to the National Commission. Still nothing. Then Marta Lamas, a prominent writer and activist, held a National Congress on Diversity in Querétaro. Octavio rose in the middle of a session and told of his experiences.

"He explicitly stated that he feared for his life, but no one offered any help. Two weeks later, he was dead."

It happened on June 21. Nadia called Octavio around 3 P.M. to discuss an event they were planning. Their conversation lasted half an hour. According to phone records, Octavio then called Martín and later a group of activists in San Luis Potosí, his final call ending around 3:45. At a quarter to five, some teenagers walked into the condonería for their scheduled counseling session with Octavio. They found him in the back room soaked in blood, stabbed multiple times in his leg, stomach, and heart.

"This wasn't a robbery," Nadia says, still stirring her untouched drink. "All of his money and credit cards were still there. The authorities say that it was a 'crime of passion,' but Octavio had lived with Martín for years. They were partners; there was no one else. No. This was a hate crime."

She has to be upset, but she speaks with the same steely distance Alberto did about being raped. I ask if she's ever been threatened, as an activist.

"My tires have been slashed. Once, they fell off as soon as I started driving. And I get threatening phone calls, no matter how many times I change my cell number. So yes, I have fear. All of us activists do. We worry that what happened to Octavio might happen to us."

These fears are not unwarranted. In 1991, Amnesty International published an exhaustive report on extrajudicial killings by police, soldiers, and military death squads in Mexico, who have used such torture tactics as covering people in honey and burying them in anthills. Ten years later, the nation's most renowned human rights attorney, activist, and nun—Digna Ochoa*—was shot in the head in her D. F. office, having previously been kidnapped (and raped) three times and forced into brief exile. Gays are also a target. According to the Citizen's Commission Against Homophobic Hate Crimes, 290 Mexicans were murdered because of their sexual orientation from 1995 to 2003. For Octavio, being both gay and an activist may have been a deadly combination.

I lay my hand atop Nadia's. She tolerates this for a moment or two, then drinks her entire mocha in one gulp.

Octavio's condonería is located on Avenida Universidad, a major city artery that runs along a canal lined with shade trees and benches. A friend and I expect the store to be blocked off by police tape, but its door is merely padlocked and lacey curtains

---

* Digna Ochoa's body was found wearing red rubber gloves inexplicably coated in starch. A note beside her was addressed to other "sons-of-bitch" human rights lawyers. Yet Mexico's special prosecutor concluded two years later that Ochoa's death was "probable suicide." Human rights groups around the world decried the ruling, and the Inter-American Commission on Human Rights later identified severe flaws in the investigation, including the failure to properly protect the crime scene and ensure chain of custody of the evidence. In addition, lawyers of the Ochoa family were denied permission to present new evidence supporting their case. See statement by Eric Olson, Americas Advocacy Director at Amnesty International on July 19, 2003, at www.amnestyusa.org.

drawn. LIC. OCTAVIO ACUÑA RUBIO* is painted across the storefront beneath a smiling condom wearing white gloves.

We circle the neighborhood a few times before entering the adjacent sporting goods store. The attendant shakes her head when we inquire about Octavio. "I don't know anything, anything at all," she says, then disappears behind the curtain leading to her back office.

Next door is a design store manned by a chavo wearing a black T-shirt emblazoned with a red swastika.† We ask him about the murder.

"I didn't hear anything that day," he says. "No gunshots or anything."

Octavio was stabbed, not shot. When I point this out, he shrugs. Has he experienced any problems with graffiti or prank calls?

"Never," he says. "Everything is tranquilo."

We continue on to the other gay-owned condonería in town, located above a dentist's office on Avenida Corregidora Norte. To enter, we must unlatch a heavy chain covered with bells. Shelves display dildos, condoms, and party gifts; a back room showcases S/M gear, including an assortment of handcuffs, which are called esposas—or wives—in Spanish. Pamphlets on HIV education and sexual orientation are stacked by the cash register, and a rainbow flag covers the back wall.

A thirty-something man in glasses approaches us with a small green bottle, dabbles its oil onto our wrists, and blows, emitting a tingly heat. "Lick it," he instructs. It tastes like a Granny Smith

---

* "Lic." stands for Licenciado, or holder of a bachelor's degree. Education is so revered in Mexico, "Licenciado" becomes part of your identity upon graduation. People often add the prefix onto business cards, and are addressed as such in formal settings.

† According to Raúl, the swastika signifies revolution to his generation—not Nazism. "It's like wearing a Che Guevara T-shirt," he says.

apple. He laughs at our animated response. Taking advantage of the light mood, I ask about Octavio. His demeanor changes completely.

"Oh no. I am sorry, but no. If you came to talk to me about Octavio, you have come in vain," he says, backing away from us and removing his glasses. "He was the leader of our community, the only one willing to take risks, to speak out. And look what happened to him. I am sorry my friends, but no. I cannot speak about this, not today. Not now."

Apologizing profusely, we maneuver toward the stairwell. Before we unlatch the chain, he speaks again. He opened this store three years ago. Querétaro had other sex shops, but his was the first to distribute sexual health information. Prank calls and graffiti haven't been a problem. "But I take no chances. I installed a siren that will blare if I pull it, and I have two chairs to block the entrance to the back room, where there is an exit. I also have eight security cameras. But if Octavio had cameras inside his store, they just would have killed him outside it."

"What was he like?"

"I can't say he was a close friend. He was more of a colleague. But when he died, I cried like he was my father. And when I think about the people in this town who need him for information about sexual health, I hurt. Badly."

Has this made him reconsider the future of his own business?

"This has been my life work of fourteen years. My family tells me to close down, but I want this struggle to continue. Yet, if a pen falls, I jump. When I come home to my partner at night, I am not allowed to touch the light switch. We keep all of our windows closed all of the time," he says, slowly walking toward us.

"I am not afraid of them killing me. That would take what—five minutes? No. I am afraid of what my death would do to my family. It would be a very slow death for them. They are so proud of me, so proud to have a son who teaches kids about sexual health."

He is standing two feet away now, staring so intently I must avert my gaze. "To come out to someone, to tell them you are gay—it is such a gift. It is a symbol of love. It is saying, here is this piece of my heart that I have decided to share with you. But if I find out for certain that Octavio was killed for reasons of homophobia, I will close my shop and move to D. F. or to Canada the next day."

CHAPTER ELEVEN

THE AMBASSADOR

A Town in Morelos,
July 2005

Investigating Octavio's murder is so chilling, I need some solace afterward. A number of people passed along their contacts in Mexico, and after surveying the list, I decide to visit the family of my friend Víctor. We met in Brooklyn four years ago, right after I moved to Park Slope. Needing help with a futon one morning, I rang the deli downstairs, and he got dispatched to my door—a moon-faced man with a bowl of black hair and the sweetest eyes. Though slight of height and build, he hoisted the mattress atop his shoulder like a floppy baby. Between my broken Spanish and his rudimentary English, he communicated that he was from a small town in the state of Morelos, just a few hours' drive from Mexico City, and his wife and daughter still lived there. He smiled upon learning I am Texan. "Cowboy!" he said, twirling an imaginary lasso.

Our paths crossed often after that, usually in the street on our bicycles. He'd be wearing a white apron and delivering hoagies; I'd be in lycra and heading to Prospect Park. We'd pantomime about life while waiting at the traffic lights, groaning about work, about being separated from our families, about this manic city that accorded its occupants no rest. One night, he brought over a DVD that his daughter Jumi sent from Mexico. My roommate—a grad student who did a Peace Corps stint in Nicaragua—and I watched it with him. Photographs of Jumi at various stages of life appeared in slow succession as "Wind Beneath My Wings" played in the background. He anticipated each photo before it appeared. "She looks a little gordita [chubby] here, right? Wait until the next one, when she's eating her mamá's tamales!"

Before I departed for Mexico, we invited Víctor upstairs for lunch. He arrived at our doorstep in a dress shirt unbuttoned just enough to reveal the Virgen de Guadalupe dangling from a gold chain. Although we'd planned a full menu, he carried fistfuls of shopping bags that included a brand-new tortilla press. "We're making sopes!" he announced. He dumped cornmeal onto the countertop, drizzled water over it, and kneaded it into a thick lump of masa from which he rolled little pellets that the press squashed flat into tortillas. After cooking one on a skillet, he showed us how to pucker its smoking-hot edges so that its future condiments wouldn't slide off. We tried but failed to do this: the sope singed our fingertips too badly. Víctor laughed good-naturedly and puckered all the sopes himself with his heat-resistant hands, then slathered them with cream and sprinkled on shredded lettuce, crumbled Oaxacan cheese, and a salsa he blended with grilled tomatoes, peppers, onions, and garlic.

Víctor left for El Norte in 1995 because his daughter needed an operation. His salary as a taxi driver couldn't foot the cost, so he crossed the Arizona desert with a coyote and fifteen pollos and traveled to Brooklyn by backroads and buses. He earned enough the first year to pay for Jumi's operation but decided to stay longer to rebuild their house. That took four years. For the past two, he'd been working to finance Jumi's private school tuition. "She is almost fourteen now. I haven't seen her in years. Es muy duro," he conceded. It is very tough.

Before Víctor left that afternoon, he pulled out a book with a crumbling map of Mexico and showed me his hometown in Morelos. Then he wrote out the address of his family in laborious script and asked if I would visit them. I promised. Cupping my hands in his, he said to please be careful.

Buses are ranked by class in Mexico: there's segunda, primera, and de lujo. If the schedule lists a 10:43 departure, they are generally out the gate by 10:44. (Arrivals are another story.) An advantage to traveling segunda is that if you spot one en route, you can wave it down—even from the shoulder of an interstate—and request a stop anywhere you please. De lujo, meanwhile, boasts cocktails served by attendants and enough legroom to touch up a pedicure (as I once watched a woman do). I tend to ride primera, which includes snacks (ham-and-jalapeño croissants saturated in butter) and entertainment (movies blasted so loud, I once asked a fellow passenger why. "Pues, so you won't fall asleep and miss your stop," he replied.)

Happy, Texas blares on the way from Querétaro to D. F. and *007: Tomorrow Never Dies* from D. F. to Morelos. The peoplescape soon rivals James Bond for my attention. Bare-chested men hack stalks of sugarcane with machetes. Rumpled children peek behind fruit trees. Pilgrims weave their way up the craggy cliffs of Tepoztlán in single-file rows, soaking in its rumored "energy vortex." At last, we pull into the station. A taxi zips me across town to Víctor's neighborhood, where the road slowly fills with potholes, children, and chickens. His street rises up at a thirty-five-degree angle and is paved with gravel and weeds. A girl with long black hair stands halfway up, watching intently.

"Jumi?" I call out.

She jumps up and down, clapping her hands before racing

toward me with hugs and kisses. She inherited her father's handsomest features: shiny black eyes, wide Mayan nose, prominent cheekbones, a jubilant smile. A cell phone is clipped to her jeans and she wears a T-shirt of a puppy with a butterfly atop its nose that says CUTIE PIE. Slipping her arm around my own, she leads me up the incline, bubbling with excitement. I have officially become Víctor's ambassador.

A tall metal gate gives way to a modest, three-walled house built around a courtyard with a stunning view of the town and the sugarcane fields surrounding it. Jumi cries out "Mamá" and a middle-aged woman appears in the open-air doorway. She grins and points skyward. "¡Ven!" Jumi commands, dragging me back through the gate before I can say hola.

"That was my Tía Vera, and over here is Tía Laura and Tía Marta." She points. She is related to nearly everyone on the block. We charge farther up the incline and bolt through another gate. "This is my house," she says grandly. It is a renovated two-story built around a courtyard full of frantically barking dogs chained to trees on foot-long leashes. We dart upstairs. A poster-size calendar of a bare-breasted Chinese woman covers one wall; on the other hangs a framed photograph of the Twin Towers with mug shots of Víctor's family superimposed in the clouds. Jumi's bedroom is loaded down with a Hewlitt Packard computer and color printer, a television set with a built-in DVD player, and a souped-up stereo system with stacks of CDs. A woman with long wavy hair and shapely legs emerges from a second bedroom. Shyly covering her mouth, she introduces herself as Judith, Jumi's mamá. She is so pretty, I am at once happy and sad for Víctor.

As if on cue, Jumi's cell phone rings. It is Víctor, making his first of half a dozen calls that day. As they talk, we walk down to the street for a taxi. I ask where we're going but don't catch the response. We pile in. The phone is passed to me and I crow on and on about how bonito everything is, to which Víctor replies "Qué bien." We pull up to a restaurant owned by a tía who embraces me before plunking down warm bowls of pozole (hominy soup with chicken, oregano, and red chile) and plates of deep-fried tacos drizzled with cream. Still chatting with her father, Jumi says that she forgot something at home and dashes into the street for another taxi. Judith and her sister, meanwhile, watch me eat, giggling behind their hands at how I scoop bits of chicken out of the soup and plop it inside my tortilla. Trying to deflect the attention, I play twenty questions with Judith: does she work (no), how does she spend her days (relaxing), where did she meet Víctor (at primaria).

"He's been gone seven years and has only come home twice to visit. The last time, Jumi was ten," she says, clearly soliciting an explanation.

I don't know how to tell her that consumerism has hijacked her husband. Víctor has seen how much flashier their life could be and wants to provide it. But when will it be enough? Jumi turns fifteen next year, which necessitates a quinceañera, or coming-out-to-society party. Then there will likely be preparatoria, some college, a wedding, grandbabies, a new house of her own. If Víctor wants his daughter to experience all those things, he might never return.

Instead, I blame the complexities of immigration for his absence: the vigilance of the Migra and the perils of the desert. I assure her that Víctor loves them, that he talks about them constantly, but that he knows they need the money and it is too risky to cross the desert for a visit.

"Ay," she sighs, stirring her pozole. "Dios."

A taxi pulls up and Jumi pops out, holding a video camera. I smile and wave into the camera, take an animated bite of pozole, and lick my lips. We all laugh. Jumi sits and continues filming me from two feet away. While I eat. While I drink. While I speak. Judith explains that she sends her papá videos like this every month or so. This is their relationship: voices on the cell phone, faces in videos.

After lunch we hail another taxi and head for the outskirts of town, where the sugarcane grows. We park beside a woman ladling something into small clay pots beneath a coconut tree. My stomach churns when I notice her handwritten sign: PULQUE RICO. An alcoholic beverage made from the fermented aguamiel, or juice, from the flowers of a maguey, pulque was used in the religious ceremonies of the Aztecs. Its hangovers are legendary. The woman pours me shots of three different flavors: oatmeal, mango, and pineapple. The liquid is highly acidic and strangely sweet. Jumi films me drinking it, which inspires me to declare a false love for it. This prompts Judith to buy me an entire potful. Gripping it with both hands, I squat beneath a coconut tree, wondering how to create a distraction so that I can empty it without anyone noticing. Unfortunately, Jumi is still filming my face. I down the contents of the pot as quickly as possible. Then we pile back into the taxi and continue down the road, passing by grazing horses and barefoot children. Feeling the need to fill in their gaps about Víctor's life, I tell them how I always see him on his bicycle, then imitate him racing about. They laugh with delight. I ask Jumi if she has a bike.

"Sí, but I'm afraid to ride it because of all the cars," she says, nodding at the barren road before us. "Is it scary riding a bicycle in New York City?"

"It's not so bad," I lie, then gush about what a hard worker Víctor is, how he darts about on important errands.

"What kind of errands?" Judith asks.

"Oh, you know . . . deliveries," I say vaguely, realizing I have no idea what Víctor tells them. Do they know that he braves Brooklyn traffic in the heat, sleet, and rain delivering veggie burgers for dollar tips? Switching topics, I describe our adventures making sopes and how Víctor could practically lay his hands flat on the skillet and not get burned.

"He cooks?" Judith asks incredulously.

"Papá comes over to your house often?" Jumi chimes in.

Can I count the times he has helped install our air conditioners? "Oh yes!" I lie again. "Constantly."

This brings the smiles I hoped for, but this conversation must end—now. "So what kind of industries do you have in town?"

"Sugarcane and construction," Judith says.

"Y ya," says the taxi driver. And that's it.

We ride in silence until a shriveled woman tending to a smoky grill appears on the side of the road. I ask what she is making, and we pull over.

"¡Elotes!" Jumi says, skipping over to the stand. Corn on the cob.

The old woman ticks off her menu on three fingers: corn, sugarcane, and coconuts. My stomach still gurgling from the pulque, I order the latter. She bends over to open a broken freezer filled with coconuts bobbing in water, fishes one out, hacks it with a machete until she strikes milk, pokes in a straw, and hands it over. The milk is cool and rich. I drain it dry. She takes it back, carves out its white flesh, then coats it with chile powder and lime juice for me to eat.

Jumi, meanwhile, is munching a spear of grilled corn dripping with chile and cream. Halfway through, she looks up. "When is Papá coming home?"

Judith, the taxi driver, and the old woman turn to me expectantly. I have been asking Víctor this since I've known him. The answer is always just a few months away. When I left for Mexico in December, he said February; during our last visit in May, he said November. When I see him this fall, he'll say next spring. "Just as soon as he can," I say lamely.

"And when are *you* coming back?"

"August," I hear myself say.

Jumi beams.

We return to town to hit the mercado, where vendors sell everything from luggage to tools to chanclas upon and beneath blue tarps. Jumi hovers over a table of wallets featuring cartoon characters like Scooby-Doo, Tigger, the Care Bears, and the Powerpuff Girls. She seems so impressed with them, I offer to buy one for her fourteenth birthday next week. She smiles at me with shining eyes, then deftly moves from the 30-peso wallets to the neighboring 150-peso T-shirt table, where she picks out two that are silk-screened with lowrider cars driven by cholos and busty brunettes against a backdrop of the American flag crowned by a bald eagle. Judith intervenes, saying that I offered to buy her a wallet, not a shirt. I admittedly feel a flash of gratitude—until she whips out a roll of hundred-peso notes and hands three to Jumi. I try to protest—that is the equivalent of five hours of bicycle deliveries for Víctor—but Jumi snatches the money and buys the shirts. Feeling like a (cheap) sucker, I steer her to a pirated CD bin and instruct her to get whichever two she wants.

My bus leaves in forty-five minutes. We hail another taxi. Jumi asks the driver to play her new CD. Daddy Yankee's "Gasolina" blasts forth. We return to the countryside, where Judith suggests we take a walk. The taxi rolls to a stop to let us out and then trails a few feet behind us, blaring the music. With Jumi filming us, it feels like we're in a music video and should be singing.

Perhaps because our time together is dwindling, Judith overcomes her shyness and asks a few direct questions, starting with my age. "I thought you were twenty!" she shouts. This reaction has more to do with my lifestyle than my looks. I anticipate her follow-up question before she even asks: "Why aren't you married?"

I explain that in New York, it is quite common to be single at thirty, forty, sixty. She stares in amazement while Jumi beams. "See, Mamá? That's why Papá wants me to go there!"

Jumi says that her best friend Beatriz got pregnant two years ago, at age thirteen. Now fifteen, she has two babies. "I don't want that happening to me," she adds.

We return to the bus station, where an entire extended family has gathered. A few look strangely familiar, but I continue chatting with Jumi and Judith until boarding time, at which point the whole family steps forth to kiss me. They are, of course, Judith's mother, sisters, and brothers. I feel terrible for not recognizing them. Each one presents me with a gift: a rose clipped from a bush, a mango picked from a tree. I have nothing to give in return—not even my attention, as I must go. I hear myself promise to return in August. They wave until my bus turns a faraway corner.

For the rest of the summer, Jumi will call my cell nearly every night. Each conversation concludes the same way: "Are you still coming to see me in August?" I always say yes—until the end of that month rolls around, and I discover that I cannot. When I break this news, her silence is so heartbreaking, I hear myself say, "But I will return . . . in December!"

"December," she repeats slowly.

I imagine what she's thinking: America is a place where everyone lies about when they're returning.

CHAPTER TWELVE

INCANTATIONS

San Cristóbal de las Casas, Chiapas, July 2005

Maybe it was the pulque. Or the pozole. Or the guilt. Soon after leaving Víctor's family, my digestive tract shreds into ribbons, and my backpack pinches a nerve in my neck, partially paralyzing me. I am spread-eagle across a friend's sofa-bed in Querétaro, wondering what to do, when the headline of an old *La Jornada* catches my eye: ZAPATISTAS* DECLARE RED ALERT. All rebel forces—both civilian and insurgent—have been called into the jungle of southern Mexico; henceforth, they shall work in a "clandestine and nomadic manner." I don't know what this means but it sounds exciting.

The Ejército Zapatista de Liberación Nacional (EZLN) snatched the international spotlight in the early morning hours of January 1, 1994, when they marched into the highlands of Chiapas wielding AK-47s and machetes and seized the city of San Cristóbal

* The Zapatistas named themselves after the 1910 revolutionary hero Emiliano Zapata, whose rallying cry was ¡Tierra y Libertad!—Land and Liberty.

de las Casas. Their timing was both symbolic (NAFTA kicked into effect that day) and strategic (the Mexican Army was still snoozing off hangovers after celebrating the New Year). And their demands were poignant: better schools, hospitals, and working conditions; access to land and power in politics and the media; autonomy; and basic dignity for the nation's twelve million indigenous people. The Mexican Army overcame the Zapatistas' uprising in less than two weeks, but not before their pipe-smoking, ski-masked spokesman, Subcomandante Marcos, became an icon of the antiglobalization movement. He began writing communiqués about the dire state of Mexican Indians—how they live on less than 250 pesos a month; how 70 percent have no sewage; how they are routinely subjected to police detention and even torture—and circulating them via the Internet from his hiding place in the jungle. He also launched some high-profile campaigns, including a cross-country caravan to D. F. to seek passage of an indigenous rights bill in 2001.* But aside from a few forays into the publishing world,† Marcos has kept quiet lately. Apparently, this is about to change.

When my former roommate Omar visits that night, I point out the Red Alert article. He is not impressed. "The Zapatistas

---

* When the Zapatistas arrived at the Zócalo in D. F. in March 2001, hundreds of thousands of supporters were waiting to greet them. Congress passed a severely watered-down version of their indigenous rights bill, however, and the Zapatistas refocused their attention on creating autonomous communities instead.

† In addition to missives, essays, and a detective novel coauthored with Paco Ignacio Taibo II, Subcomandante Marcos has published a children's book called *The Story of Colors*. The National Endowment for the Arts gave Cinco Puntos Press (an independent publishing house in El Paso, Texas) a $7,500 grant to help offset the costs of a bilingual translation, then revoked it out of fear the Zapatistas would reap the profits. In the media frenzy that followed, the J. Patrick Lannan Foundation stepped in and subsidized the project.

are just for show, Fani," he says. "They got everybody's hopes up in 1994 and did nothing with it. They're just going to do that again. They say Marcos isn't even a Mexican, but a foreigner."

Although Subcomandante Marcos has never made a public appearance without his trademark ski mask,* government investigators claim he is actually a philosophy professor named Rafael Sebastián Guillén Vicente from the Universidad Nacional Autónoma de México (UNAM) who mysteriously disappeared in the 1980s. While Marcos is most certainly a Mexican citizen (albeit perhaps a white one), people often call him a "foreigner" because he is so different from the Mayan army he represents. And that's not the only beef about him. Critics blame his antics for the disastrous 1994 peso devaluation and recession. My family in Monterrey contends that to buy weapons, he harvests marijuana in the jungle and sells it to narco-traffickers. Still others claim he uses his impoverished army as a human shield to advance his own radical political agenda. If I so much as question these assessments, people shrug and say, "Foreigners always love him."

This comment spurs déjà vu. While living in Beijing in 1998, I grew enamored with a group of writers, painters, and poets whose work was banned by the government. In my eyes, they were dissidents taking a stand against a repressive regime. My Chinese friends, however, scoffed that they created this art with the *intention* of it being banned so that foreigners like me would buy it. When I implied that maybe their government had brainwashed them to think that way, they said no, but perhaps I had been by mine. In China, being informed that I thought in a certain way because I was a foreigner simply made me feel like a

---

* When asked why he always wears a mask, Subcomandante Marcos once joked: "Well, those of us who are the most handsome must protect ourselves." He later retracted, saying he was just "making propaganda" for himself. See Andrés Oppenheimer, *Bordering on Chaos: Mexico's Roller-Coaster Journey toward Prosperity*, Little, Brown and Company, 1996.

gullible idiot. Here in Mexico, it is yet another reminder that I am an outsider peering in.

Whatever the case, I want to go to Chiapas now. Everyone in Querétaro tries to talk me out of it. It is too dangerous, they say, especially given this Red Alert. One friend even warns that the Zapatistas might kidnap me. This notion strikes me as ludicrous, certainly counter to everything I've read about them, but the fact that it comes from a twenty-eight-year-old artist who has traveled internationally gives me pause. This is her country: surely she has a deeper understanding of the Zapatistas than I do. My knowledge, after all, is based entirely on books and articles written by gringos like me.

Before I can go anywhere, my neck needs to hold my head upright again. What to do? Like forty-five million Americans, I have no health insurance. I can't afford the fees. I bought a traveler's policy on the Internet before coming here, but it primarily subsidizes getting crushed by buses—not relieving pinched nerves. Mexico has had socialized insurance plans since 1943, but access to free health care is generally limited to citizens with full-time jobs (which excludes about half the nation, as well as me). One of President Fox's major initiatives is creating a universal health insurance policy called Seguro Popular,* but foreigners can't access that either. My options are singular: Farmacias Similares.

* By early 2007, some twenty-two million Mexicans had signed up for the plan, according to *Harvard Public Health Now*. The annual premium ranges from about 650 to 10,000 pesos, depending on family income, and the poorest 20 percent of the population is exempt. Both the World Health Organization and international medical journal *Lancet* have given Seguro Popular rave reviews.

Started in 1997 by entrepreneur Víctor González Torres, Farmacias Similares takes a Wal-Mart approach to health care: low-cost, generic versions of patented drugs sold in high volumes along with clinical services. It is the scorn of multinational pharmaceutical companies but a savior to poor Mexicans (some 2.5 million of whom use the services of the 3,700 franchise branches every month) and shallow-pocketed travelers. Its mascot is Dr. Simi, a portly, mustachioed cartoon pharmacist. Employees often don oversize costumes of him and salsa in the street to draw in the crowds.

A friend drives me to a nearby branch. I stand in a brief line and am escorted into an office presided by a woman in a lab coat seated behind a desk. She takes my temperature and pulse, examines my neck, numbs it with an injection, taps out a prescription on an electric typewriter, and sends me out the door in ten minutes flat. The injection cost 170 pesos, oodles of stomach pills are 60, and the consultation fee is 20. For less than 25 bucks, my neck and digestion normalize within forty-eight hours. This is one chain we need in El Norte.

The following morning I fly out to Tuxtla Gutiérrez, the capital of Chiapas in southern Mexico near Guatemala. To my left sits a chavo wearing baggy jeans, Nikes, and a bandana. He radiates nervous energy, fiddling with his Walkman and sneaking peaks at me. I finally ask where he is headed and learn that he is returning from Miami to visit his family for the first time in seven years.

"Seven years! How old were you when you left?"

"Just a chiquito. Fourteen."

His name is Marby. For the past third of his life, he has been working double shifts in restaurants throughout the American South—Texas, Louisiana, Alabama, Florida—and sending home $200 every fifteen days so that his four younger siblings can stay in school. He has no legal papers. "But look at these!" he exclaims, opening his wallet. Tucked inside are membership cards to Blockbuster and Sam's Club, a fake driver's license and Social Security card, and scores of banking and credit cards. This visit home will be brief: his boss in Miami can only spare him two weeks, and he'll need at least half that time to cross the desert again. I ask how he'll do it. "With a coyote. You can always find one in a cantina. It's dangerous though. You never know who to trust."

He asks about my plans and laughs at my apprehension of the Red Alert. "Tranquilo. You're a foreigner. The Zapatistas love foreigners. We are the ones who have to worry about them."

We are landing now. I write down my cell number and ask him to call once he has made it back across the border, so that I know he is safe. He promises.

At the airport, I catch a taxi to San Cristóbal, a ninety-minute drive dead east. Lush green jungle cascades into valleys on one side of the road and pine-clad mountains ascend on the other. Fog hangs heavily, unveiling villages only moments before we glide past. Women kneel in the earth, weaving on back-strap looms hanging from the highest points of their huts, symbolizing their connection to Ancestors (who whisper what to weave). Barefoot boys carry mounds of wood suspended from cloth straps around their foreheads; men walk in single-file succession balancing machetes atop their heads.

San Cristóbal is a jewel of a city paved with cobblestone streets, its colonial architecture splashed with rose on purple and tangerine on green. Baroque churches glimmer in the highland light. The taxi drops me off at Rosie's, a hostel popular with independent journalists and activists. I am hoping to get the skinny on the Red Alert here, but every bed is booked. Rosie walks me up a hill to a hostel painted electric blue called Posada

Cinco, which her son Roberto owns. He is chatting with three blond and bikinied women sunning atop batiks in the garden out back, which overlooks the city and surrounding mountains. I join them. The women flew out to Chiapas from Canada and the United States as part of an international delegation to do solidarity work with the Zapatistas, but the Red Alert scrapped their itineraries when everything closed down. Rather than revolution, they are now working on their tans.

"We should go horseback riding," one says, sighing as she rubs coconut oil on her bronzed arms.

"We should go to Belize," says another, stroking her navel ring.

Roberto gives me a tour of the hostel. I choose a private room with a window framed by bougainvillea inhabited by hummingbirds. He then offers me a late breakfast: fruit salad with yogurt, honey, and amaranth plus whole-grain bread and raspberry preserves. I carry my tray to the outdoor dining nook and do a double-take at the young woman smoking a cigarette there. The Great Lakes are tattooed across her chest and neck. Artichoke vines climb one arm; doves and compasses, the other. The words WING and ROOT are stamped across her knuckles. Her silky black hair is covered with a red bandana and her eyes are outlined Cleopatra-style. She introduces herself as Natalie, another Red Alert refugee. She was studying Spanish at the language school at Oventic, the Zapatista governing center closest to San Cristóbal, when she fell ill and traveled to the city for medicine and rest. When she returned a few days later, a sign hung on the front gate of the community that said CERRADO POR ALERTA ROJA. Closed for the Red Alert.

"Everybody was gone and everything was closed: the school, the clinic, the stores, the offices. I totally freaked out because I had left all my stuff there: my plane ticket, my visa, my clothes. Everything. I thought there had either been a terrible illness, like the plague, or the paramilitaries had stormed in and killed everyone. Something drastic. But I finally found some internationals camping out in the barn. I stayed with them a couple of weeks, but it was weird. Maybe if the paramilitaries came and tried to burn everything down, we could have stopped it, but since no one was there, why would they bother? Now I'm just hanging out here, waiting to see what happens."

The Zapatistas are planning the next phase of their movement, she says, but no one knows the details. In the latest communiqué, foreigners were simply instructed to stay away, that they would be "entering rebel territory at their own risk." Natalie hopes they'll be allowed back soon; she can only stay here until the end of the summer, when she has to return to Chicago.

"Are you a student there?" I ask.

She looks me up and down, to see if I can handle it. "I'm a dominatrix," she says, stubbing out her cigarette. "I must get back to my dungeon."

Natalie gives me a tour of San Cristóbal, which capitalizes on its revolutionary past rather astutely. Sidewalk cafés serve cappuccino in clay mugs painted with Zapatista ski masks; cinemas advertise nightly screenings of Zapatista documentaries. Shops sell Zapatista postcards, posters, T-shirts, books, CDs, and satchels. A bar called Revolution is festooned with red stars. Indigenous women mill about, hawking Zapatista dolls of every size, from earrings to key chains to something you could prop against a pillow, each one ski-masked and clenching a weapon. "¡Mira, Marcos!" they cry out. Look, it's (Subcomandante) Marcos! According to journalist Andrés Oppenheimer, Indian women started ski-masking their dolls during the 1994 uprising, at the suggestion of a Spanish reporter. Another reporter wrote about the "phenomenon," and the dolls became a sensation. I once asked a vendor if she considered herself a Zapatista. She shook her head and grimaced.

As we walk the streets, Natalie talks business. She opened her dungeon in 2001 and has since turned it into a cooperative, with several other dominatrices chipping in rent and helping run the place. She cares about her submissives and they pay her well, but it gets exhausting dreaming up new ways to torment them. A few seem to be undergoing withdrawals in her absence: her cell phone rings incessantly. She snarls into the phone, then hangs up with a sigh. "They miss me." She generally does sex work for three-month stints and then travels for up to half a year, doing performance art (burlesque) and volunteering in activist hotspots (Venezuela is next).

As dusk approaches, we enter a café for our first of many café-con-leche-fueled meals. I'm under the impression that Natalie is Chicana like me, root-seeking in Mexico, but no: her mother is white and father is Vietnamese. Although she grew up eating Vietnamese food and practicing certain cultural and religious traditions, nothing was fully explained to her. Her father taught her bits of the language, but all she remembers is how to count.

"Why did you decide to come here, instead of Vietnam?"

"Mexican culture has always been more comfortable for me. And it's not the emotional mind-fuck that going back to Vietnam would be. There, I'd be coming at what should be 'my' culture from the outside, as a foreigner."

This is why I majored in Russian and ran off to China. My ancestral culture felt too intimidating, and my ambiguous appearance permitted an escape. It is surreal to hear my story tumble from the mouth of a stranger.

"Do you think you'll ever go?"

Natalie drains the last of her coffee and sighs. "Sometimes I feel like I'm traversing circles around the world and its people to ultimately end up in Vietnam, learning to be a foreigner."

"It will be worth it," I say quietly.

The moon has risen. We traipse the city's periphery back to the posada. I gradually sense that someone is following us, and sure enough—a man slips behind a light post when I whirl around. He whistles.

"He must think we're prostitutes," Natalie surmises. "Just tell him we're not working tonight. When you approach men on a business level, they leave you alone."

Dominatrices, I'm learning, make highly desirable travel mates. They expertly assess situations, nothing fazes them in the least, and they say self-deprecating things like: "But what do I know, I just pee on people for a living."

While ambling about the following day, I come upon some indigenous women standing by a storefront. Each wears a black wooly skirt tied with a colorful sash and a satinlike blouse embroidered with flowers. Their skin is dark, their cheeks are windburned, their long hair is braided and woven with ribbons. And they speak a musical language that dates back to the Classic Maya civilization they descend from: Tzotzil.* One smiles and steps aside so that I can enter the doorway. It leads into an old courtyard home with cardboard, banana leaves, coconut shells, and other organic materials piled high in every corner. A couple of Tzotzil women are designing silk screens of Mayan folk-art patterns; another two are stirring bubbling caldrons of corn husks and palm fronds. One is laying out freshly recycled paper to dry in the sun.

I duck through a doorway into a gift shop that doubles as an

* More than 400,000 Tzotziles live in Chiapas. Other Mayan descendants in the state include the Tzelzales, the Tojolobales, and the Ch'ol.

art gallery, its shelves lined with cards, calendars, and journals. But I am drawn to a handmade book with a bas-relief mask of a goddess on the cover. Her almond-shaped eyes are excised so that she gazes almost hauntingly. The title page says *Incantations*, and the three hundred pages that follow are awash in prayers, stories, poems, and spells with silk screen illustrations.

"Every word in here is traditional; we didn't invent a one," a Tzotzil woman in an apron says. She turns the pages to a poem called "To the Wildwood" written in Tzotzil and translated into English.*

Sacred Mother,
Holy Woman in Flower:
Wildwood, Sacred Pine, Holy Oak:
I'm going to build my house.
I must chop you down
and raise you up as my house post
so I'll have a place to sleep. . . .
Give me your body to make my walls
to keep the rain out, the mist, the frost, Holy Mother.
Otherwise Mother Pukuj will eat me,
Woman of the Woods will frighten me,
Monster With Its Feet on Backwards will come to visit,
along with Boogey Man With a Hat Like a Griddle,
Charcoal Cruncher, Meat Stripper,
and snake, jaguar,
coyote, fox,
owl, night hummingbird, bat.
Holy Mother, Sacred Wildwood, I need your tree, your oak,
so I'll have a place to live where I'm not afraid.

---

* Cinco Puntos Press will publish a trade paperback edition of *Incantations* in 2008. This excerpt of Xpetra Ernándes's "To the Wildwood" was used with their permission.

"Are you Xpetra Ernándes?" I ask, noting the author's name.

She smiles. "Sí, but these are the words of our ancestors. We put them together for our children and their children so they will not be forgotten."

Books have a thousand-year-old history in Mayan culture. Early writers painted on stuccoed bark, but in time they developed long sheets of paper doubled in pleats that could be folded like cloth. Mayans recorded everything back then: rituals, calendars, prophecies, history. They pierced their tongues, dripped the blood onto the manuscripts, and stored them with reverence. During the Conquest, however, the Spanish destroyed all but a handful, claiming they contained "nothing but superstitions and falsehoods of the Devil." This is what makes *Incantations* so extraordinary: it is believed to be the first book Mayan women have written in five centuries.

Just then, a foreign woman with long, graying braids and Virgen de Guadalupe bottle-cap earrings enters the store. Xpetra introduces her as Ambar Past, the founder of this artists' collective, which is called Taller Leñateros. We chat a bit and she invites me home for lunch. Her carved wooden door opens into another veritable gallery. Charcoal nudes cover the walls. Tiny paper ornaments dangle from tree branches hung on a pole. We sit at a table covered with mud cloth and lilies and share a meal of tomato soup and bitter greens.

Ambar was raised in El Paso, Texas, and learned Spanish from her family's housekeeper. She ran off to Oregon with a boyfriend in the late 1960s and became a farmer, raising peacocks, catching salmon, and otherwise foraging for sustenance. "And then one day, I said 'This is too much' and left the breakfast dishes on the table and moved to Mexico!" She laughs. "Well, actually, I went to San Francisco first."

There, she met some "bearded wilderness types" who were planning to travel across Mexico. They just needed a translator—"a Spanish-speaking Sacagawea" to join them. Ambar raised some money selling bean sprout sandwiches to college students, then journeyed south with them in a VW bus along the coast toward Mazatlán. At one stop, they saw some traditional Huichol Indians* "dressed to kill" boarding a bus to their village. On a whim, they joined them. Ambar sat by a Huichol returning home from the army for the first time in years. He advised her not to do anything in the village but sit and wait and see what happened.

"My companions were dying to get invited to do peyote with the Huicholes. They even brought along beads and trinkets to get in with them. But I took the man's advice and just sat there, and sure enough, the Huicholes started inviting me places while the guys stayed behind."

One morning, they took her to a house where a woman was giving birth. They ground up peyote to rub on her stomach, then gave some to Ambar. "And suddenly I could understand Huichol!" She laughs. "And they could read my mind. That was my first experience with Indian people here, and it was a strong one. I was twenty-three at the time, and stayed three months. The guys never got in with them, I think because they had intentions. And I did not."

From there, Ambar's group continued on to Oaxaca and then Chiapas, where they attempted to raft down a river that eventually ran dry and found themselves stuck in the bottom of a canyon. They abandoned their belongings to climb out, tying themselves to rocks to rest and sucking flowers for moisture. When they finally reached their VW van, the men called it quits. Ambar, however, decided to stay in Chiapas until she was down to her last hundred dollars. That was in December of 1974. It hasn't happened yet.

---

* Every year, the Huichol Indians make a 250-mile pilgrimage from the mountains of Jalisco to the desert surrounding Real de Catorce in San Luis Potosí, where they harvest peyote for use in ceremonies and rituals. Shamans consume it to envision cures for illnesses and for guidance in harvesting and hunting; artisans, to create their psychedelic bead-and-yarn artwork of deities like corn, blue deer, and eagles.

"My big break was when a hippie gringo ethnographer who spoke Tzotzil started introducing me to people in Chamula [a village near San Cristóbal]. It was hard at first, because they just saw me as income. Ten pesos to stay with us for the night, five pesos for a lesson in Tzotzil, five pesos to see my grandmother's huipil.* Yet the experience blew my mind. I learned to weave, I learned to spin, I learned to dye yarn for weaving. I started asking people how to do natural dyes, but the women just remembered bits and pieces from their grandmothers. So I began to experiment."

All was bliss until she contracted an acute case of appendicitis, hours from the nearest clinic. The villagers feared that if Ambar died, the military would come and investigate. So the women filled a gourd with warm charcoal and massaged her stomach with it. "And I got better," she says. "That is when they noticed that I was mortal."

In time, Ambar learned Tzotzil and realized that half of what people said was poetry. She won a grant and started recording their stories, planning to share any profits that came her way. "And what I heard was amazing, stories about the Hurricane Woman and the Butterfly Man. They would tell me songs and prayers and magical spells. And it was all said in the most gorgeous fashion, in couplets and metaphors. I kept on recording for hundreds of hours, until we had our first book."†

---

* Huipiles are colorful embroidered blouses worn primarily by indigenous women. According to Dr. Ellen Riojas Clark, a professor at the University of Texas at San Antonio, huipiles reveal a great deal about their creators, including where they are from, their marital and social status, and something about their personality. The design, style, and color of huipiles change so dramatically from village to village, they serve as a textile road map.

† *Slo 'il Jchi 'iltaktik/In Their Own Words: The Lives of Four Tzotzil Women* was published in 1978 by CADAL in San Cristóbal de las Casas, Chiapas.

Soon after its publication, a Tzotzil woman asked Ambar to teach her natural dyeing techniques. Ambar climbed to her hut on the top of a mountain and ended up staying a whole month. While Ambar lay on her gunnysack bed one night, the woman sat beside her and began exploring her entire body with her hands. "She concluded: 'You are a real woman. You could even have children someday.' That was how I made my first real Tzotzil friend."

After helping open both a weaving cooperative* and a school for natural dyes, Ambar gravitated toward paper making. In 1992, she and her Mayan friends established the paper cooperative Taller Leñateros. They produce an art and literary journal called *Jícara* as well as calendars, journals, postcards, and some twenty-five books, of which *Incantations* is the most ambitious.

"Mayans have an ancestral memory of their ancient codices and they talk about them all the time, even though they've never seen them and many can neither read nor write. They learn things from books they dream about. They have entire libraries in their hearts," she says.

And it has boosted their self-esteem to see the interest their work has generated. An article the *New York Times* wrote about *Incantations* that spring brought in thousands of e-mail inquiries and sold hundreds of copies.

"Chiapas has only been a capitalist system since 1994. Before that, the entire economy was based on the exploitation of the Indians. When I used to come to San Cristóbal with my Tzotzil friends, they would shrink as soon as we entered the city. On the sidewalk, Indians would quickly step down so you could pass. People grew up thinking their Indian culture was shameful. Sometimes when we interviewed people to join Taller Leñateros and asked if they spoke any language besides

---

* The weaving cooperative, Sna Jolobil, still operates today out of the ex-monastery attached to the Templo de Santo Domingo in San Cristóbal.

Spanish, they would say, 'Oh, no!' as if we had asked if they practiced witchcraft or beat their children. Before 1994, if you spoke to people in Mayan, they wouldn't reply. They would change out of their traditional clothes as soon as they entered the city and buy something from a store."

These revelations are uncomfortably familiar: it sounds like my elders' descriptions of growing up Mexican in South Texas. My Tío Valentine tells stories of getting smacked with a ruler for speaking Spanish in class, and of being taunted for the green stains on his jeans that labeled him a "cotton picker" or "mojado." Yet he abided by the refrain: Lo que diga El Bolillo. Whatever the White Man says. Anglos were to be addressed as "ma'am" and "sir," and their authority never questioned. Only in high school did Tío Valentine learn the word "discrimination." Before that, being tormented seemed to be Mexicans' lot in life.

"What was so significant about 1994, aside from the Zapatista uprising?" I ask.

"What more do you want? The Zapatistas completely changed Indians' perceptions of themselves and what they are capable of doing. They also put San Cristóbal on the map. Businesspeople complained they scared tourists away, but al contrario. The major benefit I see from the Zapatista uprising is that Indians realized, Oh! We are worth something."

CHAPTER THIRTEEN

MEET ME AT THE HOUR OF GOD

Acteal, Chiapas,
July 2005

"Meet me at La Hora de Dios," she says, flicking her long, auburn-streaked hair over a shoulder and widening her eyes.

La Hora de Dios. That's God's time, Mayan time, indigenous time. It is one hour later than La Hora Oficial: official time, President Fox time, mestizo time. I nod.

"We'll be traveling through Zapatista territory, so bring your passport and visa. There might be military checkpoints. We'll spend the night in Acteal, where the massacre took place. Do you have a sleeping bag?"

Zapatistas? Massacre? Sleeping bag? I shake my head vigorously.

"I'll find one for you," she promises, then glances at her watch. "I must go now. Hasta mañana." With that, she kisses my cheek and leaves.

Her name is Rebeca. A friend suggested meeting her for coffee to get the lay of the Chiapaneco landscape, and I did—expecting, at most, half an hour of her time. But coffee evolved into pastries, which became a full-fledged comida corrida, and now an invitation into Zapatista turf to attend a baptism (I didn't catch whose).

She is an ageless woman, Rebeca. Her skin is as taut as a thirty-year-old's, but she orates like a silver-haired mystic. A mestiza social worker who has aided everyone from battered women in D. F. to the Sandinistas in Nicaragua, she has been counseling the Zapatistas since their 1994 uprising. And now, it seems, she is taking on me. When I told her of my mission here in Mexico, she vowed to help—as if one's roots could be dug with a shovel. Finishing up my café-con-leche, I wander off in search of a corn grinder, the gift she deemed most appropriate for our hosts. Whoever they might be.

And what was that about a massacre?

I arrive at our designated spot near San Cristóbal's main mercado the following morning. The streets pulse with commerce. Vendors push carts of mangoes cut like pinecones and coated with bees; girls swing fistfuls of live chickens by their feet. A weathered old man in a white tunic bends almost parallel to the ground as he transports a television set atop his back, while a boy strolls about with a dozen miniature xylophones hanging from his arms, shoulders, and chest.

Rebeca appears in a huipil patterned in brightly colored pinstripes and jewelry made of clay beads and seeds—gifts from people she has counseled. We flag down a taxi and jet off, norteña music jangling through the speakers. She says we'll be visiting a village split into two warring factions: the Zapatistas and the Priistas. The latter adhere to the Partido Revolucionario

Institucional (or PRI), the political party that reigned in Mexico for seventy years in what writer Mario Vargas Llosa pegged "the perfect dictatorship." Fox's PAN party ended their monopoly in the 2000 presidential election, but in indigenous communities, the PRI remains exceedingly powerful—and often corrupt.

In the late 1990s, the Zapatistas grew so disenchanted with the Mexican government they began forming municipios libres, or autonomous municipalities. With funding from supporters domestic and abroad, they opened their own schools, clinics, coffee cooperatives, and stores and refused government assistance.* While the Mexican government officially "tolerates" these communities, they dispatched some sixty thousand troops to keep an eye on them. They also pumped money into progovernment (that is, Priista) communities to both reward their loyalty and to lure away Zapatista sympathizers. Tensions can rise high between these factions, especially over issues like land rights and development. (Generally speaking, the Zapatistas chase developers away,† while Priistas welcome them.) When Priista leaders feel threatened by the Zapatistas, they occasionally hire local vigilante groups called paramilitaries‡ who intimidate, rape, and even murder perceived

---

* According to Miguel Pickard of the San Cristóbal–based Center for Economic and Political Research for Community Action (CIEPAC), the Zapatistas do take some forms of government aid indirectly, such as vaccinations.

† The Zapatistas occasionally resort to violence to ward off development, contending it will turn their land into "an amusement park for foreigners." In 2003, machete-wielding rebels seized an ecotourism lodge owned by former Peace Corps volunteers in the southeastern part of the state, briefly kidnapping one of the (Indian) caretakers and kicking out the rest. The Americans have since reopened their hotel in the nearby town of Ocosingo.

‡ In 1998, CIEPAC documented fifteen paramilitary and armed groups in Chiapas, including Máscara Roja (Red Mask).

opponents. This is all called la guerra de baja intensidad, or the low-intensity war. And we are heading into the thick of it.

After an hour's drive through jungle mountains, we pull into the plaza of a village. In the nearby mercado, women squat behind pyramids of mangoes and pears. Rowdy men hover over a painted and numbered board, tossing centavos on top of it. (Whoever guesses which number their coin lands on gets to swipe the board.) A lone man in a corner sells whole raw chickens on one table and X-rated comics with names like *¡Puro Sexo!* on the other.

"Priistas," Rebeca mumbles.

We walk toward the trail snaking up the tree-covered hill where the Zapatista enclave lives, and climb toward the sounds of fiesta. We are soon spotted by a band of women and girls, who rush down to greet us. They wear the same pinstriped huipil as Rebeca over navy skirts cinched with red tasseled belts, plus white shawls embroidered with red flowers. Rebeca speaks to them in Tzotzil, and their laughter rings out. Two young girls slip their hands in mine and lead me to the hilltop, where men await in black wooly vests and straw hats with colorful ribbons spilling over the brims. Rebeca proceeds to shake the hand of every single person on the premises, caressing the babies' heads. I follow suit, adjusting my typical grip-and-squeeze for their gentle touch. They smile with mouths full of silver.

Beyond the dirt path a quartet, who somehow dragged a Yamaha keyboard, drums, amps, and five-foot speakers up that hill, is playing rock music on a wooden stage. I walk over to listen and am surprised to spy some foreigners milling about. Members of a Catholic church in Tennessee, they traveled here to help build a corncrib and hold workshops on dental care. "We pulled one girl's tooth right out with our bare hands!" a sunburned woman in a floppy hat exclaims.

In time, the band announces that the baptismal family has arrived. We trot down the hill to greet them. From a truck emerges

Marta,* a caramel-skinned Mexican originally from San Luis Potosí; Matthew, a soaring Irish-American; and their two sons, the younger of whom will be baptized today. Both husband and wife are enrobed in native regalia, which must have challenged the tailor, as Matthew towers two feet above even the tallest Tzotzil. We accompany them up the hill as the band cranks out a welcome song.

The padrino, or godfather, of the baptismal child grabs a microphone and invites everyone visiting the community to step forward and introduce themselves. This is a lengthy proposition, as everything must be translated into English, Spanish, and Tzotzil. One by one, the Tennessee Catholics climb the stage and say how deeply this community has touched them. Many grow emotional, and when Marta takes the microphone, she breaks down. Her niece joins her onstage, and they hug a long moment before she reveals how good she feels to be back in her tierra, her nation, her Mexico.

I am searching for a bathroom when emcee-padrino calls me to the stage. I rather enjoy public speaking so am perfectly collected when I accept the microphone. Then I look into the audience. More than a hundred Zapatistas have gathered in identical native dress. Many are barefoot, with mud-caked toes. A few are unnaturally skinny. A little girl's belly noticeably distends, her huipil badly frayed. I want to explain why I have come to Mexico, what it means to be standing among them, but they stare back so intently, a golf ball lodges in my throat. I can only croak out my name. They applaud just the same, and the band revs up another number.

The padrino then leads the way into La Iglesia del Sagrado Corazón de Jesús, a small wooden chapel with a tin-sheet

* Before marrying Matthew and moving to the United States, Marta did solidarity work with the Zapatistas. Now she brings church members here two weeks every year.

roof. Pine needles cover the floor, and incense smolders in clay urns. Benches line the walls for the nursing and the elderly, but the rest of us stand, kneel, and bow throughout the two-hour Animist-Mayan-Tzotzil-Catholic* ceremony that ensues. At one point, the priest carries out a plastic tub of water and asks the baptismal parents and padrinos to step forth. Five babies are being baptized: Marta and Matthew's blue-eyed cherub and four tiny Tzotziles. Mexican Indians spend their first years of life tied to somebody's back or breast, so they look especially vulnerable outside their second wombs. The priest takes them one by one, holds them above the tub, and using a coconut shell, pours water over their heads. They all wail in protest but the American nears hysteria and doesn't calm for the duration of the ceremony. We sing. A dozen candles are lit upon a piece of wood. We pray. Old men in tunics play a hymn with a wooden harp, miniguitar, and a gourd full of beans. We dance, shuffling our feet with our hands by our sides. Next comes the peace offering, the communion, more hymns, and the blessing, and we are released into the sun.

The women of the village spent the morning preparing a giant kettle of cabbage and beef stew over a fire. They ladle out servings with a gourd and usher us to a table set with corn tortillas, limes, chile, salt, and bottles of Coca-Cola. I hungrily eat, picking the beef bits out of my soup and plopping them into tortillas to make tacos.

"Not like that," Rebeca says, shaking her head. Placing a tortilla in the palm of her hand, she rolls it tightly with her index

---

* Chiapas is actually Mexico's least Catholic state. Evangelicals, Protestants, Muslims, and other denominations make up about 36 percent of the population, and some are severely repressed by the Catholic majority, who perceive them as an affront to tradition. Many of the shanties on the outskirts of San Cristóbal are populated by religious minorities who have been expelled from their villages.

finger and takes a dainty bite. "Mexicans eat tortillas like this."

I manage to smile as everyone laughs, but am mortified. What kind of Mexican can't eat a tortilla properly?

After lunch, we settle beneath the shade trees as the band begins another set. Young girls gather around to peer at my lapis necklace. I am trying to pantomime its Uzbek origins when a man emerges from the trees, swinging a plastic bag and hollering. He wears cowboy boots and jeans and has shoulder-length curly hair. Upon capturing everyone's attention, he pops open a beer and chugs it like a frat boy. Alcoholism runs rampant in indigenous communities: stumbling drunks are a common sight along the shoulders of highways. But the Zapatistas strictly forbid drinking in their communities. When some men approach him, he lunges as if to tackle them, loses his balance, tumbles down a slope, and crashes into a hut, his stash trailing behind him. Picking himself off the ground, he cracks another beer and begins to guzzle. Just then, his entourage—an elderly man and two painfully embarrassed women with babies strapped to their backs—appear out of the wilderness. Without a word, they slide down the slope, grab a limb, and drag him away. He serenades them with a corrido.

"Priistas," people whisper.

Rebeca takes this as our cue to leave. We bid everyone farewell with hugs and handshakes and head to the bottom of the hill. A mountain taxi soon pulls up: a truck with a tall metal cage built inside its bed, perfect for transporting people, animals, or both. We clamber aboard, secure a spot unoccupied by chickens, and hold on tight as we trek deeper into Zapatista territory. Wooden billboards depict girls wearing bandanas across the bridges of their noses, so that only their eyes are visible. Printed beside them are the rules of this rebel land: No Alcohol, No Marijuana, No Stolen Cars. Storefronts are painted with murals of Che Guevara and the Virgen de Guadalupe in black ski masks, but their doors are bolted and chained.

"The Red Alert," Rebeca shouts over the motor and wind. "No one knows when they'll reopen."

As we ride, the sky turns dark. The daily downpour is imminent. We curve around a mountain and a giant obelisk appears on the side of the road. The truck drops us off beside it. Dozens of human bodies writhe together in anguish, some twenty-five feet high. THE OLD CANNOT KILL THE YOUNG FOREVER, its plaque reads.

"La masacre," Rebeca says. The massacre.

It happened three days before Christmas in 1997. Tensions between Priistas and Zapatistas flared to an all-time high, and the members of this community—a village called Acteal—felt exceedingly vulnerable. They had recently formed a coffee cooperative that exported organic brew directly to Europe, bypassing (Priista) intermediaries. They also sympathized with Zapatista causes (although they disapproved of their use of arms). For weeks, Zapatista supporters in neighboring communities had been receiving death threats from paramilitary groups. Houses had been burned; women raped. The Fray Bartolomé Human Rights Centre of San Cristóbal circulated news releases that called the situation extremely grave.

At 10:30 A.M. on December 22, scores of Acteal villagers had gathered in their chapel for Mass when seventy paramilitaries armed with AK-47 assault rifles and machetes stormed inside. They murdered everyone they could catch, then chased the survivors into the jungle. At the entrance to the village—where Rebeca and I now stand—forty state police awaited in patrol cars. Though they could hear the sound of gunfire, they did not intervene. The army is also believed to have been within earshot. The killings continued for about six hours, until eighteen children, twenty women (four of them pregnant), and seven men were dead, either shot in the back or repeatedly slashed in the face. Their bodies were then loaded into a cargo truck and hauled away.

A few hundred feet from the obelisk is a store that appears to be open. We enter. Crates of Coca-Cola products (Coke, Strawberry Fanta, Orange Fanta, Agua Ciel bottled water) hog half the floor space, along with bags of potato chips, cookies, Ramen noodles, beans, candy, and candles. It is like a Harlem bodega: junk food for the poor. I comment upon this as we walk down the hill, and Rebeca describes the integral role Coca-Cola plays in Mayan culture.

"They used to drink posh [an alcoholic substance] during their ceremonies but have switched to Coca-Cola because it is cheaper and doesn't contribute to alcoholism," she explains. "They also believe that when they burp up the gases, evil spirits are released."

This isn't the only "alternative" use of Coca-Cola in indigenous Mexico. Ilol, or shamans, use it in a number of their curative rituals along with candles, live chickens, and raw eggs. To celebrate a baptism, parents often invite friends and family over to "hug" the baby, or share a Coke with them. The more bottles the host family accumulates, the higher their prestige. I will later meet a doctor who treats burns that have become severely infected because Coca-Cola has been poured over them, in the belief the wounds will magically heal.

We reach Acteal's housing settlements, built at varying levels of the downward-sloping hill. One has a mural of brown hands holding a cross against a backdrop of doves and bees. It is the national headquarters for Las Abejas (The Bees), a pacifist organization that supports every aspect of Zapatismo but the bearing of arms. Most residents of Acteal are members, and Indians travel from across the country to attend meetings and workshops here.

We follow the dirt and rock trail to its jungly end where a hut stands: the chapel where the massacre began. Rebeca opens the creaky wooden door. Inside is dark save for candle glow, but I can make out a Virgen dressed like a Tzotzil in a tiny white shawl embroidered with flowers. She slumps over in her glass case.

"She was shot that day too," Rebeca whispers. "The women wrapped her wounds."

After praying our respects, we walk outside. The sun is bleeding upon the horizon. We watch it from a wooden platform overlooking the highlands. A young man in a blue button-down shirt and trousers soon joins us. Rebeca greets him warmly. He is Francisco, the recently elected catequista, or moral authority figure, of Acteal. He welcomes us to pass the night in a nearby hut and escorts us over as thunder rumbles. We beat the rain by seconds. As we sit upon the raised wooden platforms that will serve as our beds, Francisco tells us about his life. The eldest of six, he only studied through primaria, as his father needed help tilling the earth. Their family once sold corn and coffee in nearby mercados, but NAFTA has driven prices so low,* it costs more to grow these crops than what they would earn by selling them. They are now subsistence farmers, tending only what their family can eat and allowing the rest to go fallow.

"Food is our biggest problem here. My family has tortillas and coffee for breakfast, lunch, and dinner. Even beans are too expensive now."

My stomach chooses this inopportune moment to roar. Rebeca covers for me: "Tell Stephanie about that day."

"I was with my family when the paramilitaries came. We were standing in front of those rocks outside, talking with our neighbors, planning our Christmas," Francisco says in a voice so soft we must lean forward. "They came at us from everywhere. Atop the mountain. Down the mountain. From the trees. We ran and hid but could hear the gunshots. The screaming. It went on so long, we didn't know what to do."

---

* According to a 2003 Carnegie Endowment report, some 1.3 million Mexican farmers have been forced to quit their fields since the implementation of NAFTA, due to the tanking of prices. The bulk have either migrated to urban areas or headed to El Norte.

"What *did* you do?" I ask.

"We prayed."

Lightning brightens the hut. "And after the paramilitaries left?"

"We prayed some more. Then we became desplazados [displaced]. But not for long. We returned to Acteal, and people from other villages came too, to protect us."

"Did you lose anyone?"

"Only my mother, María Pérez Oyalte. She was at Mass when they came."

"Only" is an appropriate qualifier, as so many lost more. Like Zenaida Pérez. In addition to being shot through her brain and permanently blinded, this four-year-old child lost her mother, father, two sisters, and brother. Pinned beneath her dead mother's body for hours, she somehow escaped notice as the paramilitaries hovered about, firing or stabbing at anything that moved.

"What was the government's response?"

"They never did anything about it, never said anything about it, never offered to help."

Perhaps because they were responsible. A year after the killings, a special federal investigator issued a report stating that police had supplied the paramilitaries with their automatic weapons. But while the interior secretary got canned, the governor of Chiapas resigned, and some high-level officials including the state attorney general were barred from public office for a minimum of eight years, only a few officials served any jail time.

"For so long, our children were afraid," Francisco says. "Anytime a dog barked, they thought the killers had returned. Now things are tranquilo. But still we have no weapons in our community."

"Why not?" I breathe.

"We're Tzotziles. We're Abejas. It is not part of our culture."

Rebeca eases the conversation to lighter topics. His four children. The weather. I take out the hunk of gingerbread stored in my backpack. Francisco accepts some for his family and wishes us a peaceful night.

"I was here in 1997 too," Rebeca says as she bites into the bread. "We were walking around one afternoon when we came upon a military outpost.* A soldier put his hand in front of my camera and told us to leave. We could see houses burning in the village below. Tortillas were left on the comales. The village had just been attacked, and the people had run away."

She faces me. "That is how people became Zapatistas. That is why they took up arms and joined the EZLN. Why return home when your house has been burned and your animals killed? To wait for it to happen again?"

Within minutes of bidding me sweet sueños, Rebeca is snoring beside me. I, however, am wide awake and fully attuned to every noise that breaks the night. Flicking on a flashlight, I examine the butcher paper that covers the walls of the hut. Groups like the Fray Bartolomé Human Rights Centre routinely send observers into these communities for periods of two weeks and more—the optimism being that the army or paramilitaries would be less likely to use force against a village inhabited by outsiders. This strategy was employed in the 1980s in Central America as well, with foreigners serving as "human shields" to protect villagers from Contra attacks. In Acteal, observers sleep in this very hut—and many have left their signature. *Ciao Chiapas!* wrote an Italian; Paola from Spain tabulated each of her fourteen days here two summers ago. A Japanese uses Kanji to inscribe a message.

How can the Abejas refuse to be armed? Ever since someone

---

* According to the Center for Political Analysis and Social and Economic Research (CAPISE) in San Cristóbal, there are 111 military outposts in Chiapas.

kicked in—but did not enter—the front door of my parents' home while we were sleeping, I've kept knives beneath my bed; my father, a gun. And nothing even happened to us. I cannot fathom the courage it would take for a village to refrain from similar protective measures after a significant portion of its members had been slain. Especially now. Wouldn't this be a prime time for the paramilitaries to return, given that so many Zapatista enclaves have closed for the Red Alert? According to the nongovernmental organizations I will later interview, only about a half dozen human rights observers are scattered around Zapatista territories at this time, and Rebeca and I are the only ones in Acteal.

What would we do if someone came? Jump in front of their convoy and snap their photo? Threaten to call someone on my out-of-range cell phone?

Roosters herald dawn. It is a relief to hear them. I walk to the overlook to watch the sun rise, startling a man in the process. Clad in a belted tunic and galoshes, he carries a Coke bottle around his waist and a hoe over his shoulder. I am wearing pajamas with a towel draped over my shoulders. We exchange a wide-eyed once-over and trade buenos días before he disappears into the banana leaves, descending to the coffee fields below.

The door of a nearby cement building opens and a young woman steps out. A pink comb is stuck in her hair in that casually defiant manner of urban youth, and she wears a huipil, embroidered skirt, and plastic sandals. Her name is Roselia, and she traveled to Acteal from her home village to study medicine. I ask about health problems in the area.

"Intestinal issues, especially among the little kids, who don't know to be careful," she says. "Women have a lot of children here—ten, thirteen, some as many as fifteen. My mother had twelve. I don't have any. I am twenty-five and single and that is how I like it. If a man wants to be with me, he can follow me around."

She must be a Zapatista.* I ask if it's unusual not to be married at her age.

"Some girls marry as young as twelve or thirteen around here. But I have too much to do. I never finished preparatoria. My mamá didn't let me. She said I needed to take care of my brothers and sisters. Now I think that I don't like that she did that."

We talk about societal pressure to get married and what a drag it is and how even our friends who've been holding out with us are starting to give in and how some are even reproducing. Then she tosses something new into the equation.

"There are also a lot of women here who have babies from men in the army," she confides.

"They fell in love with soldiers?" I ask, surprised.

"No, they were robbed," she says, using the euphemism for rape.† "It is very hard, because they have to raise the baby on

---

* The Zapatistas have recruited quite a few women through their Ley Revolucionaria de Mujeres (Women's Revolutionary Law) that—among other things—grants women the right to decide when and whom they marry.

† According to government statistics, as many as 130,000 women are raped each year in Mexico. Women's rights groups claim that only about 1 percent are punished (and, in many parts of the country, stealing a cow carries tougher penalties). A young girl often must prove she is "chaste and pure" before accusing a man of statutory rape, and in nineteen states, rape charges will be dropped if the perpetrator agrees to marry his victim. See Marion Lloyd, "Mexico to Compensate Woman Denied an Abortion after Rape," *Houston Chronicle,* March 8, 2006, A1; and Mary Jordan, "Machismo's Dark Side: Rape Often Goes Unpunished in Mexico," *Washington Post*, July 6, 2002, B3.

their own. No man will marry them. And if they are already married, they must separate."

This quiets us. Finally I ask why she thinks the army does such things to her community.

"We're at war. War over our land. War over our water. War over our liberty. But now the soldiers are leaving our area. They are abandoning their posts. We don't know why. Do you?"

She looks at me with questioning eyes, and I feel afraid for her. I shake my head as Rebeca approaches. They greet each other like old friends and the conversation takes a seemingly happier turn: Roselia's upcoming trip to Mexico City. I don't catch what she'll be doing there, but she seems worried.

"You'll be fine!" I interject. "You can visit the Zócalo, the Museum of Anthropology, Frida Kahlo's house. . . ."

"Whose?" Roselia asks.

I chatter away about the fantastical painter, happy to make the introduction. But Rebeca later tells me that Roselia is going to D. F. to search for her brother. He migrated two and a half years ago to find work, and the family hasn't heard from him since.

Roselia must go to class now. When we hug good-bye, she grips me tightly. My head fits squarely on top of hers, so that I peer down her long, ribboned braids. When we part, I cannot read her expression. A Lakota friend once told me that to be Indian is to be a little bit happy and a little bit sad every day. So seems Roselia.

"Let's go see the memorial," Rebeca suggests.

We walk along a path to the massive amphitheater built especially for Acteal's memorial services for the victims of the massacre. Held every twenty-second of the month, the services draw hundreds if not thousands, including many foreigners. We descend the steps to the memorial beneath. Along a brick wall hang framed portraits of the dead: babies, children, holy men, and women, four of whom were pregnant. One entire family was wiped out: a husband, a wife, and five little girls.

"Where are their graves?"

"Beneath us."

We descend more steps to the altar. A chalice contains the ashes of slain victims from a massacre in Guatemala, brought to Acteal as an offering of solidarity. Murals depict communities holding hands in fields of maize graced by a Virgen in bandages. JUNTOS CONSTRUIREMOS UN MUNDO DE PAZ CON JUSTICIA Y DIGNIDAD it reads. Together We Are Building a World of Peace with Justice and Dignity.

We must go now. Rebeca is needed in a Zapatista community in another part of the state. I cannot accompany her, due to the Red Alert. Packs on our shoulders, we climb up the hill to the main highway. We pass many people: children swinging machetes; grandmothers lugging firewood. We also pass the public dump: the side of a previously pristine mountain. Refuse tumbles into the jungle below.

"Their primary water source is down there too," Rebeca says, shaking her head. "But ni modo. There are no garbagemen out here."

I haven't learned much about Rebeca these past twenty-four hours. Who is she and why has she so committed herself to this work? I start asking questions. No, she isn't married. Sí, she once had a child. A son. He died a few days after he was born. "We were in Nicaragua. It was the 1980s. There was no medicine," she says evenly.

This inspires other questions, but a San Cristóbal–bound taxi appears in the distance. She waves it down for me. "We'll go to Polhó next, home of the desplazados [the displaced]," she promises. "Meet me in the mercado on Sunday at ten."

"In La Hora Oficial or La Hora de Dios?"

"De Dios, of course." She smiles. At the Hour of God.

With that, my taxi parts, leaving Rebeca on the winding highway, a lone figure that within a turn vanishes in the tropical landscape.

CHAPTER FOURTEEN

THE PEOPLE WITH NO PLACE TO GO

Oventic and Polhó, Chiapas,
July 2005

A note from Natalie awaits my return: "The Red Alert is over. Returned to Oventic. Come visit."

Each of the Zapatistas' thirty-eight municipios libres—autonomous townships—is governed by one of five caracoles. The literal translation of "caracol" is "shell," which symbolizes the opening of a heart in Mayan culture. Oventic is the caracol closest to San Cristóbal. Foreigners describe it in almost idyllic terms, as a utopian society where everyone sings and recycles. Rumor dictates that you need a letter of introduction from a "Zapatista solidarity organization" to gain entrance through the front gate, and you must then seek permission to stay from a Junta. I actually acquired such a letter from an activist group five months ago, but for an entirely different purpose. I bring it anyway, hoping it will suffice.

Combi vans and collective taxis depart from San Cristóbal's bustling mercado for a multitude of destinations. I maneuver through the crowds, calling out the name of mine. People direct me to a combi with two passengers: an Italian* with double lip piercings and an Israeli with earlobe stretchers. I know without asking that we're headed to the same place. (When I later ask Rebeca what Zapatistas think of this urban interpretation of tribal life, she says they understand that their supporters live on the fringe, like they do.) We wait an hour for the combi to fill before jetting off on a winding mountain road that steeply ascends into mist. Along the way, we pass a wickedly drunk man sprawled in the middle of the road. He swings at our tires with a tree branch. We miss him by inches. Propaganda soon proliferates. In some villages, everything from piles of rocks to storefronts are painted the colors of the Mexican flag—green, white, and red—and spell out PRI. Other villages feature billboards of ski-masked faces and quotations by Subcomandante Marcos.

Forty-five minutes later, we pull up to the front gate of Oventic. The entire community is awash in colorful murals. The nearest depicts a woman reading a book, her blue hair flowing in rivers of constellations, musical notes, corn, and fish. A twenty-something man and a middle-aged woman guard the gate: the Commission of Vigilance. The Israeli, Italian, and I approach them. They stare at us wearily. I hold out my letter. The man examines it upside down, passes it to his compañera, and asks for our passports. We hand them over, and she walks them down the hill. He points to some benches, where a clump of foreigners await. All are heavily body pierced and tattooed.

The guard returns with a notebook. We jot down our names and organizational affiliations (I make one up), and she disappears

---

* The Zapatistas have ardent fans in Italy, including the nation's famed soccer team, Inter Milan. The team donated about $6,800, an ambulance, and a jersey to the rebels in 2004 and entertained Subcomandante Marcos's challenge to a soccer match.

down the hill. More time elapses. We strike up small talk. An Italian couple flew in on their own dime to spend the month building Oventic a new Web site. An American had hoped to conduct bicycle maintenance workshops, but now that he's seen the mountainous terrain, he worries the Zapatistas might not ride much. We are discussing this dilemma when everyone suddenly silences. I turn around. A woman is walking toward us wearing an embroidered huipil over a navy skirt and a black ski mask that covers all of her face but her eyes. Something Rebeca said comes to mind: "Indigenous people are treated like they're invisible here in Mexico, so the Zapatistas wear masks so that you will see them. And there is power in the fact that you can't see them, but they can see you. You are forced to look them directly in the eye because that's all there is."

We rise to our feet.

"The General Commission will receive you," she says.

We follow her single-file down the hill and enter a cabin painted with an ear of corn composed of Zapatista kernels. Two men and a woman in black masks sit behind a table beneath a black flag with a red star and the initials EZLN. It would be intimidating if the woman's head didn't teeter so precariously against the back of her chair as she dozed in and out of sleep. As we slide into the benches before them, the spokesman selects a passport and asks whom it belongs to. The combi guys rise and say they have come to photograph the caracol.

"Our murals: sí. Our people: no," he determines. "How long you stay?"

"A month," the Italian says.

"Or two," the Israeli quickly adds.

"Sleeping bags?"

They nod.

"Bienvenidos," the spokesman says. "You may camp in the barn."

The Italian and Israeli look at each other in surprise before bolting.

My turn. I rise and (stupidly) state that I am a writer who wishes to speak with their compañeros to help spread the word about their struggle and—

"Interviews: no."

My body quivers. "I mean—I have a friend . . . in Texas . . . who owns a fair trade store. I wish to buy. . . ."

"Shopping: sí."

I relax. "How many people live here?"

"Bastante." Plenty.

"Two hundred? Five hundred?"

"Interviews: NO," he says firmly.

I beg forgiveness, reiterating that I really am here just to look around and—

"Look around: sí. Shopping: sí. Interviews: NO. Adelante."

I grab my backpack and hurry out the door. The hill is dotted with cabins called Office for the Dignity of Women, Collective Café of the Resistance, and The People's Collective Music Store (where "revolutionary CDs" are on sale, two for a hundred pesos). I enter the health clinic and wander halls decked with murals advising patients against the following: defecating in the open air, walking around barefoot, lubricating condoms with cooking oil, and allowing dogs to lick their babies. A passerby notices my notebook, darts into a room, and returns with a three-page, single-spaced list of supplies needed by the clinic—everything from soap to ultrasound machines.

Tucked behind the January 1 Autonomous Rebel Zapatista Secondary School at the bottom of the hill is the dorm for the international students who study at the language school. A scroll by the door is inscribed with hometowns: Austin, Toronto, Ishikawa, Tel Aviv, Berlin, Madrid, the Bronx. The walls are made of cinder blocks, wood, and mud and impaled with wooden planks: bunk beds. Spartan, but cozier than the barn. Natalie walks in sporting a red Zapatista shirt, en route to Spanish class. I tag along but am denied entry. Prospective students must first undergo a background check through a Zapatista solidarity organization to determine their "activist credentials." Too bad: I was curious to see how they structured their lesson plan around the tenets of Zapatismo. (Natalie jokes that while she's learned to debate neoliberalism, she still fumbles buying mangoes at the mercado.)

I amble instead to the basketball court,* where some heated games are under way. The hoops have no nets, the balls are only half inflated, and hardly anyone stands taller than five foot three. Yet, the girls in huipiles and boys in button-down shirts hustle like pros, cutting, screening, passing behind the back, even slam-dunking. Cheers resound for every basket scored, and the victors laugh as they race down the concrete court (which reads ¡DEMOCRACIA, LIBERTAD Y JUSTICIA!). When one group's ball completely deflates, the players simply step off the court, form a circle, and play a new game—catch—against a backdrop of mountains and maize.

After class, Natalie invites me to dinner, served in a nearby store. Mugs of hot atole (rice, milk, and cinnamon) and slabs of bread await on a table propped up between a fridge and a stove. She introduces her fellow students. Roger is a classically trained guitarist here compiling a book of Zapatista songs; Canadian Jen is researching her thesis on women and globalization; Canek is a Chicano anarchist studying Tzotzil. No one is certain what Alan—a Frenchman—does, as he speaks little English or Spanish, but he bows his head hospitably.

Night has fallen. The sky glitters with stars; the air feels crisp and cool. We return to the dorm, where Natalie and Roger pull

---

* In the 1980s, the governor of Chiapas decided basketball was the key to fighting alcoholism and built thousands of courts. Critics say he secretly wanted landing platforms for military helicopters in Indian communities, but the sport has caught on, even in Zapatista enclaves. See Andrés Oppenheimer, *Bordering on Chaos: Mexico's Roller-Coaster Journey toward Prosperity,* Little, Brown and Company, 1996.

out their guitars. At the first chords of music, Zapatistas appear. Natalie offers one her guitar and he launches into the "Himno Zapatista" as a duet with Roger. Everyone sings along:

> Vamos vamos vamos vamos adelante
> Para que salgamos en la lucha avante
> Porque nuestra patria grita y necesita
> ¡De todo el esfuerzo de los Zapatistas!
>
> Let's go, let's go, let's go, forward,
> Out into the struggle
> Because our native land calls out and needs
> All the strength of the Zapatistas!*

Natalie accepts back her guitar and strums Lhasa's "Con Toda Palabra" in a sultry alto. Next up is Roger; then the Zapatistas take a turn. Corridos, ballads, marches, and love songs surge forth half the night. Canek and I swing together in the hammock above some turkey chicks, humming at the moon. When sleep calls, I crash on an empty plank in the dorm.

The following dawn, I rise with the roosters and follow a trail to a row of dry latrines. A youth brigade alternates cleaning them out with buckets and brooms and spraying one another with the water hose. I swing in the hammock until the others awake, then join them in the store for a breakfast of eggs and black beans. We are washing our bowls when two women enter and exchange sharp words with the cook. An unauthorized person spent the night on

---

* Lyrics for the "Himno Zapatista" were taken from the songbook *Canciones Zapatistas*, compiled by Zapatista supporters and distributed by AK Press and Rebel Imports.

the premises: does she know who it is? My stomach churns with the realization that they are talking about me. I briefly consider fleeing but turn myself in. They aren't happy. I should have slept out in the barn, they scold, and I had no right to eat. I beg for a way to ameliorate the situation. The women discuss this in Tzotzil for such a long time, I envision scary scenarios, starting with a self-criticism before the Junta. Finally, they reach an accord: a 40-peso fine. This is two days of wages for them; seventeen minutes for me. I try not to think of this as I hand over the money, guilty as charged.

I return to San Cristóbal that afternoon and meet Rebeca at the transportation hub by the mercado the following morning. Before we can visit the desplazados, or displaced people, we must return to the baptismal village to pick up Marta (the mother of the baptismal baby) and a friend of theirs named Rafael. And to do *that*, we must fill our colectivo so the driver will make the journey. I walk out to the middle of the street and join the other drivers in shouting the name of our destination to passersby: "Yabteclum, Yabteclum, YABTECLUUUUUM." They howl in laughter, as does a nearby woman selling something hot and wet out of a giant blue pot. Atole! I buy two cups.

"Atole on Sunday morning is a very old Mexican tradition," Rebeca says as we stir the steaming liquid.

"Sí, my Abuela used to make it all the time," I hear myself say, then wince at my own audacity. My grandmother committed suicide when Mom was three years old.* She may never have even made *her* atole.

---

* The woman I grew up calling Abuelita was actually my great-grandmother. Mom was raised by her aunt and uncle, Tía Benita and Tío Ben.

Rebeca's eyes light up. "Ahhh, your Abuela," she says with a knowing smile. "Your *Mexican* Abuela."

I hide my face in the Styrofoam cup and gulp the atole, scalding my throat. Why did I just lie to Rebeca? After the tortilla incident, was I worried she would ask for proof of ID?

"I have a story about atole," she says, swirling her cup. "There once was a chavo who couldn't afford everything he wanted. So he decided: I'm going to El Norte. And he did. But then came December twelfth, the day of the Virgen de Guadalupe, and he started feeling lonely. So he decided: I'm going back to my pueblo. And he did. He showed up at his mamá's house in his new baggy Levi's, his hair covered with a bandana, carrying his headphones and laptop. And his mamá said, 'Ay, mijo, what happened to you?' And he put on his headphones. That night, she said, 'Mijo, I made you tamales, your favorite,' but he said, 'No. I want a hamburger.' Then she said, 'Mijo, I made you agua de jamaica, your favorite,' but he said, 'No. I want a Sprite.' Late that night, she made a pot of atole and poured him a cup before he went to bed. 'What's this?' he asked. 'Just stir it and drink it,' she said. And he took one sip of the sweet warm milk and said, '¡Aaaaay, Mamá!'

"You see, Stephanie, it's just like you," Rebeca concludes with a smile. "Atole will make anyone remember who they are."

As well as, apparently, who they are not.

When our colectivo finally fills, we return to the baptismal village, where our party awaits. Marta is dressed in native regalia; Rafael—a bearded mestizo who teaches economics at the university—wears blue jeans. We pile in their car and head into Zapatista territory upon the mountain highway. At one point, we pass some villagers gathered around a disconsolate child screaming into her huipil. "That must be the little girl whose family died eating wild mushrooms," Rebeca says. "Seven of them. They knew the risk but took it anyway, they were so hungry."

A billboard announces our entry into the Autonomous Rebel

Zapatista Municipality of San Pedro Polhó. We pull up to its front gate. Two young men wearing bandanas step out of the shade. Rebeca presents a permit and allows them time to examine it before slowly reading it aloud. They consult each other in Tzotzil and wander off. A new man appears. Rebeca tells our story.

"But the permit only has two names on it, and you are four," he says.

"We have come to bear witness to the strides you have made in your autonomous school, your autonomous clinic, and your autonomous church," Rebeca says grandly.

"It doesn't say that here," he insists.

She smiles angelically. They stare at each other without blinking. Rebeca wins: we're allowed to park and proceed down the hill. The long, meandering trail exposes tin-roof huts on stilts and wooden shacks splashed with murals. Comal smoke slithers through treetops. After the massacre in Acteal, some eight thousand people fled here to safety. They set up encampments of cardboard and tarps and slowly began to starve. According to Rafael, more than a third of the children here are malnourished, and the adults suffer so many stress-related cramps and ulcers, they can hardly digest.

Our destination is a three-level wooden construction. As the others file in before me, I notice a cavernous building across the road. Steel bars serve as its door. A little girl sits before it, smiling shyly. I wave and she laughs, covering her mouth. I do the same, then follow the others inside. A dozen Zapatistas and Zapatista supporters greet me, all wearing traditional dress (but no masks). Like Francisco in Acteal, they are the catequistas, or moral authority figures, of their villages. They congregate in Polhó once a month to discuss issues affecting their communities and to hear lectures by sympathetic mestizos like Rafael and Rebeca. Their meeting room feels spacious and airy due to the screenless, paneless windows. Benches face a blackboard and an altar to the Virgen de Guadalupe; a large caracol, or conch shell, decks a table. A bare lightbulb dangles from the ceiling.

We sit with the women and help shell a gunnysack of green beans. They appear to save not only the little beans but bits of shell as well. I grab a fistful and hope for the best. Every time the women peek into my bowl, they burst into laughter.

Rafael, meanwhile, lectures about Mexico's bewildering political climate, and a bearded man translates it into Tzotzil. Of foremost concern is the July 2006 presidential election. The populist mayor of Mexico City, Andrés Manuel López Obrador, leads the pack by a double-digit margin.* He represents the Partido de la Revolución Democrática (PRD) party, although Subcomandante Marcos dismisses him as a "phony leftist." At one point, Rafael calls four catequistas to the front of the room and introduces one as Subcomandante Marcos, another as Obrador, and the remaining two as "The Pueblo" (that is, The People). He makes The Pueblo stand between the other two and asks them all to hold hands. Then he tells Marcos and Obrador to pull. "This is what Marcos and Obrador are doing to our people, pulling us in opposite directions. And The Pueblo, we don't know what to do. It is like a man with two wives who just can't choose." Everyone laughs.

During the break, Rebeca gives me a tour of the facilities. The top level is the meeting room; sleeping quarters are below; and the dirt-floor bottom serves as the kitchen, with enormous kettles bubbling over a fire and oil drums filled with water. Steps descend to an outhouse hidden by banana trees.

"It is so beautiful here." I sigh.

---

* In what was widely viewed as a conspiracy to keep him off the presidential ballot, Congress voted in April to strip Obrador's official immunity and remove him from the mayor's office so that he could stand trial in a dispute over a road construction. After one million Obrador supporters flooded the Zócalo in protest, however, the attorney general who oversaw the prosecution resigned and Obrador remained in office.

Rebeca nods, then points to a nearby mountaintop. "There is a military camp up there. They have cameras and sound recorders that document everyone who enters Polhó's front gate. They give kids candies laced with drugs and violate them."

We return upstairs for another hour of discussions. Afterward, the translator looks over at us. Is there anything we wish to contribute? Marta rises. Although she is as dark and petite as the Tzotzil women and dressed almost identically, she poses a stark contrast. Her sclera and teeth glisten white; her hands and feet are uncalloused; she maintains a normal body weight. And she begins her speech by almost apologizing for this, explaining that friends presented her with these clothes and she wears them out of respect for Tzotzil culture. I'm surprised to realize that she feels like an outsider here too—and is perceived as such, despite being born-and-bred Mexican.

Marta philosophizes about how the catequistas are out planting seeds so that corn might grow, and how their road is long but a light shines at the end, and they are part of that light. Such metaphors usually strike me as glib, but Tzotzil life is so rooted in the earth, no others would suffice. Marta grows emotional as she speaks, and something churns inside me too. When I rise to speak and the catequistas turn to listen, even my own clichés sound poignant. I end by assuring everyone that people around the world hold meetings about Chiapas, watch films about Chiapas, dream about Chiapas.

The translator stands. "Many people visit us from other parts of the world and they say the same thing, that people know about us in Italy, in France, in Canada. And we wonder, how can this be? We are just poor campesinos living in the mountains. How can we not be alone? But all of you say it, so we believe it to be true. And it gives us strength."

At that, the catequista band strides to the front of the room and plucks their oversize guitars and accordion. Covering their heads with their shawls, the women sing hymns in high-pitched voices. We kneel upon the wood floor before the altar to the Virgen de Guadalupe as the eldest catequista—dressed in a ragged tunic—leads us in rounds of Hail Marys. We say them in unison to a point and then our voices commence their own journeys. I've been rattling off bedtime prayers in the same order since childhood and can recite the Hail Mary in five seconds flat. But I pray now with focus, each word enunciated instead of slurred. Suddenly we are praying so loudly, the room seems to vibrate—and then our voices trickle off, fading into a silence that we hold long moments more. We draw crosses on our chests, kiss our fingers, and stand. It is time for supper.

We file down the stairs into the kitchen. There is one kettle of coffee, another of cinnamon tea, and a third of soup: the beans we shelled plus potatoes and an onion. The women heat corn tortillas directly over the flame until they turn crispy like tostadas. These will be our (edible) spoons. We eat standing up around slender tables, the men in the back, the women and children by the fire. Rafael explains that many Tzotzil phrases revolve around the heart. To ask how someone is doing, you inquire: "How is your heart?" To express thirst, you say: "My heart is dry." For remorse, you can choose from "my heart withdraws," "my heart weeps," "my heart grows small," and "my heart becomes two." A sixteenth-century Dominican friar compiled more than eighty Tzotzil metaphors that refer to the heart. Scholars call this a testament to the ancient Mayan belief that our heart is what makes us fundamentally human.

The women laugh at my attempts to speak their language, and they sound so joyous, we all join in. By the end, I need only look at them, and we share a good laugh. We rinse our bowls in icy water and store them in a bin. Rebeca and I return upstairs. She shows me the catequista's caracol and blows into it. The resonance is surprisingly robust. "This is how indigenous people traditionally call their meetings to order. The Zapatistas adopted it as their symbol to signify that every voice is heard."

The catequistas insist that Rebeca, Marta, Rafael, and I make our bed on the small wooden platforms while they spread blankets atop straw mats or benches. The eldest sleeps smack on the floor.

At sunrise, Marta, Rebeca, and I steal off to buy breakfast for the catequistas. The little girl from yesterday remains seated by the cavernous building with the bars. Her hair is gnarled and matted, her feet caked with mud. I wave and she returns it. Rebeca tells her story in a low voice: "Her brother killed someone and got locked in that cell, but their mother set him free. Now the mother must serve his sentence." I turn around, aghast. The child waves again, cheerfully.

Polhó's grocery store offers a wall-size window with a panoramic view of the village, but its edibles are limited. We buy four bags of macaroni and continue on to the street vendors. One woman sells bruised tomatoes. Rebeca orders a kilo and inquires about business. The woman modestly covers her mouth when she speaks, then wipes her face with the hem of her huipil—exposing her bare breasts in the process.

We return to the meeting room. The little girl is standing by the bars of the prison cell, holding a pail covered with cloth. Breakfast for her mother.

While the Tzotzil women cook the pasta, I head upstairs to pack and remember the crayons and coloring books tucked in my bag. I distribute them to the catequistas' children, who pounce two to a page and color industriously for the rest of the morning. After our meal, the conch shell calls us to the main level. We pray to the Virgen and sit upon the benches for a final hour of discussion. And then it is time to go. The women present me with a beaded necklace with a tiny Zapatista doll charm. Standing on their tiptoes, they hug and kiss my neck, their hair smelling of smoke and beans. The children approach me next. From behind their backs, they produce a page ripped from the coloring book of a dancing bear wearing a red star vest. I kiss each one on the cheek.

Then the translator walks over. "We don't allow outsiders into our community because of what happened in Acteal. That is why we are so strict," he says. "But we have given you the seed of our story so that you can plant it elsewhere. That is all we ask of you."

His eyes are so sunken, his cheeks so gaunt, this nearly does me in. I take his thin hands and make this promise as my nose bristles with thorns. As we exit the facility, the little girl by the prison cell grasps that we are leaving. Jumping to her feet, she calls out to her mother, who steps into the sunlight for the first time. Her hair is completely gray and her huipil badly soiled. Her limbs are emaciated. She slips her hand through the steel bars to wave at us and manages a smile. I saved no crayons for her daughter. This realization makes me cry so hard, Rebeca has to steer me up the hill.

"Why is this happening?" I gasp.

Rafael points to an especially attractive mountain peak. "Because they want to be able to say, 'Mira, look how pretty that spot is, let's put a Holiday Inn on it,' and then do it, without worrying about who might live there. Of course, they say they will do it so that the Indians can progress, so that they can be modernized, but do you think they are going to give the Indians any of the profits? You see how the people live here. All they have is their food and their clothes, and all they want is their land and some peace."

CHAPTER FIFTEEN

THE RECONQUISTA

Oaxaca,
July 2005

Time is evaporating. I've received a yearlong fellowship that starts in late August in New Jersey, which gives me one last month to explore. Between the murdering of activists and massacring of Indians, I worry I'm getting a distorted view of Mexico. When friends travel here, they return so relaxed and tanned. Maybe I should take a break, be tranquila. Everybody raves about Oaxaca, praising its artistic culture and culinary wizardry, so I hop a flight to its capital (also called Oaxaca). My timing is auspicious: their Guelaguetza festival is under way. Women dripping in beadwork greet us at the airport, proffering schedules of the parades that will caravan through the streets and the musical concerts and puppet shows that will be performed in the plazas. My taxi driver adds that you can get blitzed for ten pesos at the Mezcal Festival, where revelers shoot distilled spirits in every conceivable flavor: pineapple, mango, cappuccino, kiwi, almond. "I'm going tonight, if you care to join me!"

Sadly I can't. Chiapas butchered my digestive tract, leaving me so disoriented, it feels like I'm walking through clouds with shackles on my feet. Mezcal would be disastrous. I lean my head against the car window as we lurch past old stone buildings painted in electric hues like jade and cobalt. Jacaranda and hibiscus blossoms drape the stuccoed walls. Bands of indigenous women shuffle past in red-and-ribboned huipiles that extend to their ankles. We're not in Mayan country anymore: this is the ancestral land of the Zapotecs, the Mixtecs, the Triquis. They sell gardenias from baskets balanced atop their heads to tourists who appear both relaxed and tanned. I came to the right place!

The cabbie drops me off at the gate of my home for the next month. I'll be renting one of five bedrooms that open to a courtyard with an exposed living room and communal kitchen. My new housemate—an American college student named Susie—is reading on a couch beneath an avocado tree. Her digestive tract is in shambles too. Cautioning me against the dangers of dehydration, she hands over a bottle of Gatorade. I collapse into bed with it.

Hours later, an explosion almost tosses me onto the floor. Cannons? Gunfire? Paramilitaries? I clutch my blanket, panicking, until cries of drunken joy chime in. Firecrackers. Another round bursts through the night, so thunderously loud it sounds like they're being launched off the roof. The whole room quakes with every explosion. Sucking down Gatorade, I wait for sleep or sunrise.

The next morning, my body is leaden. I lounge around bed much of the day but am stir-crazy by dusk. I wander outside and wind up at a Guelaguetza culinary fair where regional specialties are prepared by knowing, wrinkled hands. There are plantains sautéed plump and sweet. Corn tortillas grilled with spicy green chorizo. Tamales steamed in banana leaves. Grasshoppers deep fried with chile, onion, and garlic. Oaxaca is especially renowned for its seven kinds of mole, a chocolate-based sauce containing as many as thirty ingredients simmered for days. Women stir great pots of it, the shades ranging from yellow-orange to brick red to manchamanteles (tablecloth-staining).

For dessert, crowds swarm around a family making buñuelos. First, the father takes a ball of masa, twirls it like a pizza, and lays it atop the bald head of a blue-eyed mannequin, where it rests until the mother dunks it into a wok filled with oil. It bubbles like a pimply balloon until she pops it with tongs and drains it dry. The daughter then sprinkles it with powdered sugar dyed red and a molasses of cane sugar and anise. Buñuelos are especially tasty with atole, which is being ladled from a pot two tables away.

What arouses my appetite is the tlayuda: a giant tortilla topped with your choice of asiento (pork fat), tasajo (beef), or squash blossoms, plus string cheese, refried beans, cilantro, and buckets of salsa, then folded in half and blackened atop a comal. I order a vegetarian one without cilantro.* Five minutes later, however, I'm served one with a whole bouquet of cilantro grilled inside. What to do? Sending orders back in foreign lands is risky: in Moscow, I once got kicked out of a restaurant for doing so. But cilantro is so noxious, I go for it, raising the stakes by declaring a severe allergy to the herb.

The cook glares at me. "¿Y luego?" And?

"And . . . if I eat this, I'll get hives and . . . get sick and . . . die. Could you make me another, please?"

Everyone within earshot offers an opinion.

"She wants you to throw away that entire tlayuda? What a waste!"

"Whoever heard of someone dying over a little cilantro?"

"Make me a tlayuda with *extra* cilantro!"

---

* I know, I know. What kind of Mexican doesn't like cilantro? To me, it smells and tastes like an armpit.

At last, someone comes to my defense: the gentleman seated beside me. "She said no cilantro. I heard her myself."

With a grunt, the woman dumps the tlayuda into the trash can and makes a new one, maneuvering down the row of ingredients and finishing off with a dollop of an unidentifiable black substance. I bite into it hungrily but something tastes strange. That black stuff? Everyone is watching so intently, I can't possibly make another fuss. I swallow what I can, then head home with a gurgling belly. Rosalinda—my landlady—takes one look at me and says I should try the homeopathy she has been practicing for years. It has cured her diabetes and entails nothing more than the daily drinking of something (I don't catch what). She repeats the word several times before resorting to English: "your pee-pee." Trying not to blanch, I thank her for the tip and flop into bed.

The contractions coincide with the firecrackers, starting around midnight. Sharp pains ripple through my belly, causing me to sit up in bed and scream. Like I'm giving birth. To something slathered black and nasty, wearing a crown of cilantro. This isn't just Montezuma's revenge.* It is the Reconquista. I crawl to the bathroom and fall asleep with my face pressed against the rim of the toilet, awakening in sunlight. My lips are the color of chalk. I stagger outside. Rosalinda and Susie are visibly spooked at the sight of me. Rosalinda says that I must commence her homeopathic regimen at once; Susie says I need a doctor. I want Dr. Simi. Susie wins and half carries me to the nearby hospital, where a young doctor with galaxies of freckles and moles stretches me out on a bed and presses my abdomen.

---

* One of the many (highly disputed) legends of the Spanish Conquest says that the famed Aztec god-king Montezuma believed that conquistador Hernán Cortés was the plumed serpent god Quetzalcoatl returning to reclaim his throne. It was a fatal mistake: the Spanish shattered his civilization in two years. Gringos who experience intestinal issues in Mexico are said to suffer from "Montezuma's revenge."

"She is completely dehydrated, probably from amoebas," he surmises. "She must be admitted at once."

Admitted?! Won't that cost a fortune?

Tranquilo, the doctor says. It won't be more than a thousand pesos.

Nurses lift me into a wheelchair and cart me off for gown-changing and form-signing. I try to read the paperwork but the words blur together. Susie deciphers one as a release form for the remote control, but the rest surpass her *Lonely Planet* Spanish. I sign them anyway. A nurse attaches an IV. Within half an hour, I've lost consciousness.

I awake to darkness, my body without sensation. I call out. No one responds. I am alone. You might think barren beds and other people's weddings are the worst part of being perpetually single, but no. Being all by yourself in a hospital is. I blink in the blackness, praying for someone, anyone. And then the light snaps on. It's the young doctor. I take his spotted hand and curl up to it like a pillow, so that he is forced to bend over me.

"You have so many of these," I mumble, stroking his moles.

"Those are called lunares," he says.

Like the moon. That is much more poetic than what Mom used to call mine: "places where a little bird crapped."

I bask in the warmth of the doctor's hand, hoping he'll climb in so I can feel even more heat. He doesn't, but he takes his time removing his hand from my grip. "You'll be fine, mija, just fine," he murmurs, patting my head.

And by morning, I am. A nurse holds up a mirror: my lips are pink again. I am relieved—until a new lady enters, dressed more like a businesswoman than a nurse. "Time to pay," she announces.

"Aren't you going to take this out first?" I ask, holding up my hand and its IV tentacles.

"Not until you pay," she says, handing me the bill.

Four thousand three hundred forty-five pesos! Granted, it's a fraction of what hospitals charge in the United States, but still. I viciously protest that the doctor said it would only cost a thousand.

"You can discuss that when he returns. But that won't be until late this afternoon. If you wait that long, you'll be charged for another twenty-four-hour cycle," she says crisply.

People undoubtedly bolted in situations like this, once upon a time. This must be why I am still physically restrained. This is also why Farmacias Similares is so popular: Dr. Simi doesn't extort. I make a production of unzipping my change purse with my teeth to extract a credit card and hand it over, glowering. Before she returns for my signature, Rosalinda drops in for a visit. I tell her what happened. She smirks. "That's what you get for not having faith in me!"

It's true. I could have drunk my pee for free.

CHAPTER SIXTEEN

THE STRIKERS

Oaxaca,
July 2005

My amoebas dead and my body rehydrated, I am ready for action. Some sort of tianguis (flea market) takes up most of Calle Libres, the street adjacent to ours. I slip through a metal barricade and search for its entrance. Quite a few people are inside, but it is enclosed by fitted tarps. As I try to lift one, shouts ring out. I whirl around to see some chavos with buzz-cut hair striding toward me. Angrily. One is filming me with a video camera. I back away from the tarp with my hands in the air.

"Tranquilo," one says. "We are just workers on strike."

"What kind of strike?"

"I'd like to tell you, but I can't," he says with an impish grin. He is a beefy boy with bad skin, maybe twenty-three years old.

"But you could tell us about you," says the one behind the camera, still filming.

Strikes are a fact of life in Mexico. It is virtually the only way people can finagle pay raises or improve their working conditions. I just missed Oaxaca's infamous annual strike, when thousands of public school teachers descend upon the zócalo, pitch tents, and demand better wages. (They generally stay the whole month of May before the government concedes a few pesos.) But in the many strikes I've encountered here, the protesters hold up signs, pass out flyers, and talk with whomever will listen. Why aren't these guys? As I consider this, more young men gather around, a little too closely. The fact that three policemen are within shouting distance is equally worrisome.

"I have to go now," I blurt out, climbing over the barricade and hurrying down the street. After two blocks, I hang a right and trot to the convenience store where Tino, my Gatorade supplier, works. I ask about the strikers, and he shakes his head. "You wouldn't believe it if I told you."

The office of Oaxaca's largest circulation newspaper, *Noticias*, resides on Calle Libres. Unlike most other state (and national) media, it fiercely criticizes the local government, which the PRI has ruled for the past seven decades. During the gubernatorial election of 2004—which was bizarre even by Mexican standards—*Noticias* staunchly supported the opposition candidate (said to be a close friend of its publisher). It wrote reams about electoral fraud, including vote buying, the "escorting" of voters right into the booth, the destroying of ballots from certain districts, and returns that exceeded the number of registered voters. It also mocked the outgoing governor's efforts to drum up PRI support by staging an assassination attempt on his own life.* Nevertheless, Priista candidate Ulises Ruiz Ortiz won by a 47:45 lead.

"Everybody knows they stole the election as usual, but *Noticias* was the only paper brave enough to say so," Tino opines.

---

* According to then-governor José Murat Casab, sharpshooters attacked his car in downtown Oaxaca in March 2004. When federal prosecutors determined that his own bodyguards fired the bullets from inside the car, he accused them of "moral lynching" and claimed that the only missing evidence was his "own cadaver." A bodyguard died in the debacle.

Just one year into office, Governor Ruiz has already alienated much of his constituency with antics like tearing up the green quarry stone that once paved the capital's zócalo and replacing it with cement. "It's so ugly everyone hates it, and it is costing us millions—and we're one of the poorest states in the country! I heard he did it because his brother-in-law owns the cement factory* and he's getting a kickback," Tino says.

Noticias has minced no words criticizing such deeds, referring to Ruiz as a "fascist" and his government as "the Taliban." And Ruiz has apparently had enough. After months of threats, hundreds of men from a (Priista) workers' union called the CROC descended upon *Noticias*'s office building on the night of June 17, set up tarps and barricades, and announced that they were *Noticias* staff members going on a salary strike. (Whether any are is a major point of contention.) Thirty-one "real" *Noticias* staffers were still inside the building, however, putting the paper to bed. They remained sequestered for the next month, sleeping on the floor and e-mailing stories about their predicament to their colleagues, who opened a makeshift office elsewhere. Despite these obstacles, *Noticias* never missed an issue, and tens of thousands of citizens held marches and vigils on their behalf. Presumably, this infuriated Ruiz even more. At 8:10 P.M. on July 18 (six days before my arrival here), the CROC stormed the building and everyone inside fled in fear.†

"You mean, those chavos on Calle Libres are just *pretending* to work for *Noticias*?"

---

* I never could confirm this rumor but heard it many times, from locals and expats alike (although in some versions, it was Ruiz's uncle who owned the factory).

† According to the Committee to Protect Journalists, Mexico is the world's fifteenth most dangerous place to practice journalism. From 2000 to 2006, six journalists were killed directly because of their work, and eleven died under "unclear circumstances." In most states, however, narco-traffickers pose the greatest threat—not politicians.

"Así es."

"And the real workers can't come in because they're blocking the way?"

"Así es."

This slowly sinks in. "So what are they all doing now?"

"Waiting to see what happens next."

Two men stand guard outside the makeshift *Noticias* office on Calle Guerrero. I slip past them into the hallway, where the first folding table serves as the reception office and the next two constitute the advertising department. Metal folding chairs make up the lobby. I've arranged to meet a few staffers, but none are here yet. The receptionist lends me her copy of the national weekly magazine *Proceso*, which features *Noticias* on the front cover. Judging by the photos, this office is quite a departure from their old one on Calle Libres. Gone are the ergonomic workstations with fancy swivel chairs. Now they work upon computers that were either donated, borrowed, or bought secondhand; their Rolodexes consist of phone numbers scribbled on Post-it notes. There isn't enough space for them either: staffers are stationed in offices around town.

After flipping through *Proceso*, I dig into the bound stack of *Noticias*'s back issues. The one from June begins midmonth. When I ask the receptionist for the first half, she looks at me sideways. "We don't have them anymore." The whole history of the newspaper—from date books to archives to filing cabinets—is trapped inside the old office.

Reporter Octavio Vélez breezes in. Midforties with ample facial hair, he wears jeans and carries a black courier bag. As we ascend the stairwell to the newsroom, he expresses bafflement at their predicament. "This never happened in Uruguay, Argentina, or Chile during all those years of military occupation and dictatorship. It never happened in Africa or the Middle East. Only here."

He has worked for *Noticias* fourteen years, covering social issues as well as labor disputes. The CROC is actually a legitimate union, he says. Only this strike is not. "There isn't one *Noticias* employee among them. Some are construction workers, others are campesinos, and a lot are gangsters. We have proof that the CROC pays them a couple hundred pesos a day plus food. Besides, what strikers have portable toilets and police guards?"

I ask about the night they got sequestered. He was in his office writing a story when the CROC came. "They blocked access to the doors and started yelling at us, banging on the doors, throwing stuff through the windows. We couldn't leave because they'd take our office—and we had a paper to put out. We couldn't call the police either, because they were the ones behind it. So we just stayed inside."

They organized into work crews to keep the office clean and the kitchen in order. Anticipating that something like this might happen, they had prestocked their cafeteria with canned goods like sardines, tuna, and ham as well as bread and cookies, but their supplies ran low as time dragged on. They ate just one full meal a day and had to drink water out of the faucet, which gave them diarrhea. It grew cold in the evenings, and they had no blankets save old newspapers. Several developed bronchitis, and their diabetic photographer, Román, fell gravely ill.

"He laid on the floor and didn't move for two days. We took turns watching over him. He refused to leave because he wanted to defend the paper with us. One of our neighbors finally sent us insulin through the roof."

The psychological torment was equally damaging. According to Octavio, some of the strikers had guns and threatened to use them. They stuck cameras in their windows and photographed them. When the staffers' families came for "visits"—

that is, standing across the street and holding up signs—they chased them away.

Then, in the early evening of July 18, a neighbor called to say that the CROC appeared to be plotting something new. They had ladders now and wore ski masks. Ten minutes after eight, they invaded, breaking through the front glass doors with clubs and pipes. "They came into our newsroom and started destroying our computers, our TV sets, our printers, everything. Then they began stealing our things—our beepers, our cell phones, our tape recorders, our money, our bank cards. They took my PalmPilot, where I store the contact information of my sources. We ran out and came here."

"You didn't go home first?"

"There were too many stories to write! What they wanted was for *Noticias* to stop being printed. We had to keep going—out of pride, out of dignity. Out of self-respect."

Octavio's phone rings with a call he must take. I shake his hand and walk down the row of reporters tapping on vintage computers atop folding tables toward the office of Editorial Director Ismael Sanmartín Hernández. His deep baritone voice echoes down the hall. I rap on the door before entering. A caffeinated man in a button-down shirt and tie, he is conducting conversations on both a landline and cell phone. He motions me to the couch. Wooden ducks decorate the built-in bookcase behind him; protest signs are stacked in a corner. He hangs up both phones and declares that he has been with *Noticias* "since its first instant" twenty-nine years ago but has never experienced anything like this.

"We have always been known as the rebel paper, and we go through periods of peace and war with the government. But politicians are less willing to accept criticism now than before, I think, because the PRI has lost so much power nationally. So we are like boxers: we duck and we duck and we duck and then we punch. If we criticized the government all the time, they'd kill us. But if a paper doesn't criticize now and then, why exist? To wrap your fruit?"

He opens a scrapbook, the cover of which reads CHRONOLOGY OF AGGRESSION AGAINST *NOTICIAS,* and flips through its pages. The latest round of aggression, he says, began with Governor José Murat Casab, who ruled from 1998 to 2004. He tried to buy half of *Noticias* so he could control its contents. When the paper's owner refused to sell it, Murat's cronies began prank-calling staff members and spray painting anti-*Noticias* rhetoric across the city. "During Murat's last week in office, they even came to the warehouse where we store our paper, ink, and delivery trucks. They fought our security guards and ended up killing one of their own men, only nineteen years old. They just left him there for us to deal with," he says, shaking his head.

The next round of photos are from the marches held downtown. *Noticias* staffers are shown chained together, wearing surgical masks and holding signs that say FREEDOM OF EXPRESSION IS A HUMAN RIGHT. Other photos depict *Noticias* vendors in the bed of a truck stacked with newspapers, fending off gangs of men. "Plainclothes cops," Ismael says. "They keep stealing our papers."

Our interview ends here—his phones ring incessantly—but I spend the next two days in his office, reading the scrapbook and whatever document he tosses my way. Staffers continuously flow in and out, soliciting his advice on everything from stories to ads to page layout. He marks it all up with a pica pencil and—in between sessions—fires off e-mails to newspapers and human rights organizations around the globe, asking for their help. Whenever visitors drop by, he invites them to join me on the couch. "Sorry there isn't more room," he says cheerfully. "We're in a war zone here."

The next morning, I return to Calle Libres and steal down the sidewalk opposite the CROC strikers, stopping at a white gate and knocking. A housekeeper opens the door a crack and I slip her a business card. She disappears with it and a middle-aged woman with gold-rimmed glasses returns. Without a word, she ushers me inside her elegantly furnished home. After asking a few questions through pursed lips, she consents to an interview. I deeply respect this about Mexicans: though they fear speaking out, they almost always do it anyway. Ismael had a hunch she would; he suggested coming here.

"You can't imagine how terrible this is," she says. "Those strikers get drunk every night and the government is paying them to do it and the police are here to protect them! We can't even go out at night anymore. We're prisoners in our own home."

She excuses herself to round up the neighbors who have helped her form a Frente Civil, or Civil Front, that recently submitted a petition to local and national government officials, demanding the strikers be relocated. The dining room soon fills with women with manicured nails and salon-styled hair. Our hostess—whose name is Isabel—brings out a pitcher of agua de jamaica and a platter of cookies and we sit around her dining room table.

"When the strikers first came, they were mostly people from the country," a plump woman begins.

"Humble people," says another, cradling her grandbaby.

"Campesinos," summarizes a third.

"They turned our street into a plaza with their tomatoes and onions and chickens. . . ."

"And containers of rice and beans."

"But now they are mainly porros,"* Isabel says. "One night,

---

* Porros are gangster-style hoodlums generally affiliated with universities, which use them as an informal army to repress student strikes and the like.

they will be porros; the next night, they will be plainclothes cops; the next—drunkards."

"One time, they were homosexuals!" the plump lady interjects.

"Homosexuals," I repeat.

"Oh yes!" She crinkles her whole face. "The CROC only sends the worst!"

"It is such an escándalo!" another cries, waving a handkerchief.

I steer the conversation toward the night the strikers stormed the newspaper building. Isabel claims she saw the whole thing from her rooftop and walks me up there to prove it. Sure enough, her deck looks out directly onto *Noticias*'s, some forty feet away. She points out the shattered light fixtures and boarded-up windows.

"I watched those porros climb in on their ladders and break those windows. Such horrible noises! I could see them beating up everyone inside."

Small businesses dot the neighborhood. "See that hotel? It is usually full this time of year with Guelaguetza tourists. Now it is empty. That hair salon is suffering too. And no one sends their kids to that computer school anymore. How can they? If you walk down the street, you'll get harassed."

On our way down the stairwell, we run into another neighbor: a hefty guy my age wearing a Nike tracksuit and baseball cap. She tells him I'm researching the strike, and he sighs. "Whatever you say about those strikers, you have to admit—it is a very impressive thing they're doing. They're like the Mafia. The Godfather. And this situation will only get worse."

"What do you mean?" I ask.

"Guerrero, Michoacán, Chiapas, Oaxaca. All those states are full of guerrillas revolting against the PRI. I could see Mexico having another revolution. An ideological one, like in Vietnam."

He says this matter-of-factly, as though it were inevitable. I turn to Isabel. Removing her glasses, she nods in agreement.

Vendors await the arrival of the latest edition of *Noticias* in the courtyard of the San Agustín Convent. When I arrive at eight, scores are huddled together on the stone steps, wrapped in jackets to ward off the morning chill. Some play cards; others drink coffee. I approach the loner, who is finishing a chorizo sandwich. Young and scraggly, he is swathed in black. His eyes alight with recognition when I extend my hand in greeting. (Yesterday, I spotted him carrying a bundle of *Noticias* and chased after him. He suggested meeting here to talk.) He has been selling newspapers since he was ten, but his job turned precarious on June 2, when plainclothes policemen started snatching them. They took a hundred papers from one friend; eighty from another; and hauled *him* down to the police station. "They took everything. My ID, my money, my newspapers. They later returned my money and ID, but they kept the papers—about two hundred pesos' worth. They said I needed a permiso to sell them, but never once in fifteen years has anyone asked for one. They came again a few days later, but just got out of their car and threatened me. They didn't detain me."

We're soon joined by Armando Pérez Rivera, a representative of the vendors' own union. A salt-and-pepper seventy-year-old, he wears a cowboy hat and slacks. The other vendors gravitate toward us as he speaks, which he seems to enjoy. "I've been selling newspapers for twenty-five years, about four hundred copies a day. Mostly *Noticias*; *Imparcial* doesn't sell too well. . . ."

"And *Tiempo* sells even less because [former Governor] Murat owns it!" interjects a vendor named Clara. She is so sunbaked, even the whites of her eyes are brown.

Everyone laughs; Armando continues. "Never once in all that time have I had a problem. But after Ulises Ruiz got elected, plainclothes police started riding up on their motorcycles and stealing our papers. They took sixty-eight of my copies one day and one hundred sixty the next, and—"

"There is no justice here!" Clara shouts. "All of our media is bought by the government! Only *Noticias* is of The Pueblo [The People]!"

Armando glares at her before switching topics. "Our union wrote a complaint and took it to *Imparcial,* but they refused to print it because the government has bought them too—"

"There is no freedom of expression in Mexico!" Clara interrupts again. "We might as well be mutes!"

After thanking Armando for his time, I turn to Clara. At thirty-six, she has been selling *Noticias* with her mother for a quarter century. They arrive here around 4:30 A.M. each day to ensure a good spot in line. It generally takes four hours to sell a stack of three hundred; they profit one peso from each. "During the repression, the paper sometimes didn't arrive until four P.M., and we had been waiting since four A.M. But we waited because we wanted to support *Noticias.* All of us vendors marched at their protest. If we don't defend each other, who will?"

Everyone returns to the stone steps. I join them for the wait. Around nine thirty, the sun peeks out from the clouds. Top layers shed; coffee cups refill. An hour later, a plane flies overhead. "Here they come!" they shout, pointing it out to me. "*Noticias* is on the way!"

An unmarked van pulls up half an hour later and is unloaded in ten minutes flat. "It always comes in a different van, to lessen the chances of getting robbed," Clara whispers.

Side by side, the vendors rapidly assemble their stacks of papers, tie them into bundles, and bolt—some on foot; others on bicycles. Two men pile theirs atop the backseat of a motorcycle, and one sits upon the stack, his feet barely touching the seat. When his partner revs up the engine, he bends over to grip his shoulders for balance. It looks so dangerous, I cringe.

"Ayo, Silver!" someone shouts.

With a triumphant beep of the horn, they wave and roar away.

Perhaps because I am not affiliated with an official news agency (or anything, for that matter), my calls to the office of Governor Ruiz go nowhere. I've met politicians in other cities by simply dropping in, but that isn't so feasible here. Soon after taking power, Ruiz moved the House of Government from the zócalo downtown to Santa María Coyotepec, a town half an hour away. (So many protests were fomenting beneath his old office window, he said he wished to "avoid distractions.") Instead, I pursue David Robles, PRI lawmaker and the leader of the CROC. Supposedly he visits the strikers on Calle Libres twice a day, but whenever I show up at the specified time, I'm told to return several hours later. When I do, they say that I just missed him; can I come back mañana? After two weeks of stonewalling, I declare a strike myself, grabbing hold of their barricade and refusing to leave until I meet with him. This unnerves his gatekeeper enough to make a few phone calls. Meanwhile, a brawny boy with a buzz cut is sent over with plastic chairs. We sit upon them on the street curb beneath the shade. I halfheartedly ask if he really works for *Noticias* and he halfheartedly says sí. We are quiet for a long time, until his curiosity leaks. Who am I and why do I keep coming back?

"I've always wanted to do that, study languages and travel," he says after I share my story. "But I didn't pass the university exam. Hardly anybody does. If five hundred take it, only like seventy will pass—and those who do usually bribe someone. The system here is so corrupt. If you don't have money, you can't get a degree, and without a degree, you can't get a good job, and without a good job . . ." His voice trails off, but his meaning is clear: without a good job, you end up here, pretending to be an employee on strike.

The gatekeeper walks over to say that Robles is in D. F. and won't be back for several days. I peer hard into her eyes: they look exhausted. Twenty feet away, the guy with the video camera emerges from the tarp. He would probably rather be a filmmaker.

You can get deported for working as a journalist on a tourist visa in Mexico, but I can't help myself. Stories are my vice. So when I stumble upon the headquarters of the CROC one day—identifiable by its logo of a fist holding a torch—I park upon its couch. Ninety minutes later, two men with the universal look of politicians (proud, moneyed, slick) walk in. The *Noticias* vendors had cracked jokes about Robles's panza (belly), and sure enough, one has a giant girth enrobed in his leather jacket. He bids his companion well with a hug-turned-double-slap-on-the-back* and breezes by to his office. A secretary follows with my business card and then invites me inside.

Robles's desk is cluttered with a pen set, three statues of Don Quixote, and a stack of papers, which he thumbs through as he speaks. "This is a labor issue. It has nothing whatsoever to do with freedom of expression. Workers have the right to strike, yet we have been attacked for it on a worldwide scale. I'm leaving for Caracas tomorrow and Geneva and Paris after that to repair the CROC's reputation."

"How long will the strike last?"

"A long time."

"Weeks? Months? Years?"

---

* This style of abrazo, or hug, is said to date back to Pancho Villa days, when men wanted to determine if their compañeros were armed.

"Months."

I ask about the night of July 18, and he shakes his head. "That was pure telenovela. Those journalists were not sequestered; they could have left anytime they wanted. And they did. We have photographs of some participating in marches when they supposedly were sequestered inside their office. The night we entered, there were only sixteen left—not thirty-one."

"And what happened?"

"Nothing. They say we destroyed their equipment, but it isn't true. We only broke two of their glass doors in order to get inside. A public notary investigated afterward and certified that nothing else was destroyed—not a single thing." To prove it, he opens the folder of what appears to be a notarized document, points to a highlighted sentence, and snaps it shut.

I smile with all of my teeth. "Why don't you let me inside so I can see for myself?"

He stares back so stonily, I change the subject. How many strikers are actually *Noticias* employees? Fifty-six, he says, including administrative personnel and reporters. He refuses to release anyone's name, however, and my follow-up questions go nowhere. When I rise to shake his hand, I take advantage of my obvious linguistic disability. "Oh, and Señor Robles? What's a porro?"

"Porros? They are university students who get paid to make problems. Why?"

I allow my eyes to widen. "Really? That's what everyone calls your strikers!"

His eyes narrow. "You've been to Calle Libres; you've seen the strikers yourself. Do they look like porros to you?"

CHAPTER SEVENTEEN

THE RESISTANCE

Oaxaca and Tehuantepec,
July 2005

You'd never guess Oaxaca's main newspaper is under siege by strolling across the city. Everyone is too busy celebrating the Guelaguetza—in so many ways, you needn't keep track. Sip a coffee at an outdoor café and a parade will march by. Drop in a store and someone will pour you a shot of mezcal. Walk down Calle Alcalá,* the main pedestrian strip, and hear a different concert from a faraway land every forty feet, piped in through hidden speakers. Snuggle into bed and get tossed out by firecrackers.

The Guelaguetza's prized event is a song-and-dance pageant of indigenous groups from the seven regions of Oaxaca.

---

* Calle Alcalá is named after Macedonia Alcalá Prieto, an accomplished Oaxacan violinist, pianist, and songwriter whose inability to support his family with his art drove him to the bottle. He is best loved for a waltz called "Dios Nunca Muere," God Never Dies, composed in honor of the Virgen. More than 150 years later, Oaxaqueños still stand when it is performed in public.

Tickets are steep—four hundred pesos—but I go anyway, thinking it will be a nice introduction to local culture.* The grounds of the Auditorio Guelaguetza swarm with vendors hawking tchotchkes. At the front gate, a woman plops on my head a straw hat that says GUELAGUETZA 2005 on one side and COCA-COLA on the other. The amphitheater is slammed-packed, but I find an empty patch of cement one aisle over from the performers, most of whom appear to be from fifteen to twenty-five years old. The guys wear white campesino pantsuits with red bandanas and huaraches; the ladies are an onslaught of accoutrement: ribbons, lace, beads, embroidery, and colorful rebozos. Gold jewelry shimmers from their arms, and fresh flowers are woven through their hair.

Once everyone settles in, adolescent boys crisscross the stage blowing caracoles in the cardinal directions as a girl representing the goddess Centeotl blesses the festivities with a golden stalk of maize. Then women in ruffled skirts seize the stage, each balancing a basket of flowers atop her head. They waltz a tune or two before detonating the firecrackers buried inside their baskets. Everyone jumps to their feet—first in alarm, then in cheer—as the women whirl through the sparks and smoke, their charred flowers flying.

The dancers that follow do so sedately, shuffling about with props ranging from machetes to live turkeys to pineapples for interminable intervals. But no one leaves, for in between acts, the Zapotec tradition of Guelaguetza (or gift giving) kicks in. After their bow, the dancers grab fistfuls of food—coffee, tamales, bananas, beets, cilantro—from the baskets they dragged

---

* I will later learn that these prices stir controversy in Oaxaca, as the Guelaguetza used to be free. Now, only the "nosebleed" section is gratis, and you must arrive at the crack of dawn to be guaranteed entry. Local activists boycott the event, claiming it is more for tourists than Oaxaqueños.

onstage and toss them into the audience, which leap like fans for drumsticks at rock concerts. I lack the hand/eye coordination to catch anything and everyone notices. A dancer from the neighboring aisle passes over a tortilla in cellophane packaging; a mother of four hands over a fifth apple. Before long, our whole section is sharing its booty, ripping off a hunk of each item before passing it down the row.

When the pageant ends two and a half hours later, it seems to have been a success. The amphitheater filled to capacity; people leave with armloads of groceries. It occurs to me that the vast majority of spectators are tourists—both foreign and domestic—rather than locals, and that the performers appear to be more mestizo than indigenous. But I leave with the impression that indigenous culture is not only respected but also celebrated here in Oaxaca. Just as the Tourist Bureau hoped I would.

Even after living here for six months, Mexican time eludes me. Sometimes I arrive at the predetermined hour and the person I'm meeting is either exceedingly late or doesn't show. Other times I dawdle and end up insulting someone. There is no discernible pattern: people who jot down their appointments are just as likely to blow them off as people who don't, and whenever I try to predict what someone will do, I am wrong.

Like now. Tino, dispenser of Gatorade and acumen, notices my Zapatista necklace and says that Oaxaca has indigenous resistance groups too. His friend does solidarity work with them in the countryside. "Come by mañana around this time and I'll give you his phone number."

By mañana, I assume he means "sometime in the future,

maybe," so I wait a few days before returning. "Where have you been?" Tino cries when I do. "My friend came all the way here to meet you and you never showed up!"

I apologize to no avail. In Tino's eyes, I am now a flake. He does, however, give me the acronyms of some local groups, including OPIZ, MULT, and CIPO, though he doesn't know how to reach any of them. "Their work is very dangerous, so they operate underground," he says. "Nobody can find them."

Except Google. Though little has been published about them online, I find a few e-mail addresses and dash off some inquiries. To my surprise, my in-box fills with responses. Juan Sosa Maldonado from Organización de Pueblos Indígenas Zapotecos (OPIZ) offers to meet the following afternoon in front of Oaxaca's chief landmark, the Santo Domingo Church. I arrive five minutes early and he walks right up, looking exactly as you'd imagine a resistance leader would: like Emiliano Zapata (minus the rifle). His handlebar mustache and caterpillar eyebrows are flecked with silver; his eyes are large and somber, as is his smile. We walk to a nearby café. Unsure how to begin, I start chattering about the Guelaguetza. He sips his black coffee before politely interrupting.

"Sí, Oaxaca has a pretty Guelaguetza. A very pretty Guelaguetza. But if you visit our communities, you won't find anything pretty at all. The indigenous in Oaxaca have nothing: no water, no electricity, floors made of dirt."

Oaxaca is Mexico's second poorest state. A *New York Times* reporter once interviewed a priest who declared that hunger is so rampant here, infants have died in his arms as he baptized them. As in Chiapas, parts of the countryside are embroiled in "low-intensity warfare" with the government, especially in the Zapotec town of San Agustín Loxicha in the Sierra Madre mountains, a five-hour drive from the state capital. Troubles here began in the summer of 1996, around the first anniversary of the slaying of campesinos by police in the neighboring state of Guerrero.* Claiming retribution for the killings, a rebel insurgent group called the Ejército Revolucionario Popular (EPR) launched multiple attacks on police and military posts in Guerrero and Oaxaca. According to wire reports, at least eleven died in the shoot-outs. When police discovered one guerrilla was the former tax collector of San Agustín Loxicha, they swooped upon the town and arrested scores of its citizens—including the bulk of its elected officials and several teachers—whom they suspected of being EPR supporters.† In protest, dozens of families packed their bags, traveled here to the state capital, pitched tents on the zócalo, and declared a plantón. Under this type of protest, participants hunker down until they are forcibly removed or their demands are met—whichever comes first. In this case, the families cooked their meals, reared their children, slept atop cardboard, and staged hunger strikes in the zócalo for four and a half years, from June 10, 1997, to December 24, 2001, until the government convinced them to move into a nearby shelter rent-free.

Meanwhile, back in San Agustín Loxicha, more leaders were rounded up.

---

* On June 28, 1995, seventeen campesinos affiliated with a land rights group set out on a march demanding the release of a local activist as well as improved schools, roads, and water. At a roadblock, Guerrero state police shot every single one of them dead and then planted weapons in their hands and photographed them, so they could claim self-defense. Eight months later, Televisa aired a tape of the killings, which became known as the Massacre at Aguas Blancas. The Governor of Guerrero was forced to step down, but rather than serve jail time, he retired to his South Florida estate. See Linda Diebel, *Betrayed: Assassination of Digna Ochoa* (New York, NY: Carroll & Graf, 2006).

† Just how many got arrested is hard to verify. A review of newspaper archives shows that the *Washington Post* reported 24; the *Irish Times*, 82; the Inter Press Service, 150.

"The government would bribe people, telling them, 'If you say so-and-so is a comandante of the EPR, we will pay you a thousand pesos.' These are poor people, so of course they gave in. And that caused a lot of hostility within the communities," Juan says.

One by one, his compañeros disappeared, and in July of 1998—after two policemen died in another EPR attack—it happened to him.* He was waiting for his wife outside a store one day when a car pulled up and three men jumped out. One yanked a shirt over Juan's head and tossed him into the car, where they handcuffed him and then drove away. A couple of hours and vehicle changes later, they arrived at a house. There, the torture began.

"They wanted to know everything. Who my family was, what we all did. When I said nothing, they beat me up, starved me, blasted loud music in my ears. They made me stay awake for days with blinds over my eyes. They poured chile water in my mouth and nose so that I blacked out, and when I awoke, they threatened to electrocute me. They wanted me to admit to killing those policemen, but I refused to go to jail for something I did not do. But when they started threatening to get my wife and my son, I accepted the fact that I would have to say that I committed the crime, so they would be spared. I signed the papers they wanted me to sign—except, there was nothing written on them. They had me sign blank pages so that they could write whatever they wanted on top."

After twenty-five days of torture, Juan was allowed to bathe and dress in clean clothes. Then his captors handcuffed and blindfolded him, drove him to a clinic for a brief health inspection, and dropped him off at a maximum security prison. His cell consisted of four walls, a low ceiling, and a cement floor,

* What follows is Juan Sosa Maldonado's version of events. The details proved impossible to confirm.

with neither a plank for a bed nor a bucket for a toilet. After nine days of solitary confinement, a visitor arrived: his wife. She had spent the past month filing formal denuncias (complaints) with the local and state government as well as human rights groups here and abroad.

"She said she didn't want me to take the blame for the killings. She was willing to risk whatever might happen to her or to our family. So we did."

Juan remained under constant surveillance in solitary confinement for forty-five days. The guards allowed him only one restroom break per day and a change of clothes once a week. Meals were slid beneath the door and were barely edible.

"How did you survive?"

"I felt very strongly that this just could not happen again. I could see the struggle ahead and I had to be a part of it."

From solitary confinement, he was transferred to another ward for five months and then to a federal prison in the state of Mexico for fifteen. His wife, meanwhile, rallied help from international human rights organizations. Finally, on May 11, 2001, Juan was released.

"Why?"

"Those papers they made me sign that day. I had to make a thumbprint on them, and you could see where my fingers had been cut during the torture. I could use that as evidence, because I didn't have those cuts before."

As vice president of OPIZ, Juan now spends much of his time appealing the cases of his still-imprisoned compañeros to the Human Rights Commission in D. F. "Guelaguetza is supposed to represent giving, so every year we ask our government for our liberty, but we never get it. There are still twenty-one of us in prison. Thirteen have been accused of federal crimes and eight of local crimes. They've even imprisoned one of our women."

I wonder aloud why I have never heard of Oaxaca's resistance movement before.

"The government learned their lesson after the Zapatista uprising in 1994. Anyone who tries to help us gets disappeared too: teachers, organizers, lawyers, journalists.* We have the exact same problems with detentions, assassinations, and paramilitaries as they do in Chiapas. But ours is a silent war."

I call for the check and we walk down Calle Alcalá. Every other building is an art gallery, a bookstore, a mezcal shop, or a boutique, and tourists flit about, pollinating each. We reach the zócalo, where the Loxicha families staged their plantón beneath the shade of Indian laurel trees. "The children bathed over here"—Juan nods toward a sidewalk café full of foreigners drinking hot chocolate—"and the women tended fires for their tortillas back there. The smoke would drift up to the governor's window. He didn't like that at all!"

We cut across the plaza and continue walking many blocks before reaching the concrete complex that houses the families left over from the plantón. (Their husbands remain in prison here, which is why they haven't returned home to San Agustín Loxicha.) Two dilapidated cars are beached upon the driveway; hens cluck from a coop. Three women in aprons and their numerous children stand in an outdoor kitchen equipped with mud ovens fitted with comales, halfway through their daily production of twelve kilos of tortillas the size of medium pizzas. They use them for everything: scrambling their eggs, wiping their hands and spills, filling their bellies and pockets. Neighbors drop by to purchase some, but the bulk are sold by the children. Soon after our arrival, a seven-year-old named Libertad rides in on a

---

* An editor of a Oaxacan weekly was kidnapped, threatened, and "roughed up" for twenty hours after attending a clandestine guerrilla news conference in September 1996. He later told reporters that he suspected his abductors were either police or part of a security agency. See Nancy Nusser, "Mexico's Anti-Rebel Military Drive Fueling Peasants' Anger," *Atlanta Journal-Constitution*, September 22, 1996, 3A.

bicycle from her afternoon deliveries and throws herself into a chair, demanding a box of milk.

The women smile hospitably as Juan introduces us but are reluctant to speak. When I ask about the plantón, they only say it was "muy duro," very difficult.

"What do you remember most?" I press.

One pauses in her kneading to reflect. "The baptism."

Juan explains that a sympathetic bishop once collectively baptized thirty babies from the plantón. Prominent Oaxacan artists, politicians, and journalists served as the padrinos and hundreds attended the service. Opening a photo album, he proceeds to show me images from the plantón and other incidents in OPIZ history. One depicts an outdoor meeting where everyone wears ski masks or bandanas. Juan ticks off their fates: "He is in prison now. He's just been released. He was disappeared for six months. He was killed." The women and children gather around when their loved ones' photos appear, then return to their masa kneading and tortilla flipping. He closes the album and searches for a positive note. "The mothers here teach their children Zapotec so they won't forget their roots. These kids remember their culture; they remember where they come from."

Seated in a high chair next to me is a toddler. His body is the size of an eighteen-month-old but his head rivals my own. He moves like a tortoise. It takes him several minutes to notice me, but when he does, a smile slides across his face. He slowly reaches out to me, and when I meet him halfway, he wheezes with happiness. His name is Ever Ambrosia Antonio and he was born during the plantón. His mother left the zócalo just long enough to physically deliver him in a hospital, then wrapped him in a blanket and returned to the square. I ask what is medically wrong with him. Everyone shrugs.

"They have no health care," Juan explains. "There are clinics, of course, but indigenous people usually can't afford the fee, much less the medicine. So they go without."

I am one anecdote away from tossing myself onto the hot comal. In a whisper, I ask Juan if I can do anything for the families. After some prodding, he concedes that "some beans or rice might be nice." I round up three of the girls—Libertad, Érica, and Basilia—and head out the gate. The latter two are in their teens and wear long pleated skirts and conservative blouses that might have belonged to a secretary once. Excited by the prospect of a shopping spree, they slip their hands in mine and confide their families' needs. Libertad struts ahead of us. Her hair is cut short like a boy's, and she sports blue jeans embroidered with butterflies. It suits her sassy demeanor.

Rather than the mercado I'm envisioning, the girls lead me to an upscale megaplex with television sets displayed in the windows and washers and dryers stacked by the entryway. I grab a cart—which Libertad climbs into—and beeline to the food department. The girls engage in comparative shopping as we tour the aisles. "This costs 7.56 pesos per kilo, but this costs 6.98 pesos, so it is más económico!" The cart fills with laundry detergent, five bags of rice and beans, cooking oil, sugar and salt, apples and oranges, and a new set of plastic dishes. Everyone stares as we unload at the checkout in a flurry of broken Spanish and Zapotec. The cashier swipes several of our items twice. I ask her to print out the receipt before I pay and sure enough, she has overcharged us.* I react as if she is single-handedly responsible for the oppression of Mexican Indians. Érica and Basilia practically shrink into the floorboards, but Libertad stands beside me, her bony shoulders flared. A manager comes running and knocks fifty pesos off the bill. We hail a taxi home, which thoroughly impresses Libertad. She sits up straight on the edge of the seat, soaking everything in with unblinking eyes.

Back at the house, the mothers do not acknowledge the pile

* According to Juan, this often happens to indigenous people, who are assumed to be illiterate and/or too humble to make a fuss.

of groceries that amasses at their feet. This happened at the baptism in Chiapas too: the recipients of my corn grinder did not react when I gave it to them. It is actually considered rude to do otherwise. Guests should be made to feel appreciated for their presence, not their gifts. Érica and Basilia hurry back to work and don't reestablish eye contact for the duration of my visit. Only Libertad continues to chat, introducing me to each of the hens.

Juan emerges from a doorway. "Remember how I told you that a Loxicha woman is in prison? Her sister is here."

He leads me into the community room that doubles as OPIZ headquarters. Tucked in a corner is Luciana Almaraz Matias: twenty-three years old and count-my-ribs skinny with a long, scowling face. On her lap is a curly-haired toddler clutching a plastic luchador. Juan and I sit across the table from them. Luciana says the repression began in her community in late August 1996. "They started taking people right off the street and throwing them in jail or torturing them or killing them or raping them, if they were a woman. My sister got taken on June 25, 2002."

At that time, their family was here in the capital, caring for their gravely ill mother at a hospital (as there are none in San Agustín Loxicha). Isabel left early one evening to feed and bathe her little girls—ages three and one—and didn't return. Luciana thought nothing of it; her sister needed the rest. The following morning, however, she bought a copy of *Noticias* and was horrified to see a familiar face in the Police Section. Though the mug shot identified her sister as someone else, the story said she had been arrested for kidnapping.

"They accused her of taking a little boy with two men she didn't even know," Juan says. "They told her that if she didn't sign a confession, they would take her girls away. So she did—but they took them anyway."

The family's lawyer located the girls in a shelter a month later and Luciana has been raising them ever since. She seems so downtrodden, I try to think of a lighter topic. "What does your son's father do?"

"He is in prison too," she says flatly.

"The men's and women's cells are very close to each other, so if you visit a woman, you will also see a lot of men," Juan explains. "One of the men accused in the kidnapping doesn't have any family out here, so . . ."

So Luciana started visiting him too. And she stayed longer and longer and later and later until a child was conceived in a warm cot behind cold bars. A curly-haired one, who is currently squirming his way right out of her lap.

It is Sunday afternoon, and Juan is taking me to prison. The Santa María Ixcotel Central Penitentiary is surprisingly close to downtown, just a bus ride and several-block walk away. "This follows the tradition of the pueblos, where jails are in the town plaza by the municipal buildings," he explains. "It is good for the families, so they can visit more easily."

As we near the entrance, the surrounding brick fence transitions to chain-link topped with barbed wire, and armed guards appear. The waiting area—a stretch of covered seating that resembles a bus stop—teems with families, most of whom are indigenous. Many bear gifts: tortas wrapped in embroidered cloths, sacks of fruit, toilet paper, a birthday pastel wrapped in butcher paper, clothes. The prison supplies its inmates with just enough food so that they don't starve and enough clothes so they aren't naked. Rural families who wish to support imprisoned family members often have to sell their farms and animals and relocate to the big cities, where most prisons are located. Of course, this scenario isn't unique to Mexico. For years, an aunt of mine has been following her sons across Texas as they get transferred from one prison to the next. She would actually fit in well here: poor, brown, and anxious—as are so many prison families in the world.

At the front desk, a guard digs through my bag and extracts the sole cosmetic I brought to Mexico: a tube of Aveda lipstick. I pass it to Juan, who wedges it between two planks in the roof above the waiting area. Another guard leads me into a windowless room where she spreads me like a starfish and pats me down. A second door opens to a reception area where a woman with a visitors' log asks who I wish to see. I exchange my passport for a poker chip, walk through another set of doors, and am suddenly inside the prison. A mob of skinny men descend upon me. One wields a toilet paper dispenser covered with beaded bracelets; another shoves a clock emblazoned with a woman's bare ass in my face. A third grabs my hand and begs to be my hired guide.

"They let vendors inside prison?" I ask Juan, fending them off.

"They're not vendors. They're inmates."

Inmates?! Why aren't they locked behind bars? Or at least in handcuffs, or in uniforms? Where are the guards? The only one in sight is kicked back in a chair, licking an ice pop. A watchtower looms overhead with nobody in it. Prison movies flood my brain. We're going to get stabbed, raped, trampled in a riot, killed! All my instincts say to run away screaming.

But no. These guys just want to sell us something. Badly. When Juan turns them down, they bound off to the next clump of visitors. Gripping me by the elbow, he leads me past the basketball courts—where half a dozen heated games are under way—to a labyrinth of concrete and chain-link partitions. I feel exceedingly vulnerable walking among so many out-of-cell inmates, but no one pays us much attention. They are too busy sewing soccer balls (for retail) in the shadow cast by the prison wall. There is no ceiling here: the sun beats unobstructedly.

We turn a corner and spy a dignified-looking man in a pressed shirt and jeans knitting a Rastafarian coin purse. Juan introduces him as Agustín Luna Valencia, the former municipal president of San Agustín Loxicha. He was arrested at a roadblock in September of 1996, while driving to the capital to meet with state officials. He told his captors that he was home celebrating the festival of a patron saint during the EPR attack and had hundreds of witnesses to prove it. Yet he has been imprisoned ever since. I ask about the living conditions here.

"Not favorable, but at least we have a space to rest. We are respected because of the way we conduct ourselves, but we are subjected to much injustice." He shakes his head in disgust, then resumes his knitting. His family brings him arts-and-crafts materials once a month and then sells his creations at a nearby mercado. It is their primary source of income now that he is in jail.

We move on. Juan points out the cell shared by the Loxichas. It resembles a Chinese university dormitory, with four bunk beds, laundry lines, and little wiggle room. An outdated calendar of a blonde in a bikini decorates one wall and hot plates, cutlery, and cookery stock the shelves. Weapons abound—sewing kits, steak knives—but plainly they aren't used as such.

"Inmates try to return to their community once they are free, but they can never find work. First because there isn't any, and second because of their record. Even if there were jobs, no one would hire them because they've been in prison. So they usually go to El Norte afterward, como mojado. The families are never reunited," Juan says. "That is why people stay silent in Mexico. The threat of prison is so strong."

We reach our destination: the women's division where Luciana's sister, Isabel Almaraz Matias, resides. We sign another ledger and pass through a door to a small open courtyard dripping with laundry. An inmate greets us with eerily urgent eyes. Machete scars cover her arms and legs, and she appears to have lost a substantial piece of her neck. The other inmates seem downright homely, their long hair worn in plaits. We ask for Isabel and they shout out her name. A Zapotec woman emerges from the doorway in a white cotton pantsuit embroidered with foliage. Clasping her hands are her two little girls dressed in Sunday best, their pigtails ribboned and bowed. We follow them into the community room and squeeze into a picnic table between a painting class and a family eating Kentucky Fried Chicken from a bucket. I ask what happened the evening of June 25, 2002.

"I was about to return to my family at the hospital when the police came. I told them I didn't know anything about the kidnapping of the little boy, but they took me and my girls anyway. I knew it was a mistake, so I thought I would just be held a few days. But I am still here, three years later."

She never saw her mother again. She asked for permission to visit her before she died but was denied. Her husband has since abandoned her, and she only sees her daughters when Luciana makes the journey. She passes time taking secretarial classes and knitting handbags. "There are ninety-four women in this prison. Most of us are indigenous people accused of doing things we didn't. We have no way to defend ourselves."

Human Rights Watch estimates that more than 40 percent of Mexico's prison population hasn't even been convicted of a crime. Torture-induced confessions are employed to solve about one-third of cases, and defendants are rarely granted much access to the judges who decide their fate. The justice system also tends to persecute the wrong people. In D. F., for instance, more than half of the 22,000 prisoners committed crimes as heinous as stealing a loaf of bread. Politicians and businessmen who pilfer millions, meanwhile, either slip by unpunished or bribe their way to freedom. As the martyred Salvadoran archbishop Óscar Romero once noted, "The law is like a serpent. It bites the feet which have no shoes on."

I buy Isabel's handbag collection and then we must go: visiting hours are over. At the exit, Juan and I redeem our poker chips for passports. The security guard barely looks up as we walk out the door. Back in the waiting area, my lipstick is still lodged between the beams. Juan retrieves it with a smile that is sad but sweet. "Nobody ever steals here."

Back in Chiapas, I attended a forum on the Zapatista Red Alert. One of the panelists—a mestizo activist named Javier—impressed me with his human rights work in the Isthmus of Tehuantepec in southeastern Oaxaca, another troubled area. He invited me to visit his organization, so I catch a five-hour bus that arrives late this afternoon. He meets me at the station dressed in a safari-style vest and hat. As we drive toward his home in his Volkswagen Beetle, he says that an emergency has arisen in one of their communities. "I must go there at once. But you are welcome to stay at my place until I return. It shouldn't be more than a few days."

"Can't I go with you?"

He glances at me sideways. "No. It is too dangerous."

We turn down a dirt road and park by a gate. The door flings open to a yard overgrown with weeds and rubbish. Of the two modest houses, one is padlocked and the other is barren, with bedsheets covering the furniture and a hammock for a bed.

"Where is your family?" I ask. He mentioned a wife and kids in an e-mail.

"At my in-laws. You aren't afraid to stay by yourself, are you?"

Can I admit that to a man who camps in paramilitary-infested forests?

He chuckles. "Don't worry. If you scream, one of my neighbors will hear."

With that, he drops a ring of keys in my hands and jets off in the Beetle. I squat atop a pile of rocks and wonder what to do. Five minutes later, a bent-over woman raps at the gate. "Javier told me to look after you," she croaks. At age sixty-five, Inessa has never married, dedicating her life to the care of her parents. She walks me through the neighborhood, which consists entirely of high fences and metal gates. I load up on oranges and crackers at a hole-in-the-wall tienda and escort her home. Her father waves from the courtyard as she opens the gate. He is collapsed in a chair with a bum leg, surrounded by chickens. I return to Javier's and bolt-and-chain myself in.

That night I lay in the hammock with every light ablaze, cursing myself. When did fear creep into my life? Nine years ago in Moscow, I thought nothing of sleeping in the mafiosi apartment of my boyfriend's best friend, a freelance hit man. A year later, I traveled across war-ravaged Colombia with a second (raging alcoholic) boyfriend without a worry. But now, the littlest thing unsettles me. Like that spider crawling up the wall. Or the thought that Javier is on someone's to-be-disappeared list and tonight is the night they come to fetch him. Am I inherently afraid of Mexico? Or does each passing year of life take another layer of nerve with it?

Around midnight, a storm rolls in. The rain is almost deafening, and water soon seeps into the house. I pile everything on top of a table and face a new fear: flash floods followed by drowning. But the waters recede at daybreak, and by noon the road is dry enough to tread upon. I check on Inessa's family. Her father is knee-deep in mud. "It wasn't so bad. You should have seen the storm last week, ¡Híjole! It nearly floated us away."

I catch a cab to Tepeyac, the human rights organization where Javier works. A young woman in slim-fitting jeans welcomes me inside the office, a converted courtyard house decorated with political flyers and woven textiles. Her name is Rosa and she is a mestiza lawyer who defends indigenous communities. We talk awhile before heading into the kitchen to join her colleagues, also young women in jeans. They take turns cooking lunch for one another, and today someone has prepared a hearty stew of beef and vegetables plus a stack of corn tortillas. Back at my old nonprofit in New York City, we could barely agree upon pizza toppings at staff meetings. But Mexicans share such a strong culinary tradition, they can serve anything from cow brain tacos to spicy mole lamb chops and rest assured that their compañeros will enjoy it.

As we eat, the women discuss their major project: defending communities impacted by Plan Puebla-Panamá, a multibillion-dollar development plan that would integrate Mexico's southern region with Central America and Colombia through a series of large-scale infrastructure projects to better facilitate trade. One of its more controversial projects would build thousands of miles of new roads linking the nations.

"These highways divide our communities in two. The residents can't use them because they don't have cars. And even if they did, they wouldn't be able to afford the toll. If they want to cross the highway by foot, they have to walk up to five kilometers to the nearest crossover. They can't cross the highway itself. The traffic moves too fast," Rosa begins.

"And their animals get killed crossing it," another adds.

"They don't want a highway, they want something they can ride their bicycles across. But the government only cares about transnational business," Rosa says.

One of the many benefits touted by Plan Puebla-Panamá is its development of local economies, including the creation of new jobs. When I mention this, the women nearly spit out their stew.

"Don't believe a word of that!" they cry.

"The government always says that, but unions inevitably get the best jobs while the indigenous people get stuck breaking rocks under the sun all day long," one says, dumping chopped chiles into her soup and wincing.

"Plus, their mountains are dynamited—sometimes even their sacred ones—and the government hardly pays anything for the use of their land," Rosa adds. "The community would make much more money off the agriculture they would normally produce: corn, papaya, watermelon, squash. If they have no land, where will they do their dances, their rituals, their traditions? Without land, they will die—if not their bodies, their culture."

Their arguments are sounding increasingly familiar. Critics make nearly the same points against the proposed Trans-Texas Corridor. This $183 billion plan would create a four-thousand-mile network of corridors measuring up to a quarter mile in width across the United States. Opponents say it would wreak havoc on the environment, snatch land from ranchers and farmers, and devastate small towns. Supporters say it would be great for business.

I am also struck by the fact that I have met so many mestizos dedicating their lives to defending the indigenous: Rebeca, Rafael, and Marta in Chiapas; Juan, Javier, and these women in Oaxaca. How are they accepted by the communities they serve? Does nationality unite them more than blood divides them?

"What does it mean to be indigenous, exactly?" I ask.

A honey-skinned woman named María slowly repeats my question, as though weighing its words. "It is someone who identifies as being indigenous, who says, 'I am what I am.'"

"So physical appearance isn't important? Like skin color?"

The women respond in unison: "Skin color is not important here!"

Mexicans often claim there is no racism in their homeland, that their society is free from the prejudice that pervades El Norte. What matters here is class, they say—disregarding the link between the two.

"I am not indigenous because I just don't feel that way," María continues. "I don't dress that way, I don't practice those traditions, I don't speak that language. My Abuela is indigenous, but I am not."

"Does that make you sad?"

"Not at all. I am proud to be mestiza, to have a mother who is Zapotec and a father who is from the city," she says, then reconsiders. "Well, when I was in primaria, I wanted to be indigenous because all of my peers spoke Zapotec and dressed Zapotec and I felt left out."

"Let's say you learned to speak the language and started dressing that way. Would you be Zapotec then?" I press, her answers becoming increasingly important. Bloodwise, I am as Mexican as she is Zapotec.

"Being part of an identity is a mixture of things," she says, "but it is mostly what you believe in. Indigenous people have their own gods—of the land, of the water, of the trees, of fertility—and they pass down these beliefs through the generations. But in my family, these traditions stopped with my grandparents. My Abuela's dying regret was that I never learned Zapotec. I told her it wasn't her fault. If I wanted to, I could have learned it. But I didn't, so I am mestiza."

Another lawyer tells a story about an aunt who moved to the Bronx years ago. Her teenage daughter has refused to acculturate to El Norte, insisting on speaking Spanish and buying nopales at the market. She dreams of returning to Mexico someday and becoming a doctor. "Meanwhile, my aunt just wants to forget where she's from. When she returns to Tehuantepec, her daughter has to translate for her, because she has totally disassociated from this place."

Everyone shakes their head as they rise to clear the table. They've witnessed this in their communities too: when the indigenous emigrate to Los Estados Unidos, they invariably forget their dialects and traditions. They return total strangers, get shunned by their old community, and permanently relocate to California, Illinois, Georgia.

Rosa lays a hand on my shoulder. Earlier, I shared my personal reasons for coming to Mexico. She senses how raw this conversation has left me. "The important thing is that you realize what you have lost," she says quietly. "Now it is only a matter of fighting to regain it."

CHAPTER EIGHTEEN

LITTLE ZAPOTEC GIRL

Oaxaca,
August 2005

Like every South Texas Mexican, I grew up Catholic, and—despite my wildly divergent views on everything from abortion to the Vatican—still claim to be one. But I'm wary of contacting Padre Murcio. Of the two priests I encountered during confirmation classes in high school (the only time I've regularly attended Mass), one yanked us out of the pews by our ears and banished us to Monkey Row for talking, while the other terrorized us with the pains of hell. Rebeca urged me to meet him, however, so I drop by his parish across from the zócalo. A sexagenarian with a fuzzy white beard, he wears glasses, tennis shoes, and a shirt embroidered with children holding hands around the globe. And he walks extremely fast.

"Ya vámonos," he says, charging down the cobbled street.

I trot to keep up with him.

"Over there is a shelter for Triqui youth. They always need volunteers." He points. "This here is a group that works with women, mostly indigenous. In that building, a group teaches herbal medicine to village doctors. Ay, so much to do!"

A Liberation theologian, much of Padre Murcio's work revolves around social justice. He has led hunger strikes, marched for indigenous rights, ministered to the families from the Massacre at Aguas Blancas and the police sweeps of San Agustín Loxicha. After giving me a whirlwind tour of Oaxaca's charitable organizations, he stops at a chichi boutique called Mediterraneo Moda, where a bleached blonde models slinky tops for her boyfriend. I am confused—until a small, dark woman in a long white dress peeks out from behind a curtain. She winks at us with laughing eyes.

"That's Franci," Padre Murcio whispers before departing. "She'll take care of you."

I sit in a chair and watch Franci in action. She convinces the blonde to try on half the store and within twenty minutes nails a 2,000-peso sale. After escorting her out the door, she perches on a chair and removes the chopsticks holding a bun at the nape of her neck. Ebony locks tumble halfway to the floor. "Tell me . . . do you like children?"

She does. So much that she and Padre Murcio are building an orphanage in the Loxicha region on the land she inherited from her grandparents with the funds from her boutique. By her estimate, about a thousand children have no parents there. Some died in the "low-intensity war"; others from illnesses like diarrhea and the flu. The orphanage is still far from complete, but Franci plans to populate it with 365 children, "one for every day of the year." She has already taken in the first: a little Zapotec girl named Claudia whose mother recently died of pneumonia.

"Her father was an alcoholic who beat her. We heard that he planned to sell her as soon as she reached puberty," she says. "This happens a lot in rural communities, especially in the mountains. Young girls are traded as wives for money, cattle, even bottles of mezcal. It is not unusual to see a seventy-year-old man with a twelve-year-old bride out there. So we decided to intervene."

Just then, a guy our age pokes his head into the boutique. It's

Beto, Franci's friend from preparatoria. He is home on holiday from Spain, where he studies identity politics in grad school. He invites us to lunch at the café across the street. After ordering a round of Negra Modelos, I ask Franci if she plans to put the future residents of her orphanage up for adoption. This is a fiercely controversial topic in Latin America—especially in neighboring Guatemala, where nearly one in every hundred children is adopted by a family from the United States. Stories abound of babies being kidnapped and sold to unsuspecting couples abroad.

While Franci is actively seeking adoptive parents for Claudia, she hasn't decided about the others. "Of course a foreigner could offer a Loxicha child a lot, but I don't know if taking them away from their community is the best thing. They will probably never return, and what would that do to their cultural identity?"

I love this about southern Mexico: people here obsess about cultural identity as much as I do. Remembering my conversation with the young lawyers in Tehuantepec, I ask Franci and Beto if they feel accepted by indigenous communities.

"Even if you learned their language and lived among them for years, you would never be *fully* accepted," Franci says. "They take one look at me and say I am mestiza."

It is even worse in Europe, Beto says. "All my life, people have told me that I am half Spanish and half Indian, but I have lived in Spain for two years now and can tell you it is not true! Indians are the ones I relate to. Only, they don't relate to me."

"Here in Mexico, the Indians say we are European," Franci sums. "Over in Europe, everyone says we are Indian. In reality, we are not accepted by either."

Of course I am confused about what it means to be Mexican. They are too! This nation is biracial by definition. Cultural schizophrenia is encoded in our DNA. Raising my bottle of Negra Modelo, I propose a toast. "To existential identity crisis."

"¡Salud!" We clink one another's glasses.

We return to the boutique just as Franci's mother drops off

Claudia. She runs up to Franci and hugs her waist. Between five and seven years of age (no one knows for certain), she is mocha-skinned with a wide, flat Zapotec nose and silky black hair sprouted into pigtails. Having been trapped inside all day, she is clearly ready to play, but Franci must tend to the customers streaming in. I offer to take her out, and we wind up at an ice cream parlor. She orders a bag of potato skins and squirts a whole package of liquefied chile on top.

"Claudia, I think that is too—"

"¡Pica!" she gasps, twirling her tongue. Hot!

Before I can snatch the package away, she sticks it in her mouth and sucks it dry. "I like pica."

I buy her a pecan ice pop to curb the burn.

"We don't have pecan trees where I'm from, but we have guanábanas, mangoes, manzanas, frijoles, sugar, coffee," she ticks off the list. "And a burro."

I can't help but ask about her family.

"Mamá weaved clothes and washed them too. And she swept because we had a floor made of dirt. One day it rained very hard and she died. We washed her and changed her into a pretty dress and buried her in the earth. Then I weaved clothes and washed them too but Papá still beat me so I went to a house and told a Señor and he said, 'Do you want to live there?' and I said no so he brought me here and now I live with Franci." She takes a big bite of ice pop. "Can you say pecan in Zapotec?"

I shake my head and she shouts it out gleefully, flinging her hands in the air. I ask if she can say it in English. She shakes her head vigorously, and I repeat her gesture. A game is born. We finish the ice pops and continue down the street, teaching each other words like "tortilla," "sun," and "moon." Claudia takes my hand, pulls me down to her eye level, makes me repeat the Zapotec words until I pronounce them correctly, then throws her arms around me, laughing like the rain. With the exception of a six-month volunteer stint at a children's shelter in Moscow and occasional visits with my niece and nephew, my life is largely devoid of kids. Not until I am in their radiance do I realize this loss. Claudia and I spend much of the evening together, strolling about the city. By the time we return to the boutique, her hand is clasped in mine.

Franci, meanwhile, is persuading a brunette to buy a leopard-print blouse. After appealing to her vanity, she adds that the proceeds go toward constructing an orphanage, then hands her a pamphlet. I take one too. Its simple illustrations make me smile: I've just thought of a small way to help.

My sister is coming to visit, and the morning of her arrival feels like the eve of a blind date. Six years wedge between us. She was tearing around on roller skates while I was figuring out how to walk, and I've never caught up. She moved away to college when I started junior high, got married when I enrolled in college, bore her first child when I lived in Moscow, and her second when I moved to Beijing. For a whole decade, we primarily saw each other at Christmas, talking so seldom in the interim that I panicked whenever she did call, assuming something dreadful had happened to our parents.

People occasionally mistake Barbara and me for twins. We are quite alike—from our looks (brown hair, indigo eyes) to our professions (she's a poet) to our diets (spotty vegetarians). And while our Mexican heritage played little role in our childhood, we have both rediscovered it as adults. We read Latino literature, decorate our homes with Mexican art, cook Tex-Mex meals, primarily date (and in her case marry) Latinos. Yet Barbara was once denied a job promotion because she wasn't considered "Mexican enough" to fill their quota. This would have crushed me, but she laughed it off. My sister never stresses about anything, which is how she does things like earn a PhD in three years while raising two kids and holding a full-time job.

Some of my closest friends are decades older than my sister, and I have dated men her age. Yet in my eyes, Barbara is always the "biggest" person in the room—the wittiest, the wisest, the most mature. And I am "little" around her. I break wineglasses; I say inappropriate things. One Christmas, I failed to secure the lid of her blender before mixing hot chocolate and ended up scalding her children and soiling her kitchen.

Maybe this is what it means to be the younger sister.

So while I'm excited to host her visit, I'm nervous as well. We haven't been alone together since the morning of her wedding, when we drove to the salon to get our hair and nails done. And I've never spent much time with her husband, Alex, before. What will we say, do? They have bartered in Mexico's border towns and honeymooned on its beaches, but this will be their first venture into the interior. Should I take them to Calle Libres to heckle the CROC? To the prison to shop for handbags? I pour through *Lonely Planet* and stacks of tourist brochures, outlining sample itineraries. Then I lay a bottle of mezcal on their pillow and catch a shuttle to the airport. An angst-ridden hour passes before Alex's brawny frame maneuvers into line at custom's. (A member of San Antonio's SWAT Team, he also runs triathlons.) Barbara is right behind him, standing on her tiptoes and peeking beyond the gate. We wave as if we were shipwrecked. They move a few feet in line and we do it again. Yes, we are really here!

In the ten days that follow, we will climb the hilltop ruins of the ancient Zapotec capital of Monte Albán. Haggle for textiles in village mercados. Sprinkle our nachos with fried grasshoppers and sample six of Oaxaca's seven prized moles. Pass languid hours in cafés with bottomless mugs of micheladas. Relax. Get tanned.

But that first night, we steal into the corner of a restaurant just to talk. About our childhood, our families, ourselves. Stories we've never told our mother. Laughing till it hurts. Brothers and sisters in a land both foreign and familial. A new closeness takes root, flourishes.

Barbara and Alex run a part-time photography business and have—as I hoped—brought their gear. I tell them about the orphanage and they agree to do a photo shoot of Claudia so that Franci can spruce up her promotional materials. We spend an afternoon searching for the right backdrop and settle on El Pochote, a traditional courtyard home built around a pond and enclosed by high stone arches. Formerly an artist's residence, El Pochote screens nightly art-house films and hosts weekend farmers' markets, but during the day, no one is about.

Claudia holds statue-still as Barbara arranges her into poses, and when Alex says to smile her whole face alights. One hundred shots and lens changes later, he offers to take some of me with Claudia. We stand together beneath the stone arches, my hand on her shoulder. Click. She smiles up at me like a pumpkin. Click. He treats us to a slide show on his digital screen. We look so happy together. We are. We return to the boutique, her hand snapped into mine like a puzzle piece. I translate a conversation between Franci and my sister. Yes, she is looking for someone to adopt Claudia. Does she know of anyone? Barbara promises to consult her network back home.

That night, the three of us dine on a balcony overlooking the zócalo. We are strangely subdued: Claudia's absence is palpable. Down below, dozens of vendors sell globos (balloon toys) to children. The most popular kind is tubular and can be blown up to fifteen feet in length. The kids launch them like rockets into the night sky and shriek with joy as they gracefully flutter back.

"We should buy some of those for Jordan and Analina," Barbara murmurs, referring to her kids.

I was thinking the same thing—only of Claudia.

After a few drinks, we walk back to our guesthouse. As I unlatch the gate, Barbara says something extraordinary: "If you want to adopt her, Stephanie, we would look after her whenever you traveled."

I sit up in bed half the night—and many hereafter—trying to envision what this would be like. Baking Christmas cookies on those tin platters my mother once used, sneaking tastes of the raw butter dough. Placing a cool cloth on her forehead when she breaks a fever. Charging through the streets of fashionable cities, wearing sunglasses and scarves.

Then my inner inquisition begins. How could I possibly adopt a child? Not only do they require money I plainly don't have, but they also need stability—and my mail has been forwarded to nine different addresses in the last six years. There is no way Claudia could go to school, learn English, and make friends with a mother like me. I would need to settle, build a home, find a reasonable job. I've actually been open to such notions for years now, but the imagined incentive has always been a man. Never a child.

And how could I justify removing Claudia from a culture so rich? Identity is this nation's bedrock. Though I could conceivably provide her with shelter and sustenance, I could never instill her with that.

What, in the end, does a little Zapotec girl need: a community where she looks and speaks like everyone else? Or a surrogate parent who loves her?

Barbara and Alex fly home, and a week later, I must as well. El Norte beckons.

My last Oaxacan morning begins with a cup of hot chocolate

in the zócalo. A governor's convention is being held today, so downtown looks especially festive, with sprays of flowers in giant clay pots. The meeting ends as I walk to Franci's boutique and a floral free-for-all ensues. I see Claudia darting in and out of the crowds, her arms full of gladiolas, chrysanthemums, and violets. She snatches flowers right out of people's hands, leaving them gaping.

This girl could make it in New York City. She could make it anywhere.

She runs over to greet me. I stick a yellow chrysanthemum in her hair, and we walk to Los Cuiles for soy burgers. People stare as we pass—some smiling, some not. I try to make eye contact with a Zapotec woman selling rebozos. What would she think if I adopted Claudia? Her expression is not discernible.

Given our mutually limited Spanish, I worry that Claudia and I have exhausted our discussion topics. But no—we haven't even gotten to colors yet. She has difficulty pronouncing "yellow" but quickly masters "PEENK." We cover the color wheel at Los Cuiles, then return to the boutique, twirling each other like swing dancers. Franci tells Claudia that I am leaving tomorrow and she begs to come along, to fly a silver plane into the blue sky.

There are so many reasons to try to make this happen. So Barbara and I will continue growing close. So my parents will have another grandchild. So I will feel more deeply connected to this country, this heritage, this identity. So I will be less alone in the world. But aren't they all selfish, illegitimate?

Claudia is a tough little girl. A Zapotec. A survivor. She will be fine without me. The question is whether she would be happier with me.

I turn to Claudia, but she is already running out the door. She has just noticed a pot of flowers on the steps to Santo Domingo. There is one gladiola left, and she is going to get it.

CHAPTER NINETEEN

VALLEY MANTRAS

Texas-Mexico Border,
December 2005

Mexico awaits me in Jersey. Everywhere I look, undocumented workers are hammering nails, installing carpets. Manning counters at the fish market, the pastry shop, the grocery store. Scrubbing, gutting, pruning, baking. Building. Child rearing. Lingering around parking lots so someone can hire them to do more.

The nation notices them too, and their presence ignites furious debate.* They are berated on radio talk shows for stealing jobs; praised in editorials for their work ethic. Vigilantes park lawn chairs along the Río Grande and wait for them to cross, gun in hand, while missionaries lug bottles of water into the desert for them to drink. They explode membership in anti-immigration groups by some 600 percent and inspire the creation

---

* At various points in 1890, 1920, 1950, 1970, and 1990, immigrants have been blamed for stealing jobs, depressing wages, deteriorating working conditions, and overwhelming public health systems. See David G. Gutiérrez, *Walls and Mirrors: Mexican Americans, Mexican Immigrants, and the Politics of Ethnicity* (Berkeley, CA: University of California Press, 1995).

of new advocacy organizations. The U.S. House of Representatives draws a bill that would construct a seven hundred-mile fence along the border to keep them out and penalize anyone who aids them, including church groups. The Senate counters with one that would not only welcome them as "guest workers" but enable them to become citizens after a lengthy, costly process. While Congress dukes it out, state legislators introduce hundreds of bills that would strip them from access to government benefits and fine their employers and landlords.

I feel hopelessly disconnected watching these events unfold from a laptop in Princeton, New Jersey. When the holidays roll around, I hightail home to Texas and convince Greg—the artist who introduced me to Querétaro—to join me on a border road trip. From Corpus, we take a street called Weber until it becomes Way Out Weber and then a two-lane highway, and soon we're blazing trails so flat, you could roll a bowling ball to Mexico. Barns are caving in; downtowns are boarded up. There are taco stands called Leticia's and auto-repair shops called Positive Attitudes and fireworks stands called BUY 1, GET 5 FREE!!! Oil wells bob up and down like praying mantises. Cacti bloom on rooftops.

"If I lived out here, I'd drink a lot of beer," Greg muses.

He needn't leave his truck to do so. Liquor barns will roll a keg of Miller Genuine Draft right into your truck bed at the drive-thru. This is beer-chugging country, which perhaps accounts for the myriad memorials speckling the highway, each crucifix marking the spot where another soul fast departed.

Like all good Tejanos commencing a journey, we head first to Falfurrias to pay respects to the famed Mexican curandero Don Pedrito Jaramillo. He traveled to El Norte from Jalisco in 1881 and was informed of his power to heal the sick by Dios himself. For the next twenty-six years, he made house and rancho calls on foot or donkey-back between the Nueces River and the Río Grande, treating the rural poor. His statue greets you inside the doorway of the memorial: a Mexican gnome with a white beard spilling down a black suit. I pat his shiny head, then kneel at the altar upon cushions sunken thin and gaze at the walls where generations of pilgrims have posted photographs, business cards, graduation programs, driver's licenses, braids of hair, and the occasional pair of crutches.

One hundred miles later, we are nearing the border. Exit signs to Mexico ripple past. Restaurant marquees advertise FREE BEANS WITH EVERY ORDER; motels offer weekly, monthly, and "seasonal" rates. This hunk of Texas is known as the Valley. Comprised of cities like Brownsville, McAllen, and Harlingen, it is populated by fifth- and sixth-generation Mexican-American families, undocumented workers, and a smattering of white "winter Texans." We head to Weslaco, where my friend Hector lives. Although he and his mother and sisters are U.S. citizens, his mom's live-in boyfriend, Ramiro, has been sidestepping the Migra for a decade and counting.* He agrees to share his story at their suburban home in this town of 30,000 (about 85 percent of whom are Latino).

A ruggedly handsome cowboy from a rancho in Nuevo León, Ramiro speaks so softly, Greg and I must lean forward on the couch to hear him. He has worked in every industry in the Valley—cement, nurseries, carpentry, irrigation—but mostly in the citrus groves, where he puts in twenty-four-hour shifts for $5.15 an hour. I ask what the groves are like.

"Pues, fine, except when the coyotes pass through. They steal our cars to transport their pollos and we have to walk up to eight miles back to headquarters to tell the Patrón what happened. Then we have to go out and buy another car. The Patrón never lends us his. And sometimes the narcos dump their bodies

---

* According to the Pew Hispanic Center, an estimated 3.1 million children who are U.S. citizens by birth live in families with at least one "unauthorized" parent.

in the groves. Last year, my compañeros were picking oranges and noticed some hair growing out of the ground. They started digging and found a whole woman buried beneath."

Another time, Ramiro came upon five Guatemalans hiding behind a clump of trees. It was a cold December morning but they wore only T-shirts. "I asked where were their jackets and they said they'd been stolen in Reynosa. You have to be careful on the border. Thieves dress so well, they appear to be respectful people, but it's because they steal from the pollos! One of those guys lost a shoe while crossing the river and made it all the way to Houston wearing just one shoe."

I ask for his thoughts on the legislation being debated in Congress. Greg and I will hear his refrain so often, we peg it the "Valley Mantra": "If Congress passed laws that punished our employers, this whole Valley would empty. Commerce would stop. The economy would collapse."

"What about the Senate bill? Would you like to start the path to citizenship?"

He shakes his head. "I don't believe I'll ever get my papers. It used to be my New Year's wish every year, but I've given up trying, given up hope. I have no faith in this system anymore."

He says this matter-of-factly, for Weslaco is his home now. He has a family here. Children. If the Migra made him march across that bridge tomorrow, he'd sneak back the following morning. And he doubts even *that* would happen. He used to hide when Border Patrol jeeps drove by, but he's learned to play it tranquilo. "Just act like you're supposed to be here, and nothing will happen," he advises, a smile playing on his sun-dried lips.

Growing up, Nuevo Laredo—the Mexican sister city of Laredo, Texas—was my parents' favorite border town. We drove there on lazy Sundays to load up on cheap drugs (acne medication and penicillin), cajeta (a caramel-like spread made of goat milk) and—if it was Easter time—crates of cascarones (confetti-filled eggs that you smash on your primos' heads). Then we'd order enchilada platters and I'd sneak off for a quick swig of a $1 margarita. (On the border, if you're old enough to buy it, you're old enough to drink it.)

Violence between the warring "Gulf" and "Sinaloa" drug cartels has all but folded this town.* As homicide has skyrocketed (176 slayings this year alone), tourism has plummeted, and most of the old hangouts have shuttered. No one we know has returned in ages. But when the Laredo Border Patrol station invites us on a night tour of their patrol routes, Greg and I eagerly accept. Not only is this region the future site of a segment of the seven-hundred-mile wall that Congress is contemplating, it neighbors the area targeted by Operation Streamline. Announced by the Department of Homeland Security two weeks ago, this program aims to punish migrants caught crossing the Del Río Border Patrol sector with up to 180 days of incarceration.

Greg and I drive north and west, passing through towns like San Benito—where hometown hero Freddie Fender emblazons the water tower—and plenty of "colonias." These unincorporated communities came about in the 1960s, when crooked developers began hawking cheap plots of land that had no sewage, running water, electricity hookups, or paved roads to poor (and overwhelmingly Mexican) families. Unclaimed by any county, most still lack these basic services. One of the more famous colonias—Cameron Park in Brownsville—was recently named the most impoverished

---

* According to *Los Angeles Times* reporter Héctor Tobar, violence and intimidation have created a "culture of silence" in Nuevo Laredo. So many journalists have been threatened, kidnapped, and even killed here, they are reluctant to report about narco-trafficking, and municipal officials hardly ever comment publicly anymore.

community in the United States, with residents earning an average of $4,103 a year.*

As we near Laredo, even the humblest structures start sprouting bars on their windows and barbed wire around its yards, presumably to dissuade late-night crossers. Every now and then, a drug chieftain's castle peeks out from behind a high fence of reinforced steel, but most of the area is exceedingly poor. Dollar stores line the railroad tracks alongside mom-and-pop shops with names like Pancho Villa Meat Market.

We pull up to the Border Patrol station at 8 P.M. sharp. An agent named Scott awaits outside. Short and stout, he has a dirty-blond mustache and wears a forest green uniform. We climb into his Ford Expedition, which smells like leather shoes. Gloria Estefan croons through the speakers; gadgets and switches soup up the dashboard.

"Sorry, but I can't go 'Code Three' on you," he says, exiting out of the parking lot and turning onto the street. "We don't do high-speed chases anymore. Too dangerous."

Originally from California, Scott grew up in an agricultural family and spent his summers working alongside undocumented laborers in the fields. He studied horticulture in college until a friend announced that he was becoming a Border Patrol agent. It sounded so adventurous, he signed up too. In addition to physicals and Spanish language exams, he underwent an extensive background check. "They interview everyone who ever knew you, right down to your kindergarten teacher," he says. The application process normally takes two years but agents were in such demand, he got cleared in "just ten months."

I ask for more Border Patrol lingo like "Code Three."

---

* *Texas Monthly* staff writer Cecilia Ballí gave us a tour of Cameron Park, and we found it quite vibrant, boasting a community center, Boys and Girls Club, health clinic, a number of social services, and a dedicated army of community activists.

He laughs. "Well, the smugglers are called 'coyotes' or 'lookouts' or 'scouts' or 'guides.' And the people they transport are called 'aliens.'"

"What do they call you?"

"Jalapeños. I guess because our uniforms are green. They also call us bolillos [bread rolls] because a lot of us are white. Or just plain Migra."

Scott has worked in Laredo for eighteen years now. When he first started, agents apprehended between three hundred to four hundred people a day. Today, they average between thirty and forty. These statistics make him proud. "Our best days are when we don't catch a single one. That means we have deterred them."

"Aliens" aren't their principal concern in Laredo though. "Too bad you weren't here for the last shift. They caught someone floating down the river with three hundred pounds of pot. They are always transporting something—weapons, coke, hash—piled high on rafts and inner tubes," Scott says.

We cut through a HEB parking lot and charge down a rocky slope. Brush comes clear up to the windshield, so thick we can only see a few feet ahead. "You think you're all alone out here and suddenly a guy with an AK-47 jumps out and bullets whiz overhead. Or you come upon some aliens and the smuggler will grab some woman's baby and throw it into the river to distract you. You go in after the baby while everyone else runs away. We have to confront people every day who we don't know if they have a machete on them or a backpack full of food."

We reach a clearing. The Río Grande stretches out before us, a glittering abyss. We proceed along its bank toward the glow of the International Bridge. "You see that patrol jeep up ahead? You know why it's parked beneath that bridge instead of off to the side? Because the people up top will throw trash and rocks down at them!" he says, a bit indignant. "I've heard that in California, a lot of agents don't drive home in their uniform because they will get spat on or cursed at. It is like we are the opposing basketball team coming to town."

He parks by the river and faces me, his glasses reflecting the lights off the bridge. "Yet, we go out of our way to help the aliens. We'll come upon someone who hasn't eaten in two days and we'll share our lunches with them. We'll see someone lost in the water and we'll fish them out. We'll find them stranded in the desert and we'll give them water. We're like . . . we're like lifeguards."

"So how does it feel to apprehend them?" I ask.

He tells a story by way of reply. "One time I caught a young smuggler, a trainee, coming through with a group of mostly women. He had a really good attitude, very happy-go-lucky, and we got to talking. When I dropped them off at the bridge, I said, 'Maybe I'll see you tomorrow.' And sure enough, I did. They just laughed when I caught them and put them in the truck. I introduced myself and said I'd see them the next day—and sure enough, I caught them again! Then two days later, I came upon their tracks but lost them in an arroyo covered with ladybugs. But the next day, I caught up with them again, and they said: 'Haha, we saw you yesterday, but you didn't see us!' This went on a whole week. I caught the same group of people five or six times and kept driving them back to Mexico. But finally one afternoon, I found their tracks and followed them all the way to the highway, where they disappeared. And you know what? I was glad. They tried so hard, I was glad they finally made it. Any human being wants to see another human being succeed, to not be in poverty."

He leans back in the driver's seat to stroke his mustache, then shakes his head. "But I have a job I'm sworn to uphold, and I will do all I can to do it well."

He certainly has the funds to do it. Aside from the military itself, the U.S. Border Patrol is now the largest arms-bearing branch of the government, with an annual budget of more than

$1.4 billion. President Bush will soon pledge to add six thousand National Guard troops to their force. It seems like such a tragic waste: desperate migrants investing their life savings trying to cross the border while the United States squanders billions trying to stop them. I ask Scott for his thoughts on the pending congressional legislation.

"I can tell you one thing: that wall would never work," he grumbles, revving up the engine. "It would be very expensive and taxpayers like me would end up footing the bill."

That's true: the Congressional Budget Office has estimated the wall will cost approximately $3 million a mile. "What about the guest-worker program?"

He doesn't support that either. "The ideal situation would be to keep out the bad people and allow the good ones to stay inside. But who knows how to do that?"

We drive back to the station and enter via the same caged walkway "aliens" use after being apprehended. A poster of a man crumpled in the desert hangs in the foyer, scolding: NO MÁS CRUCES EN LA FRONTERA! No more crosses (that is, crucifixes) at the border. The walls of the processing center are painted white and brightly lit. Twelve computers with Department of Homeland Security screen savers form a pod in the center of the room. The agents relax in swivel chairs, swapping Christmas stories. Scott shows us the hacky-sack-size camera that snaps photos of the migrants and the little box that records their fingerprints. Within minutes, agents can ascertain how many times someone has been apprehended and whether or not they have a criminal record. If their slate is clean and they are Mexican, they are generally shipped to the International Bridge within hours and forced to walk across it. Migrants who are "other than Mexican" (OTM), meanwhile, are detained until a judge grants a hearing.

Cinder block cells surround the processing center. Generations of detainees have inscribed their names in the whitewash paint. Only one cell is occupied tonight, by a young Colombian wrapped in a blanket. Pressing his face against the window, he mimes scooping something out of a bowl and into his mouth. An agent promptly nukes a burrito and brings it to him. While Scott checks in with his colleagues, Greg and I chat with an agent who once taught elementary school in Georgia. "They chewed me up and spit me out, those little kids. I'd much rather be out here with the narcos!"

Scott gains permission to show us the "surveillance room." There, half a dozen cubicles cluster around a wall of TV screens. A few broadcast CNN and FOX News, but most stream live footage from cameras hidden along riverbanks and highways. As we watch, one zooms in on a suspiciously quaking bush. After a suspenseful moment, a cat saunters out.

"It is two days after Christmas," Scott says. "Everyone is home for the holidays. But come January, they'll be back."

In the spring of 2006, the migrants rise. They call for a nationwide workers' strike on May 1, beseeching their supporters to take the day off, join a march, and refrain from spending money. I travel to New York City that morning, arriving at Union Square by noon. It is sated with mothers pushing baby strollers and fathers with their sons. Busboys brandish flags of both their native and adopted countries; nannies and construction workers flash signs with slogans like: WE'RE NOT CRIMINALS, WE'RE WORKERS; WE ARE ALSO AMERICANS; WE ALSO HAVE A DREAM. While the majority of the strikers are Latino, every nationality is represented. Afghans, Koreans, Chinese. Pakistanis. Jamaicans. Filipinos. Irish. They flood the streets of lower Manhattan and head toward City Hall. Thai cooks flash the victory sign through their take-out windows. Yarmulke-covered rabbis step out of stores to applaud. Everyone chants the United Farm Workers'

battle cry of "Sí, se puede (Yes we can)," even the non-Spanish speakers. It is a quintessential New York moment—and it is unfolding in cities across the country. Some 400,000 people strike in Chicago; one-sixth of the population does in Denver. Nearly half of the 100,000 undocumented farmworkers employed by Florida Fruit & Vegetable Association ditch the fields. Seventy-two thousand students walk out of their classrooms in the Los Angeles Unified School District.

For a brief moment, there is hope. A proposed Senate bill would allow undocumented workers who have labored in this nation for five or more years to commence the path toward citizenship after paying fines and back taxes. Under this "documented" status, they could periodically visit their families back home—and return to El Norte by bus rather than by foot or stuffed in the trunk of a car. Meanwhile, aspiring laborers could legally apply for guest worker visas. This would help curb the human tide at the border, enabling agents like Scott to invest their time and resources into chasing narcos, gangsters, and other threats to national security rather than people who want to scrub some dishes.

None of the legislative bills address the root of the problem, of course. None hold Mexico accountable for the abhorrent corruption that condemns so many to poverty. None call for a reflection upon the impact of neoliberal economic policies and trade agreements like NAFTA that have destabilized Mexico's agricultural industry and contributed to the reasons so many must migrate in the first place. None address the concerns of poor black, Latino, and white U.S. citizens, who fear that immigrants are depressing their wages (if not swiping their jobs altogether). The bills do nothing for frustrated schoolteachers whose classrooms are inundated with children who speak little or no English, or physicians whose clinics swell with the uninsured.

The legislation would, however, give millions of people who

are desperate to work a chance to do so with a little more dignity and a lot more safety. But due to a dearth of shared vision—and fear of the fast-approaching November elections—members of Congress kill the bills in committee.* The main measure they approve is the construction of a billion-dollar wall that will physically separate the United States from its second-largest trading partner.†

My cell phone rings one night with an unfamiliar number. "¿Qué onda, Esteffie? ¡Soy Marby!" someone cries.

Marby. He is the young worker I met on the plane ride to Chiapas last summer. Since then, he has been mugged by a coyote who filched his credit cards and nearly $500 in cash. He has been apprehended by the Migra (four times) and detained for weeks in a cinder block cell. He has crossed the Arizona desert with a bottle of water and sack of dry tortillas. But at last he is on a ranch in southern Wisconsin, earning $8.50 an hour caring for cattle six days a week and supporting five family members back in Chiapas.

Marby wants to know what's happening in La Casa Blanca, the White House. He hears so many contrary reports on the local Spanish talk radio station. "Everybody says there will be a raid here next Monday. Do you think if we boarded up the windows, they wouldn't come in?"

Politically pressured to beef up their enforcement, immigration officials are indeed plucking migrants off the street and seizing them from their homes. According to the *New York Times,* 221,664 illegal immigrants get banished from the United States

---

* A similar congressional measure offering legal status and a path to citizenship for millions of illegals tanked on June 28, 2007.

† Local officials will be able to decide whether to build actual or "virtual" fences in their districts. The former would be fifteen-foot-high double fences with an access road in between them; the latter would consist of stadium lighting, ground sensors, cameras, and observation towers.

in 2006, an increase of about 20 percent from the year before. I'm contemplating a response when Marby receives an incoming call. It's his Patrón; he must go.

"I promised I would call to say I am here, and I am here!" he crows before hanging up.

For a long while afterward, I stare at my cell phone as Marby's number blinks off and on. I don't know whether to be happy or sad for him.

CHAPTER TWENTY

REBEL YELL

D. F., Morelos, Oaxaca, Querétaro, D. F.,
June–July, 2006

As summer approaches, alarming reports from Mexico fill my in-box. Of violent uprisings among flower vendors in Atenco and miners in Michoacán. Of military incursions in Chiapas. Of teachers shedding blood during their annual labor strike in Oaxaca. Nothing is confirmable: mainstream U.S. media barely mention these events, while every independent media outlet and solidarity organization releases a different set of figures. I e-mail Franci and Padre Murcio in Oaxaca and Rebeca in Chiapas but receive no response. By mid-June, I can't stand it any longer and catch a plane to Mexico City. Raúl meets me at the airport looking as über-stylish as ever, his shirt unbuttoned to reveal just enough chest hair. Accompanying him is a gorgeous man named Danel who is eager to meet me.

"Raúl says you're from Corpus Christi. Is it true?" he asks.

When I nod, he launches into one of Selena's greatest hits, performing her signature hip-swiveling moves.

"Is he yours?" I whisper to Raúl as we stand back to watch.

"Not now, but he used to be." He grins. "Selena is his hero."

They take me to La Zona Rosa for lunch at an outdoor café broadcasting the World Cup match between Australia and Croatia on five television screens. Every male passerby stops to glimpse a few plays and cheers no matter who scores. I ask our waiter if Mexico has a stake in this particular game. "No," he says, plunking down our micheladas. "We just like to yell."

I am dying to talk about the presidential election, which will be held in two weeks. Vicente Fox staged a democratic revolution in 2000 when he uprooted the PRI's seventy-year reign. Who will lead the nation next? The fiery populist of the PRD party, Andrés Manuel López Obrador, held a double-digit lead until Felipe Calderón of Fox's conservative PAN party crept onto the scene. Among other things, the former pledges to renegotiate sections of NAFTA in favor of campesinos, while the latter promotes free trade as the nation's best hope for the future. The two run neck and neck with a trail of potential spoilers behind them. Subcomandante Marcos, meanwhile, is conducting an "Other Campaign," traveling to every state in the nation and holding community meetings where citizens step forward to file their grievances about local injustices while the Zapatistas take notes and listen.

Danel, however, wants to hear my Selena stories, and Raúl says he will explode unless he tells me about his new boyfriend. I relent for a bit—Sí, she got shot at a hotel* a mile from my parents' house; Sí, he sounds wonderful—before launching in. This is the most contentious presidential election in history: who are they voting for?

---

* Tejana superstar Selena Quintanilla-Pérez was slain by the president of her fan club at the Days Inn in Corpus Christi on March 31, 1995. Tens of thousands of fans filed past her coffin at Memorial Coliseum, leaving letters and white roses. The posthumous release of her album *Dreaming of You* sold 175,000 copies on its first day.

"The PAN," they say in unison.

"Aren't they homophobic?"

"Yes, but no way do we vote for the PRD," Raúl says firmly. "We say here in Mexico that Obrador is like the cat food Whiskas. Eight out of ten gatos prefer him."

Gato, or cat, is a (derogatory) term for Mexico's "humble" population, which indeed forms Obrador's support base.* Raúl, meanwhile, is the son of doctors who own multiple cars and homes and occasionally vacation in Europe. Class allegiance overrides sexual identity in this country. As we throw back micheladas, they dish on the other presidential candidates, including Víctor González Torres, owner of Mexico's (and my) favorite pharmacy, Similares.

"Can you believe it? A man who makes a living selling condoms is running for our president." Raúl shakes his head. "I've really lost a lot of respect for us."

They both adore Patricia Mercado from the Partido Alternativa Socialdemócrata, a progressive who advocates for gay and abortion rights, but they don't want to waste their vote on her.

"If the PRD wins, it's all over," Danel says ominously.

"There will be riots and bloodshed," Raúl adds.

"Why do you say that?"

Too late: the soccer match just ended and the house band is firing up a ranchera called "No me queda más" that Selena once covered. Within two chords, the boys are swooning to the lyrics.

> No me queda más
> Que perderme en un abismo de tristeza y
>   lágrimas

---

* Two of Obrador's campaign slogans are: "First Mexico, later foreigners," and "For the good of all, first the poor."

I have no choice
But to lose myself in an abyss of sadness and
tears

"Bring me a tequila. A double, with no ice," Raúl says, pretending to slit his wrists. They flick open their cell phones to gaze at photos of their boyfriends and send them text messages. This is reassuring, somehow. Even when civil unrest is on the table, love trumps all.

Hours later, we part. Danel grabs my shoulders and peers into my eyes. "Promise me you'll take a rose, a white rose, to Selena's memorial* and tell her Danel from D. F. misses her. Promise me you will!"

I do.

There is another promise I must keep. Víctor's daughter, Jumi, is turning fifteen. Last week, he quit his job of seven years at the deli in Brooklyn to fly home for her quinceañera. I've sworn to bear witness.

The following morning I travel through the state of Morelos and hail a cab to Víctor's. He is chatting with a primo at the foot of the hill. Out of apron and off of bicycle with no hefty cartons upon his shoulders, he looks rested and happy. We warmly embrace, then walk up the hill and through a metal gate. A dozen people flock upon us with kisses. Víctor leads me past

* The city of Corpus Christi erected a memorial to Selena two years after her death on North Shoreline Boulevard by the Peoples T-head. The life-size statue stares out to sea, microphone in hand. I've driven by at all hours of the day and night: Selena is almost never alone.

the tree-chained dogs to Abuela's three-walled home, currently serving as the quinceañera storage facility. Cases of beer and tequila are stacked five feet high and twelve feet wide alongside several hundred three-liter bottles of Coca-Cola.

"How many people are coming tomorrow?" I gasp.

"Quién sabe," says Judith. Who knows.

"Three or four hundred," Víctor says, trying to be helpful. "Maybe even five hundred. Six hundred. We'll see."

I ask for Jumi, but she's at a dance lesson. Do I want to go watch? I do, envisioning her waltzing with a gallant young man across a hardwood floor beneath the hawk eyes of a viejita in a hair bun. We walk to Salón Esmeralda, an open-air banquet hall with a cement floor and a soundstage at one end. A young woman runs toward me. It takes a moment to realize she is Jumi. Gone is the girl in the puppy-dog shirt. Grown and curved in all directions, she is wholly chola now, draped in a baggy T-shirt of Jesus Christ bloodied by thorns, camouflage pants, high-top sneakers, and silver hoop earrings. We hug and laugh until someone claps us to attention. A ponytailed man in a leopard-patterned shirt strides across the floor. The dance instructor. "Places, places everyone," he exclaims, flailing his arms about. You could balance shot glasses on his cheekbones.

Jumi's dance partners are six of her (male) primos. One wears a Metallica T-shirt and dog collar studded with silver spikes; the others are clad in hip-hop gear, their boxer shorts peeking above their jeans. Collectively they are the caballeros—or gentlemen—of the festivities. They gather into formation as the dance instructor blasts Cher's "Believe" through the speakers and lowers himself into a thigh-defying squat. "Feel it, move it, BE IT!" he commands between sucks on a cigarette.

Judith and Víctor beam as their daughter gyrates on the dance floor. Víctor tries to snuggle as they exchange whispers, but Judith nudges him away, giggling. After so many lonely nights, their reunion must be salty sweet.

The quinceañera court practices another full hour before the dance instructor releases them. Jumi links her arm through mine, and we charge a block ahead of the others to gossip. The boy she likes is coming tomorrow. "There's a girl who wants to fight me for him but I don't think any boy is worth fighting for, they should fight for you, don't you think?"

I secretly admire a system where you either kick someone's ass for love or get your own kicked, and that's the end of it. I assure Jumi that by tomorrow night, every chavo in town will be throwing punches for her. She squeals at the thought.

After dinner, it simultaneously occurs to everyone that we'll be feeding and liquoring up to six hundred people tomorrow. We whirl into activity. Jumi and I tackle the geraniums amassed in Abuela's backyard, covering each plastic pot with aluminum foil. The tías crochet serapes for the tequila bottles while Judith stalks around with a hot glue gun and Víctor and the caballeros lift heavy objects. First there are twenty of us and then there are thirty, all bustling about. The night grows warm but the wind keeps us cool. I have just wrapped my thirty-eighth pot when a tía brings me a plate of sliced mango. "Remember how we picked them from my tree last year?" She smiles.

As we share the tangy fruit, I ask after her family. She points to the Metallica caballero and claims him as a son. Since there are no men her age here save Víctor, I ask if her husband is in El Norte. Her forehead creases. "He left us years ago. I am still suffering, but ni modo. What else can I do, wake up every morning and think about how my son's father is a perro [dog]? You have to move on, mija."

A woman appears at the gate with a makeup kit. The nail stylist. All the little girls and I gather around the kitchen table to watch Jumi's hands transform into those of a woman. She opts for the Dragon Lady look, with nails half the length of her fingers. The stylist adorns them with silver tinsel, rhinestones, and tiny stars. Televisa* blares in the background, its political ads out-dramatizing its telenovelas. In one, an attractive urban professional has a nightmare about police in riot gear battling an onslaught of anarchists. After jerking awake at her office desk, she whips out a ballot and votes for the PAN. So this is where Raúl and Danel got their doomsday ideas about a PRD victory. Pundits will later contend that Obrador fatally erred by not immediately countering commercials like these that compared him to Venezuelan President Hugo Chávez (whom many Mexicans consider to be frighteningly radical) and otherwise declared him a "danger" to Mexico.† Yet his shoestring budget didn't allow it.

Around midnight, Jumi mentions that she will take her preparatoria entrance exams at 7 A.M. Her score will determine not only which (if any) school she can attend but also the type of profession she can pursue. Yet her new nails are so unwieldy, she can barely grasp a pencil. No one seems to fret this except me. What is an exam compared to womanhood?

I retire to Jumi's bedroom—which we're sharing—around 1 A.M. The entire extended family waves good night from their workstations. When I return seven hours later, they are still there, wearing the same clothes and finishing up their projects. Dozens more boxes have arrived. One is filled with five hundred shot glasses engraved with Jumi's name and MIS QUINCE AÑOS (My Fifteen Years); another has five hundred highball glasses.

---

*The largest media conglomerate in Latin America, Televisa has its hands in everything from TV production and broadcasting to feature films, radio, book publishing, professional sports promotion, paging services, satellite services, and the Internet. Its power and influence in Mexico is formidable.

† Mexico's electoral commission eventually ordered such advertisements off the air. See Manuel Roig-Franzia, "Chávez's Image Becomes Tool for Attack in Mexican Presidential Race," *Washington Post*, June 28, 2006.

There are hundreds of monogrammed salsa pots, salt and pepper shakers, napkin holders, and tortilla covers, plus place settings featuring Jumi's name embedded in lace and netting. The beer and tequila, meanwhile, multiplied overnight and birthed two buckets of limes.

Commotion erupts at the front gate. The pickup truck is here. Strangers appear out of nowhere to load it. I join them on the ride to Salón Esmeralda, balancing precariously on the bed rail. At the banquet hall, a lone worker single-handedly sets up seating for five hundred. I don't see how everything will be ready on time, but everybody seems tranquilo. I return to the house just as Jumi does from her three-hour exam, mentally spent. We retreat to her bedroom, where I pour her into a corset and she steps into puddles of petticoats.

"¡JUMI!" Judith shouts.

We race downstairs. The hairstylist has arrived. Jumi sits beneath the avocado tree as she constructs wonder curls in a halo around her head with bobby pins and Aqua Net. Then the caballeros dart in, decked out in uniforms modeled off the Spanish Conquest: long white double-breasted coats trimmed with gold braid, white gloves, swords, and soldier hats. "¡Jumi! We're going to be late." I grab her train, and we rush out the gate. The whole barrio has gathered outside. They clap as we dash past. The caballeros cram into one car; Víctor, Judith, Jumi, and I into the other. Our driver is a peroxide blonde who says she once lived in Milwaukee.

The church is forty-five minutes away; Mass starts in thirty. The blonde lady slams it. The giant pink bow on our car hood grants us the right of way: everyone honks in felicidades as we swerve past. At the church, the caballeros form an archway with their swords. Father and daughter duck beneath it as the mariachis play a joyous tune and everyone in the pews rises to their feet. Jumi kneels alone at the altar, clutching her fake calla lilies, until someone whispers to Víctor and Judith that the seats beside her are theirs. They scramble forward.

The priest concludes Mass by asking Jumi for the name of her best friend.

"Mi mamá y mi papá," she replies.

"That's right, Jumi," he coos. "Your parents will always be there for you."

At that, he asks the three to stand and face the audience. Víctor smiles not just with his lips but his eyes, his chest, his whole being. After a few photos, we roar back to Salón Esmeralda, where several hundred people await in a salon magically transformed into a quinceañera banquet hall, complete with streamers and balloons. So many party favors and aluminum-covered flower pots deck the tables, the guests must crane their necks to see one another.

"Where are the security guards?" Judith hisses.

I stare at her blankly.

"There might be fights," she explains.

The tequila is another concern: they don't want to stack it on the bar "because people will steal it and drink it and then we'll really have problems." The blonde offers her car. We stuff the cases inside.

"And the presents?" Víctor whispers.

A caballero is stationed beside them.

May the fiesta begin! The first of two bands saunters onto the stage in norteño chic (cowboy hats, cowboy boots, and rump-sculpting jeans) and fires up some cumbias. After slamming a few beers, couples of all ages and sizes take to the floor as the single, divorced, and widowed people look on. The sole soloist dances with an open container of salsa balanced atop her head. We all watch, mesmerized, as she defies gravity and sense. "Qué loca," the tías whisper.

An hour before midnight, the house lights blacken and opera music blasts forth. The caballeros appear in a spotlight carrying an enormous blinking star. Jumi sits yogi-style inside of it. They lower her onto the dance floor, now ablaze with the light of twelve candelabras. Jumi tries to step out of the star gracefully but her petticoats intervene. The caballeros break her fall and somehow scoop her out. She strides across the floor with her head held high. We clap. Céline Dion belts out "Power of Love" as the court begins their recital, which primarily consists of the caballeros bowing on one knee whenever Jumi glides past.

Then the padrinos line up. One by one, they proffer gifts to Jumi upon a red velvet pillow: a tiara (which shows she is a princess before God), a bracelet (representing the unending circle of life), earrings (to hear the word of God), a Bible (to read it), a scepter (to symbolize the responsibility she has acquired as a new adult), and a four-inch pair of stiletto heels. She slips on the heels and tiara and looks around for her father so they can share a dance. He is nowhere to be seen. We chant his name to no avail. Finally, the house lights flicker on. Víctor and Judith are spotted way in the back, guarding the bar. The dance instructor swiftly retrieves them.

When Víctor takes his daughter into his arms, something stirs within me. Maybe it's the knowledge of what he sacrificed for tonight. Or the aesthetic of a father dancing with his little girl-turned-woman. Or the tequila I just shot. Whatever. Tears leak as I rise to my feet in applause. Others join me for a standing ovation. The moment is tender but brief: according to tradition, Jumi must now waltz with every adult on the premises. This takes over an hour, after which she breaks for the bathroom for a costume change. She and the caballeros return in high-top sneakers and sideways baseball caps to perform the Kumbia Kings' techno-mariachi-hip-hop hit "Pachuco." The crowd goes wild as they shake their asses and pretend to shoot one another. For the encore (Cher's "Believe") Jumi pours back into her corset and a ruffled skirt that commences four inches beneath her pubic bone and ripples down the back. Strobe lights and disco smoke shroud the choreography, but no matter—here come the fireworks! The words MIS QUINCE AÑOS shower the eight-tiered birthday cake with debris as the guests dart away, coughing.

And with that, my cost analysis of this event smashes through the roof. A journalist will later tell me that Mexican families traditionally spend the equivalent of three years' salary on their daughters' quinceañeras. In Víctor terms, that is roughly 12,000 bicycle deliveries of 20,000 bagel-and-egg sandwiches prepared over a hot griddle 2,300 miles from home. And the man is still hustling, bringing his guests plates of food and bottles of beer as Judith trails behind. Never do I see them dancing or laughing or even sitting, opting instead to pass out party favors their guests are too blitzed to notice. I soon cease drinking altogether. It is like guzzling his sweat.

Víctor could have spent this hard-earned money on any number of things. A college fund for Jumi. A small business. A car. Investments that could have shaped their future. He elected instead to give his daughter the spotlight, to elevate her status in the community. (No doubt, this also proved his worth as a father. He may have abandoned Jumi for seven years, but look at her now, a veritable princess!) Which would she have preferred, though: this one night—or all those missing years with him?

In *Labyrinth of Solitude*, Octavio Paz writes, "How could a poor Mexican live without the two or three annual fiestas that make up for his poverty and misery? Fiestas are our only luxury. . . . [It] is not merely a return to an original state of formless and normless liberty: the Mexican is not seeking to return, but to escape from himself, to exceed himself." Mexicans believe in the here and now; they strive for the delectable moments of being. And tonight has been chock-full of them. Certainly, Víctor's money could have been more wisely spent. But not more memorably. No girl ever forgets the night she became a woman.

By 3:30 A.M., most of the guests have straggled home. Salón Esmeralda is a train wreck, and la familia gets to clean it. This is no small order. We have been partying for eleven hours straight. Our heads are throbbing, our ears are ringing. The temperature has dropped thirty degrees. But we are Mexican. We aguantar. Like that seven-year-old walking by. Her eyes are glazed as doughnuts, but she has an empty beer bottle in one hand and a drained shot glass in the other. If she can hack this, I can too. I grab a stack of Styrofoam plates and march toward the Dumpster.

Half an hour later, I join Abuela at a table. We are going to be here until dawn. Maybe even tomorrow afternoon. I plop my head atop a stack of napkins that say JUMI. Leaving now would be unforgivable. It would break family code. If I'm too exhausted to clean, I should at least patiently snooze while the others do it.

By 4:30 A.M., I reach acceptance. I am not a Mexican who can aguantar. I am an American who wants to go home. Full of shame, I ask Víctor for the house keys. He hands them over, nimble as a zombie. I search around for Jumi. She is sprawled across three chairs, wearing eight inches of skirt and heels. I help her up and we teeter into the street for a taxi. A passing drunkard does a double-take at Jumi. Though only half conscious, she pulls up her rebozo.

"My quinceañera . . . is it over?" she mumbles.

"It's over," I reply. "Congratulations, Jumi. You're officially a woman."

From Víctor's place, I hop a bus back to D. F. to catch a discussion about the recent bloodshed in San Salvador Atenco. Located eighteen miles northeast of Mexico City, Atenco has a community of five thousand farmers who till land swiped from the rich and granted to the poor by none other than Emiliano Zapata. In 2002, engineers showed up unannounced and started measuring their cornfields. The Fox government had chosen their homeland as the future site of a $2.3 billion state-of-the-art airport for the nation's capital but had neglected to inform them. When the farmers were offered as little as seven pesos per square meter of land, they declared war, hijacking and torching government vehicles and kidnapping public officials, nineteen of whom they threatened to tie to gasoline tankers and detonate. The government tried to ameliorate the situation by offering up to fifty pesos per square meter of land as well as jobs at the new airport, but it was too late. Clenching their machetes in their hands, the farmers declared that the runways could only be built over their dead bodies. A humiliated Fox withdrew, and the citizens of Atenco became heroes of civil resistance to some; adversaries of badly needed economic development to others.

It is unclear what sparked the latest violence in their community. Most news reports blame a scuffle between police and unauthorized flower vendors, while blogs either say it was an anti–Wal-Mart demonstration or a police attempt to block a tour stop of Subcomandante Marcos's Other Campaign. Whatever the case, armed police battled machete-wielding, Molotov-cocktail-throwing civilians in multiple locations on May 3, including at a market in nearby Texcoco and a highway outside Atenco. Then, in the early morning hours of May 4, several thousand riot police stormed Atenco's town square and—after quashing its defenders—beat civilians indiscriminately. All told, scores on both sides sustained severe injuries and two died: a fourteen-year-old boy and a twenty-year-old college student. Two hundred and forty-one protesters were arrested, and five foreigners deported.

The crowd at the Círculo Teatral near Chapultepec Park is artsy and activist. Half a dozen speakers sit before us; tabby cats prowl the aisles of the theater. A Spaniard opens the panel by announcing that a commission of human rights activists from seven countries will investigate the tragedy. Then she gives the floor to her copresenters, who include Ángel Benhumea, one of the fathers of the dead.

"For eleven hours we waited for medical help. My son lay dying, but help did not come," he says, lifting his glasses to dab his eyes. "We live in a terrorist state here in Mexico. The entire republic has been militarized and the president can commit whatever crime he wants with impunity."

The women panelists describe another abuse endured that weekend. En route to the detention center, police officers are said to have sexually assaulted some two dozen protesters (including foreigners*) and raped at least seven. They have also been accused of sodomizing a boy with a baton. The women now suffer vaginal infections, the panelists say, and worry about pregnancy.

Forty-five minutes into the presentation, the theater doors swing open. Heads turn as the citizens of Atenco file in, each wearing a red bandana around their neck and holding a machete in the air. The audience scrunches together to make room for them, many relinquishing their seats. Atenco fills the aisles and the floor and the spaces in between and then begins to speak.

"All we have is our land and our identity. And if they take away our land, they take away our identity," says a woman braced against the railing on the upper level. "The key is to organize. The key is solidarity. The key is continuing the struggle. The key is resistance."

"TODOS SOMOS ATENCO," the audience responds. We are all Atenco.

Afterward, I pounce on a man the size of a linebacker who represents a group called Frente de Pueblos en Defensa de la Tierra (Popular Front to Defend the Land). He got detained that weekend in Atenco. "We received no medical attention in prison. We had no water to drink or clean ourselves with. They made us stand against the wall with our arms over our heads and they beat us on the back. My family paid fourteen thousand pesos to get me out but thirty of our compañeros remain inside."

He rises then, for his community is leaving. I wish him luck. He solemnly nods and walks away, his machete high in the air.

---

* Among the women sexually abused by police was a Chilean cinematography student named Valentina Palma Novoa, who traveled to Atenco to document the protests. Her chilling account of being assaulted, arrested, and deported can be found at NarcoNews.com.

While in D. F., I try to wrap my head around the recent events in Oaxaca. As I witnessed last summer, their populist rebellion has been fomenting for years, but it shifted into high gear in May, when tens of thousands of public school teachers from across the state sprang upon the capital's zócalo to demand a pay raise, as they have annually for the past twenty-six years. Because this is an election year, their plantón lasted longer than usual, which threatened to upset Guelaguetza tourism in the capital as well as leave 1.3 million students without a teacher once classes resumed. In the predawn hours of June 14, Governor Ulises Ruiz dispatched 1,700 state police to the zócalo to clear them out. Pandemonium ensued as helicopters dropped canisters of tear gas, but the teachers defended their turf with sticks and stones, aided by sympathetic residents as well as worker, indigenous, student, and activist groups who later form a coalition called Asamblea Popular de los Pueblos de Oaxaca (Popular Assembly of the Peoples of Oaxaca, or APPO). The police fled the city, and the protesters have held it ever since.

One morning, the radio announces that a delegation of Oaxacan teachers has just arrived in D. F. to deliver more than one million signatures to the federal government. I find them behind the Legislative Assembly of the Federal District near the Zócalo on Calle Tacuba. About two hundred in number, they squat in the shadows of the building, holding banners that read ULISES: YOUR GOVERNMENT IN OAXACA IS HELL and JUNE 14: WE'LL NEVER FORGET. Police nearly outnumber them, but the officers look more bored than menacing, lounging in buses across the street. I walk among the teachers with a notebook in my hands.

"Pardon," someone carefully enunciates in English. "You write about us?"

He is an effeminate man with a sweater tied across his shoulders. A name tag identifies him as a teacher from the Mixteca region of western Oaxaca. When I nod, he launches into his story, tilting his umbrella so it shields us both from the sun. "I teach twenty-two students. They are ages three to six. We have not enough crayons or paper. Our school is remote. Our bus has no road. We have no plumbing or electricity. And for this, we make two thousand pesos every fifteen days!"

I ask about the death toll on June 14. He heard that a pregnant woman miscarried after escaping the tear gas but doesn't know of any other casualties.* At that, a portly woman stalks over. "Eight died that day," she shouts, shaking her fist. "They burned our blankets and hurt our children. Taxi drivers had to rescue us."

The gates of the Legislative Assembly swing open. The teachers' representatives successfully delivered their signatures. Everyone rushes forth to greet them. "We march tomorrow in Oaxaca," the first teacher calls over his shoulder. "One-half million people. You march too?"

Before I can respond, someone thrusts something into my face and shakes it: a centerfold from *Noticias* featuring a full-color collage of images from June 14. Blood streaks a man's face. Riot police storm through smoke. Teachers flee calamity.

"Do you know what is happening in our city?" she demands.

I tell her I'll be at the march tomorrow. She snatches back the centerfold and throws her fist in the air. "YA CAYÓ, YA CAYÓ. ¡ULISES YA CAYÓ!"

The crowd repeats: He's already fallen, he's already fallen. Ulises has already fallen.

---

* Union leader Enrique Rueda told the Agence France-Presse that four were killed on June 14, including a child. Pacifica Radio's "Democracy Now!" show interviewed strikers who said eleven died, including two children. The local Red Cross only confirmed injuries, of which the *Los Angeles Times* reported sixty-six.

The midnight bus to Oaxaca pulls into the terminal at 6:15 A.M. I stagger outside and into a taxi. The driver is annoyed to learn that I've traveled all the way here for the march. "Those teachers complain they don't get paid well, but look at them! They only work a few hours a day and don't even do a good job and they earn two thousand pesos every fifteen days, plus health insurance and paid vacation!" he grumbles. "Meanwhile, I'm out here twelve hours a day making only five hundred pesos more. But who comes to interview me?"

I crash a few hours at a hotel, then head downtown. It is a shock to see. Windows are shattered. Pavement is broken. Nearly every standing structure—fences, benches, storefronts, sides of stone buildings, even street curbs—is tagged with anti-Ulises graffiti like ULISES ASESINO DE MAESTROS Y DE NIÑOS. (Ulises Murdered Teachers and Children.) In the accompanying illustrations, Ulises is portrayed as a dog, a burro, a rat, a pig, a raccoon, an octopus, a snake—even fly-infested shit.

Then there is the plantón. Plastic sheeting forms a canopy over much of downtown, and thousands of people camp beneath it upon cardboard and blankets. The artistically inclined hunch over poster board, preparing signs for the march ahead. Designated cooks flip tortillas atop portable stoves. The men take charge of security, fortifying the end of each city block with tin sheet, rocks, and concrete and standing guard throughout the night. Sanitation committees monitor the waste.

"Compañeros, I need help here," a woman shouts after sweeping a mound of refuse. People promptly gather to help scoop it into bags.

The zócalo appears to be headquarters for the teachers' supporters, collectively known as APPO. Some sleep in tents; others, in the indentations of trees. Banners of Marx, Engels, and Lenin hang from the gazebo, and bulletin boards dripping with news updates dot the plaza. College students pass out flyers printed on tissue-thin paper. Many of the surrounding sidewalk cafés are boarded shut, but not my favorite one. I order chicken mole enchiladas and ask the waitress about the plantón. She grimaces. "It's been thirty-seven days now! All the tourists are gone. I don't know how we'll make it. You're my only customer all morning. I understand why they're doing it, but we're all suffering because of it."

In the turbulent months ahead, many Oaxacan restaurants, boutiques, and hotels* will fold from the near collapse in tourism. The city's underground economy, however, flourishes. Corn-on-the-cob vendors and ice pop peddlers fill their pockets off profits from the strikers, and indigenous artisans fare well too. The governor kicked them off the zócalo last year, deeming them an eyesore for tourists, but now that the police are gone, they can sell their wares wherever they please.

After breakfast, I wander over to Alameda de León and settle on a fountain to take in the scene. A middle-aged couple sits on a nearby bench. We exchange nods in greeting and they ask why I am still here, as most foreigners have evacuated. When I reveal my interest in the plantón, they introduce themselves as primary school teachers from Huajuapan de León in northwestern Oaxaca. They instruct forty students apiece, levels one through six.†

"It is too great an age range. We can't give them enough attention," says the wife, Guadalupe, as she straightens her Dallas

---

* In August 2006, the *New York Times* reported that more than a thousand hotel workers were laid off in Oaxaca that summer, and the hotel industry lost about $150 million in revenue, with reservations canceled well into 2007.

† Twenty-one percent of primary schools in Mexico have one teacher assigned to all six grades. This is especially prevalent in indigenous schools (26 percent) and rural schools (20 percent). See Fernando Remiers, "Educational Opportunity and Policy in Latin America," *Unequal Schools, Unequal Chances* (Cambridge, MA: Harvard University Press, 2000).

Cowboys baseball cap. "Our students experience emotional problems because their fathers go to El Norte and abandon them for months and years at a time. They need psychologists and social workers, but there is no money to hire them."

Does the government offer any aid?

Her husband, Ignacio, guffaws. "They bring us beans and rice in the weeks before the election so they will get our vote."

This inspires a discussion of the presidential candidates.

"Everyone here is rooting for El Peje,"* Guadalupe says, using Obrador's nickname. "But the PAN will win because they have so much more money for advertising. People are very uneducated in Mexico. If they see something on TV, they believe it."

We chat until their group leader announces it is time to leave for the march.

"¡Vámonos!" They smile at me, extending a hand. Let's go.

But how? According to *Noticias*, public transportation halted at 2 P.M. today,† and taxis to the rallying point near the airport would be expensive. We walk to the zócalo to confer with others. Rumor has it, some local organizations are sending alternative transportation, but no one knows the details. We continue walking until a bright yellow pickup truck turns a distant corner and barrels toward us. Guadalupe grabs my hand and we jump into the cab as Ignacio and the others pile into the bed. Those who don't fit slap the railing as if wishing us luck. We lurch through the street and turn onto the main highway, which resembles a massive tailgate party—only, sober. The road chokes with cars and trucks overflowing with demonstrators brandishing signs scribed

---

* El Peje is short for peje lagarto, an alligator-type creature commonly eaten for breakfast in Obrador's home state of Tabasco. People say he shares its tough exterior but tender meat.

† Ignacio blames this on the governor's attempt to keep demonstrators from reaching the march's gathering point near the airport, six kilometers away.

in schoolteacher penmanship. Everyone is honking; everyone is chanting. Guadalupe rolls down the window and waves.

A police roadblock appears ahead. Our driver cuts a sharp corner and doglegs through a residential area, past viejitas selling tortillas and children chasing chickens. I ask Guadalupe if she is nervous. (I am.) She shakes her head. "The only thing I am thinking of now is the injustice between the social classes here in Mexico. That makes me so mad, it numbs me to everything else."

The truck halts, and we all spill out. We've reached the section of highway where the other teachers from Huajuapan are gathering. The protesters nearest the airport have already started marching toward us; we are to remain here until they pass and then file in behind them so we can march as a collective to the rallying point at a stadium many miles away. We lean against a fence and within an hour are sitting against it atop plastic bags. Guadalupe asks about my work.

"We want to write too," she says, "but we don't know how to express ourselves because we've never been given the chance. We have always been taught to respect our elders. We have a culture of listening, not speaking."

"But you're speaking out now, at this protest."

"Here, we are only expressing ourselves physically. And there are many of us. Four hundred thousand, five hundred thousand. Maybe even a million. But we can never do it individually," she says.

A band of black-clad youth approach us wearing bandanas and surgical masks. Spray paint in hand, they tag the adjacent fence with ULISES ASESINO. Ulises Is a Murderer.

Guadalupe smiles. "This too is a form of expression. But they do it as a group. Never alone."

A clap of thunder is chased by rain. Poncho vendors appear like genies. I open my umbrella, and Guadalupe and Ignacio slip beneath. Finally, around 4 P.M., the first wave of marchers flows by, twenty people across and hours deep. We gather on the street curb and cheer as if at a parade. There are college students wearing Che Guevara shirts. Triquis wearing ankle-length huipiles. Campesinos in straw hats and threadbare trousers.

"Here comes Huajuapan!" Ignacio shouts.

Time to merge into the march. Though I'm at least a head taller than everyone, I must hustle to keep up. Marchers do the wave, engage in call-and-response, sing, chant, pray. When gaps form within the masses, they gallop forth to fill them. A crush of spectators clap from the sidelines and overpasses, to which the marchers respond: "Yes, we see/Yes, we see/The support of the people, we see."

At mile two, we pass a man holding a papier-mâché helicopter flown by a miniature Ulises. "Like the helicopters from June fourteenth," Guadalupe explains. "They dropped tear gas on us and—¡oye! ¡Cuidado!"

Too late. Helicopter Man has just released a lever over my head. Flour plops out, blanketing my hair, clothes, and camera lens. The spectators double over in laughter. "At least it's not tear gas!" he says when I glare at him.

Around 9 P.M., we reach downtown. What a relief: I'm exhausted.

"¡Qué bien!" Guadalupe exclaims. "We're halfway there."

Ask anyone who knows me. "High energy" will be one of the first adjectives they pick to describe me, guaranteed. But in Mexico, I can't even keep up with people who have been camping atop cardboard for thirty-seven days. However badly I want to complete this march, I simply cannot aguantar. I apologize to Guadalupe and Ignacio, who make me promise to visit them in Huajuapan someday. "You can stay with us in our house for a week. Two weeks. A month! As long as you want. We will make you mole!"

The streets leading to the zócalo are vacant. In the plaza by the cathedral, however, thick crowds swarm DVD vendors screening their hottest item: home videos of the June 14 crackdown. Tonight they offer forty minutes of footage for fifteen pesos. By tomorrow afternoon, they'll be burning three hours for thirty pesos that include segments from today's march. It is a postmodern concept, filming your own struggle and selling it immediately afterward to the people struggling alongside you. Yet legitimizing—and weirdly empowering.

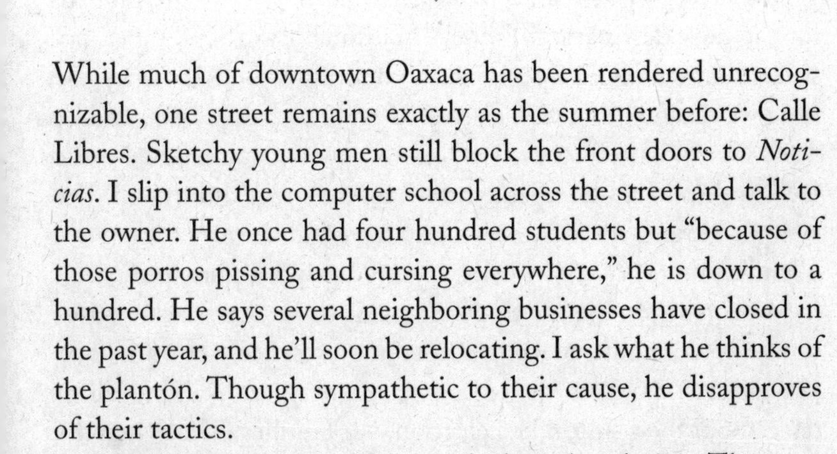

While much of downtown Oaxaca has been rendered unrecognizable, one street remains exactly as the summer before: Calle Libres. Sketchy young men still block the front doors to *Noticias*. I slip into the computer school across the street and talk to the owner. He once had four hundred students but "because of those porros pissing and cursing everywhere," he is down to a hundred. He says several neighboring businesses have closed in the past year, and he'll soon be relocating. I ask what he thinks of the plantón. Though sympathetic to their cause, he disapproves of their tactics.

"Those teachers aren't entirely here by choice. They get fined by their union if they don't show up to strike," he says. "One of my cousins lives an eighty-peso bus ride away but she still must come into the city every morning to strike or else pay a fee."

From there, I walk to *Noticias*'s latest headquarters on Calle Independencia. The receptionist escorts me to the office of editor Ismael Sanmartín Hernández. He rises, dimpled and smiling, holding the morning edition like a trophy. ¡HISTÓRICO! the front-page headline declares over a full-color crowd shot.

"Twenty percent of Oaxaca's population took to the streets yesterday," he says. "The thermometer of the social climate of this country is right here. And we're having a rebellion. A popular rebellion."

He still has no idea when his own paper's "strike" will end.* A PRD win on Sunday could send the porros packing, but Ismael isn't confident the party will pull through, despite Obrador's popularity. "The government completely controls our elections. They manipulate the process, buying votes with food, T-shirts, cement. The PRI used to pay people five hundred pesos for sneaking out blank ballots. I'm not convinced this won't happen again."

After our visit, I walk to a nearby park to mentally prepare for my next destination: Franci's boutique. Last September, my sister found a friend interested in adopting Claudia, but by the time we reached Franci, a Zapotec family had already taken her. This was wonderful news, of course, but I couldn't shake the feeling that I had let Claudia down somehow. And myself. I've e-mailed Franci several times for updates, but she never responds. Claudia's memory, meanwhile, haunts me like a phantom.

I peek inside the boutique. Franci is slipping a sparkly outfit onto a mannequin. Sensing someone's presence, she turns and squeals. We fall into an embrace, laughing and talking all at once about the plantón, the election, our families, life. When the conversation shifts to Claudia, however, her shining eyes dim. The Zapotec family adored her, but she refused to go to school, claiming the other kids beat her up. She also had nightmares that grew increasingly violent. They didn't know how to handle her. Then the family patriarch died of heart failure. Unable to care for a troubled child amid their own grief, they sent her to a home for street girls six months ago.

Guilt comes on like a hurricane. I am mired in it, drenched. I've worked in children's shelters before. Even the best ones

---

*There is more drama to come. On August 10, 2006, two hooded gunmen storm into the office of *Noticias*, demanding to see the publisher. They fire at the ceiling and equipment, critically injuring two employees. The CROC doesn't end its strike until that December.

crush kids' innocence, their vitality. Franci tries to console me. "She has twenty-five new sisters now. They are just like her. They understand her."

She promises to take me there Saturday morning.

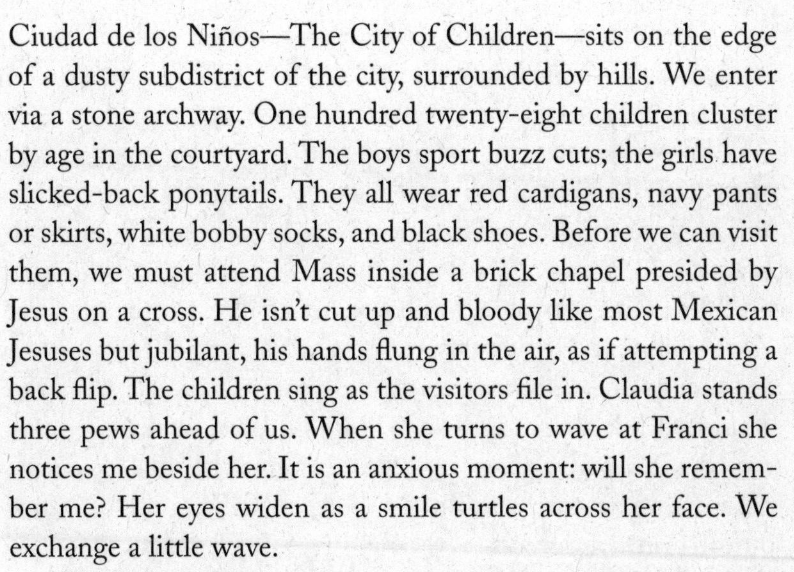

Ciudad de los Niños—The City of Children—sits on the edge of a dusty subdistrict of the city, surrounded by hills. We enter via a stone archway. One hundred twenty-eight children cluster by age in the courtyard. The boys sport buzz cuts; the girls have slicked-back ponytails. They all wear red cardigans, navy pants or skirts, white bobby socks, and black shoes. Before we can visit them, we must attend Mass inside a brick chapel presided by Jesus on a cross. He isn't cut up and bloody like most Mexican Jesuses but jubilant, his hands flung in the air, as if attempting a back flip. The children sing as the visitors file in. Claudia stands three pews ahead of us. When she turns to wave at Franci she notices me beside her. It is an anxious moment: will she remember me? Her eyes widen as a smile turtles across her face. We exchange a little wave.

The minute Mass ends, the other visitors bolt for the door. I soon see why: the screening process is interminable. An hour passes before Franci and I gain admittance to the community room, where families reunite upon picnic benches. A nun brings in Claudia, who grasps a fruit drink in one fist and a lollipop in the other. She hugs Franci hello and slips the sucker into her mouth. Most of her front teeth are now missing and the back ones have rotted gray.

Franci asks if she remembers me.

"No," she snaps, without even looking.

"Sure you do," Franci coos, stroking her hair. "Remember how she and her sister took photos of you at El Pochote?"

"No."

"Yes you do, Claudia. They brought you a doll!"

She shakes her head virulently.

This is so painful. Pulling out a notebook, I ask Claudia if she's learned how to write her name. She scrawls it out carefully, then adds vowels and the numbers one through ten. I reward her with a bag of twenty-six hair clips—one for her and all of her "friends."

"They are not my friends," she snaps. "They have lice."

"Claudia," Franci says tiredly. "You know that is not true."

"Tell us how you spend your days," I say.

"We wake up at five and take a cold shower and go to classes and clean and work in the garden and cook and clean some more and study and clean and then we sleep. I want to go home with Franci."

But Franci can't take on this responsibility. Neither can the Zapotec family. Neither can I. And Claudia knows it.

Our twenty allotted minutes evaporate. Claudia hugs me good-bye, but numbly. The daily blur of social workers, priests, nurses, nuns, and teachers have already taught her to detach. She has a hardness now, a wariness. We leave Cuidad de los Niños on the brink of depression. Franci suggests we pray. I envy this quality in the religious—how they can extract so much comfort through prayer, even believe it will generate good. In situations like this, I just wallow in guilt.

A bus drops us off at Padre Murcio's church. The zócalo is almost empty now, as the teachers have returned to their hometowns to vote in tomorrow's presidential election. We walk through the courtyard and into the church where Padre Murcio is holding Mass and position ourselves upon a wooden kneeler. Franci prays so devoutly, she practically floats, but I am weighted and heavy. Could I have prevented what happened to Claudia?

After a time, I sink into the pew and try to follow the sermon. Padre Murcio has dedicated the whole Mass to the election. "Don't sell your vote!" he shouts after the parishioners as they depart. We follow him through the courtyard and up the stairs to the dining quarters, where he serves us sliced papaya. I ask if he heard the gunfire on June 14.

"Heard it? Tear gas filled our courtyard!" he exclaims. "The teachers started banging on the doors, begging to be allowed inside."

The priests held a quick meeting and Padre Murcio persuaded them to open the doors. They have since sheltered about 1,300 people. "The consciousness of Oaxaca has awakened," he says. "And tomorrow, we will rise."

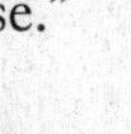

I catch the midnight bus back to D. F., arriving at dawn on Sunday, July 2. Election placards sway from the telephone wires, the light posts, the balconies, the trees; they coat the sides of buildings six layers deep. A taxi drops me off beneath a giant PAN billboard in an artsy colonia called Coyoacán, where I will spend two nights with the family of someone I happily dated in Jersey—until he got deported.*

Yolande, the matriarch, meets me at the front gate, elegant even in a bathrobe and slippers: dark-haired and ivory-skinned with heavily outlined eyes. Leading me into the dining nook, she prepares a pot of café-con-leche and admits to being so nervous about the election, she didn't sleep last night. (A psychology professor at UNAM, she ardently supports Obrador.) After breakfast, I tag along to her polling station set right inside the housing complex, spread across two parking spaces and covered in plastic wrap reading EL VOTO ES LIBRE Y SECRETO. The Vote Is Free and Secret. She explains the process while we wait. First

* Long story. Wouldn't fit in a footnote.

you hand over your voting card, which includes your photo and thumbprint along with the election years (which get indented so the card cannot be reused that year). After the officials check your card against the ledger, they rip out color-coded ballots from a booklet. Party logos* are stamped across each page along with the names of the candidates. Simply draw an *X* across your party of choice, fold the ballot, and stuff it into its corresponding color-coordinated box. No hanging chads, no electronic foul-ups. Before you leave, an official paints your right thumb with an ink that won't wear off for twenty-four hours so you can't vote again† and returns your card. As we wait, four voters fold their ballots outside the booth, revealing their *X*s. Two vote for the PAN and two for the PRD.

I join the family at a fancy courtyard restaurant that evening. Yolande asks the maître d' if they honor the 10 percent voter's discount that most restaurants grant customers with inky thumbs on election day.

"Only if you voted for the PAN," a nearby diner replies.

Yolande laughs politely, then turns to us and glowers. "Not on your life."

I grill the family about their party affiliations as we eat. Yolande's daughter, a college student, also voted PRD; Yolande's boyfriend, Juan, voted for the PAN. "I'm a businessman," he reasons. Though fiscally conservative, he is socially progressive. He supports open borders, takes pride that Mexico has no death penalty, and believes that drugs should be legalized.

"*All* drugs?" I ask.

"Of course! How else will we ever stop this bloodshed?"

---

* The PRI's colors are green, white, and red (like the Mexican flag), the PAN's are blue and white, and the PRD's are yellow and black. Supporters wear these colors on election day as a way of rooting for their party.

† This is why Mexican politicians often flash their thumbs in photographs. They are saying: "I've just voted and you should too. For me."

Plenty of Mexicans support the legalization of drugs, including politicians. The United States recently browbeat President Fox into scrapping a popular bill that would have decriminalized the possession of a small bounty of drugs, including five grams of pot, half a gram of cocaine, several hits of LSD, a couple of ecstasy pills, and a kilo of peyote. The only downside Juan could predict in full drug legalization is that narcos might stop paying their taxes.

"Businessmen always try to sneak out of paying taxes,* but not the narcos. They *want* to pay taxes because it cleans their money. No, mija, the narcos are *great* for our economy!"

Five minutes before the election results are announced at 11 P.M., I climb into bed with Yolande and Juan. After the station's countdown, Luis Carlos Ugalde, president of the Federal Electoral Institute, appears and—after applauding the republic for their patience—says the election is too close to call. They will not release the results of their exit poll. Officials will count every vote and declare a winner, hopefully by Wednesday. President Fox appears next, wooden as a puppet. He too praises the republic for their comportment and assures them that "each one of your votes will be duly counted and respected."

Cameras then turn to Obrador seizing the podium at his campaign headquarters. Glistening in sweat, he looks agitated but victorious. "We triumphed, we won."

Two seconds later, Calderón appears on the screen—equally sweaty but polished. "The quick counts signal that we have won the presidential election." He beams.

Yolande, Juan, and I stare at one another in astonishment.

---

* A 2002 study showed that about 40 percent of businesses and 70 percent of small-business owners and professionals either cheat on their taxes or skip out altogether. See James C. McKinley Jr., "In Race for Mexico's Presidency, Populist Tilts at a Privileged Elite," *New York Times*, June 17, 2006, A1.

By Thursday, turmoil seems imminent. Conservative media claim that Calderón won by a hairline while liberal and independent media report electoral fraud, including bags of Obrador ballots found in garbage cans. I am in Querétaro now, passing a long afternoon at Café Al Fondo, where the mood induces déjà vu. The chain-smoking, chess-playing, Obrador-supporting crowd wears the same look of anger/disillusionment/grief that their counterparts did in cafés across Brooklyn after George W. Bush's elections. They talk the same way too, in half sentences that trail off into space.

"We were so certain . . ."

"It doesn't seem possible . . ."

"There is just no way . . ."

After finishing my tea, I drop in on Elsa, the owner of the café. A thick-haired woman with a commanding presence, she sits on a swivel chair in the back office while her friend Fidelina slurps an ice pop on the couch. As members of Alianza Cívica, a nonpartisan voters' rights and education organization, both women worked as election monitors on Sunday.

"So many irregularities," Elsa says, sighing as she stirs her coffee. Polls closed down too early in some districts; in others, police tore down the results too quickly.* Her group counted ten instances where the same voter card appeared twice in a registration ledger with the same information but different photographs—in just four pages. What disturbs her most, however, is the vote buying she witnessed prior to July 2.

---

* As soon as votes have been tabulated at polling stations, results are publicly posted.

"The PAN handed out construction materials* right before the election in the poorest regions of Jalpan," she says. "Of course, they officially did so as the government so they could say it had nothing to do with the PAN. But why do they only distribute goods around election time and never during the rest of the sexenio [the six-year duration of a presidential term]? Why do they paint everything blue and white [the colors of the PAN logo]?"

Fidelina lowers her ice pop and leans forward, as if to gossip. "And they frightened people by manipulating their faith. They convinced people that a vote for the PRD was a vote against Christ. At my church in Huimilpan, the priest said, 'Go out there and vote for the party with the same colors as the sky, the home of our Lord, Jesus Christ.' He never said PAN, but you knew exactly who he was talking about! And the next day at the polls, I overheard a woman say, 'At least I am good with the Lord now.' I asked what she meant and she said, 'I voted and now I am without sin.'"

She bursts out laughing as Elsa unearths a copy of the newspaper *Diario de Querétaro* and tosses it onto my lap. The main headline from the June 27 edition reads PECADO NO VOTAR—It Is a Sin Not to Vote.

"If the PAN won by one vote and it is a legitimate count—fine. We'll accept it. But count those votes already! Otherwise, we'll take to the streets," Fidelina says. Obrador will hold a meeting for his supporters in the Zócalo in D. F. this Saturday, and she plans to attend. "I'm ready to fight!"

---

* Two groups—Alianza Cívica and the Center for Higher Study of Social Anthropology—published studies prior to the 2006 election documenting how millions of poor, rural Mexicans were threatened with being kicked off social assistance programs and health care if they didn't vote for particular candidates. Others were offered between four hundred and six hundred pesos for their votes. See Manuel Roig-Franzia, "As Presidential Vote Nears, Studies Suggest Coercive Tactics Are Still Pervasive," *Washington Post,* June 26, 2006, A16.

Dusk has fallen by the time I leave Café Al Fondo. As I wait at the bus stop, some luxury cars—SUVS, a Mercedes, Jeeps—zoom by with PAN flags fluttering out the windows. The drivers flash their thumbs and honk their horns. The Federal Electoral Institute has announced that Calderón won by 244,000 votes out of 41 million cast.

"Look at them, the rich getting richer," the man beside me mutters.

"They only win through fraud," his companion says. "But this time, we won't let them."

While strolling along Avenida Universidad the following morning, I notice that the old condonería of Octavio Acuña—the gay activist slain last summer—has reopened. AIDS prevention posters cover its walls; books like *Papá, Mamá, Soy Gay* and *Manual de Sexo Lésbico* line its shelves. I introduce myself to the staff—a gay man and an older woman—and they invite me into their side office for tea as they call Martín, Octavio's partner of seven years. An index card that says POLICÍA and lists several phone numbers hangs on a bulletin board; a crucifix suspends from the doorway.

Martín is a lion of a man, upbeat and gregarious with a curly mane. His polo depicts the store logo, which is a smiling condom wearing gloves. He leads me to the upstairs office where Octavio used to hold counseling sessions behind a stately oak desk. I sit upon the couch as Martín digs out photographs of Octavio—a tall, sienna-skinned man with a long, oval face and ears that might flap. They met in college. Martín studied languages; Octavio, psychology. An activist even then, Octavio organized campus-wide events like "Diversity Week" and conducted workshops about AIDS. By twenty-eight, he had earned four diplomas and a master's degree. The two evolved from friends to lovers to life partners within two years. They moved in together, painted their house, decorated it with plants, adopted a puppy. "In all that time, we never said a bad word to each other, never hit each other, not even once. Once I said guey [a crude form of 'dude'] but that's it."

After the couple got harassed by police in Jardín Guerrero in September 2004, Octavio spent the better part of a year filing denuncias. Martín supported his crusade, though he feared what might come of it. The condom shop was the target of too many prank calls and homophobic graffiti to brush it off as coincidence.

On June 21, 2005, Octavio left the house at 6 A.M. He called Martín at 3 P.M. to check in. They decided to travel to D. F. that weekend to march in the Gay Pride Parade. "Then he told me how much he loved me, how happy he was with me. An hour later, I had the urge to call him again, but there was no answer. I called again and again, like nine times. I only worked ten minutes away, so I decided to walk over."

As he stepped out of his office door, a friend ran up, panicked. Something was happening at the condonería. Martín grabbed some colleagues and hurried down the street. Patrol cars and ambulances were everywhere. "By then, I knew something had happened to Octavio. Fire was just running through my body. When the police figured out who I was, one asked me really loudly, in front of the entire crowd, who was the mujercita [little woman] in our relationship." Meaning: who received the penetration.* A teacher standing among the onlookers accused the officer of violating Martín's rights, not to mention his dignity, and later helped file a denuncia against him. (The officer got suspended for two days.)

---

* In Mexico (and much of Latin America), men who engage in homosexual relations often categorize themselves as activo (active) or pasivo (passive). Many only consider the latter to be gay.

In the months that followed, Martín had to not only cope with his grief but also fight to retain their home and business—rights he was not accorded as a same-sex partner. He hoped the killer would be found and brought to justice, but the crime was written off as one "of passion." Three days before the first-year anniversary of Octavio's death, however, *Diario de Querétaro* ran a page-one story announcing the culprit had been caught. Six color photos depicted a juvenile delinquent named Miguel Ángel Palacios Ríos confessing to police and demonstrating how he did it.

"The police said a transvestite sent him here to give Octavio a scare. That chavo was only supposed to rob him, but he said Octavio resisted and that's why he died. But he wasn't just stabbed once. It was five times! And the chavo said he did it in the front room, but Octavio's body was found in the back, and there was no blood in between. It doesn't make sense. And the transvestite later came out and said that police threatened her to say those things."

Martín's face is blotchy now but he is remarkably restrained—especially considering that this "confession" occurred only two and a half weeks ago. The case has officially been closed, and he is more afraid than ever. "The police are always coming by here. We have been silent lately because we are so afraid something will happen to us or to our families. It would be very easy for them to get rid of us, to kidnap one of us, to create an 'accident' while we are out walking."

Closing the shop is unfathomable. It was Octavio's dream. No. Martín instead takes every possible precaution. No fewer than two staffers work at any time. They installed surveillance cameras in every room and posted emergency phone numbers throughout. He says he has a passport and a suitcase ready to go. "We know there will be more Octavios. There will be more blood. Because this is a war. But a war worth fighting for."

My friend Rogelio and I agree to "meet at the meeting" in Mexico City's Zócalo on Saturday afternoon, and I realize the idiocy of this plan as my subway train approaches downtown and scores of people in yellow and black pack in. Some wear official PRD attire, but most have mixed and matched from their closets, donning leopard-skin blouses with black rebozos and fluorescent yellow caps. Obrador bumper stickers are slapped upon their chests, hats, and backs. The whole train empties at the Zócalo station. I cast myself adrift in the human current, beaching on a stairwell lined with police in riot gear. The Zócalo is hemorrhaging people. Families with picnic baskets and folding chairs are planted in the shadows of buildings. A nearby school bus spells out the word FRAUDE in its windows; wooden crates form a Trojan horse. Vendors are out in force, selling everything from Obrador paraphernalia to fresh quesadillas out of a pail.

I call Rogelio but can't hear a word he says. The streets vibrate Obrador's refrain for a nationwide recount: VOTO POR VOTO; CASILLA POR CASILLA—Vote Per Vote; Polling Station Per Polling Station. We revert to text-messaging. He is trapped on Calle Cinco de Mayo. That would normally be a seven-minute stroll away, but in this crowd, it could take an hour. I weave my way through, passing a horde of luchadores clad in yellow tights and black capes. Traffic comes to a standstill on Plaza de la Constitución. I brace myself against a stone arch and text my coordinates, wondering how demonstrators ever found one another in the 1960s. Thunder rumbles.

By sheer chance, I glimpse Rogelio riding in on a wave ten feet away. I scream his name but only the woman slammed against me hears. She joins me on the second round and a dozen people are soon helping. A father gives a countdown with his fingers—uno, dos, tres—before we shout in unison: ¡ROGELIO! He jerks his head toward us and thrusts out his hand. People push me toward him.

"Unbelievable!" he cries, wrapping his arms around me. "I never would have thought so many would come!"

The son of a successful businessman, Rogelio has traveled extensively throughout North America and once lived in Quebec, where he learned French as a chef at a sushi restaurant. Although he voted for the PAN, he empathizes with Obrador's supporters. I am relieved to find him: not only is he great company, but at six feet tall, he serves as a protective shield against the bone-crunching masses. Gripping each other tightly, we maneuver toward the Zócalo's center. A Televisa news crew tries to film crowd shots, but people keep jumping in front of their cameras to heckle them. "¡FUERA TELEVISA! ¡MUERA TELEVISA!" Get Out, Televisa! Die, Televisa!

We are a few yards from the flagpole in the belly of the Zócalo when a face appears on the sole video screen. Everyone shushes, but the sound system is practically inaudible. When Obrador takes the stage, the crowd goes wild. "¡PRESIDENTE!" they chant as he waves. "¡NO ESTÁS SOLO! ¡NO ESTÁS SOLO!" You Are Not Alone.

The bulk of the crowd seems to be working-class families and college students, plus a smattering of groupies—including the plump women in front of us.

"¡Ay, papacito!" one says, fanning herself at the sight of Obrador.

"He's so cute!" her friend exclaims, reapplying her lipstick.

Obrador's own campaign materials might exaggerate his Bugs Bunny front teeth when he's drawn as a cartoon, but he is without doubt a caudillo, or strong man. (And Latin America has endured a tragically long love affair with those.) Throughout Obrador's campaign, supporters presented him with live roosters to symbolize his cockiness.

Halfway through Obrador's speech, someone to our far left shouts out "¡MÉDICO!" All heads automatically whip to the right and echo it: "¡MÉDICO!"

"Someone must be sick," Rogelio says, standing on his toes.

My heart goes out to them. No medical team could penetrate this crowd. Five minutes later, however, paramedics are scaling a nearby barricade. Rogelio and another man lock hands so they can climb down.

"¿Dónde?" one of the paramedics shouts, a stethoscope around her neck. Where?

A hundred hands point the way as everyone squishes together, allowing them passage. Even when it seems utterly manic, Mexico is secretly orderly.

The meeting wraps up. Obrador asks everyone to return next Sunday.

"¿A QUÉ HORA?" What time?

"¿A LAS ONCE?" How about eleven?

"¡ME PARECE BIEN!" they cheer. Sounds good to me!

As Rogelio and I swamp to the subway, we try to estimate a crowd count. (The police later say 280,000.)

"Whatever it is, this will be as big as it gets," Rogelio predicts. "Only half as many will come next week, and it will die out from there."

In much of the world, that would be true. After a close election, the opposition would rally while the wound was raw, then gradually admit defeat. But this is Mexico. The resistance has just begun.

Obrador holds his meeting the following weekend. The police estimate crowds of 1.1 million, and he implores them to commit acts of "peaceful civil resistance" to force a vote-by-vote recount. At the end of July, a plantón is declared—albeit a far cry from the typical cardboard-on-concrete kind. Truckloads of white party tents are pitched along Paseo de la Reforma, one of the capital's major arteries, along with concert stages, portable toilets, merry-go-rounds, roller coasters, even a lucha libre wrestling ring. Traffic hits gridlock as Obrador supporters salsa to live music in the middle of the boulevard. Even those who initially sympathized with Obrador soon resent his strong-arm tactics, while his supporters further radicalize.

In September, the Federal Electoral Tribunal agrees to open the sealed voting packets in fewer than 12,000 of the nation's 130,400 polling stations. Calderón's 0.58 percent winning margin stands, the tiniest in Mexico's history. Days before his swearing-in ceremony on December 1, PRD lawmakers declare a pseudo-plantón of their own, camping out in the aisles to block Calderón's passage to the podium. PAN lawmakers unroll their bedding alongside them, and the factions pelt one another with Coca-Cola cans, Domino's pizza boxes, chairs, and fists. On inauguration day, Calderón must slip in through a back door. Amid jeers and cheers, he accepts the presidential sash from Fox and swears to defend the constitution before bodyguards whisk him away.

Meanwhile in Oaxaca, the rebellion perseveres. Governor Ulises Ruiz eventually concedes to a few of the teachers' demands and most return to their home villages, but the APPO refuses to end the plantón until he resigns. On October 27, armed plainclothes government agents combat APPO protesters at a barricade in a residential neighborhood. Gunfire erupts, and two bullets strike a thirty-six-year-old American named Bradley Will who flew to Mexico as a journalist for the news center Indymedia.org. He films his own shooting, dying with his camera in his hands.* Four Mexicans die from injuries received that day as well. President Fox responds by dispatching 4,500 Federal Preventative Police, an elite military force. Hun-

* Despite considerable evidence—including photographs, bullets, and scores of witnesses—the investigation into Bradley Will's death has gone nowhere. The two men accused in the shooting were released on December 1, 2006, after a state judge ruled they were standing too far away to have shot him.

dreds of protesters are arrested, including innocent bystanders who fit APPO's profile (that is, hippie-looking young men with ponytails). Many are beaten. The police occupy downtown until late December. All told, the conflict claims at least twenty lives, most of them protesters.

These battles are not my own. But watching them from a laptop in El Norte is agonizing. I can't help but compare Mexico's 2006 presidential election with ours in 2000. I believed as fervently in Al Gore as Obrador's supporters believed in him and harbor similar feelings about President Bush that Oaxaqueños do about Governor Ruiz. Yet what did I do about it? Attended a few protests, wrote some checks, and crawled into bed in defeat. And Mexicans face such steeper consequences: death squads, paramilitaries, brutal crackdowns by police. But time and again, they swallow their fear. They roll out their cardboard and refuse to budge. Not just "leftist radicals," but mothers. Teachers. Students. Workers. Farmers. Citizens who have been squeezed until they bellowed and will now gamble with death for their land, their rights, their dignity.

All of this awes me—and worries me to no end. Late at night I scour the Internet for headlines, downloading videos off Indymedia and CNN. Moaning every time I recognize a building (or a face). Trying to convince myself that—no matter how bad that riot looks—twelve miles away, lovers are sharing fruit water beneath a shade tree. Mariachis are singing. A little Zapotec girl is dreaming.

EPILOGUE

MEXICAN ENOUGH

It is Saturday night in San Juan, Puerto Rico, and I've been eyeing a certain puertorriqueño for four days now. We're two of four thousand attendees at a conference on Latin American affairs, but our paths keep crossing, and we've just spotted each other by the front doors of the hotel ballroom. Inside, a band is revving up for the Gran Baile. We introduce ourselves and are flirting within an instant. Outrageously. In Spanish. It's sexy as hell. The doors swing open and he extends his hand. "Do you salsa?"

My face burns flush. "Kind of but not—"

He is off like a comet, abandoning me at the entrance.

Salsa. I meant to learn how in Querétaro, but La Jotería was a disco-only establishment. I vow to take a class back home. And do. But I can't help wondering when this Mexification process will end. I have already learned the language, traveled the land. Must I now take cooking lessons? Enroll in Ballet Folklórico? Will I ever be Mexican enough?

It goes without saying that I will never be truly Mexican, not even if I moved there for the rest of my life and acquired the requisite customs and traditions. Because what binds a people are their bedtime stories. The songs they sing on road trips. Political and historical events. Fads and crazes. Shared memories. Not skills that can be acquired, like language or dance. Which isn't to say such pursuits are worthless endeavors. Cultural preservation is sacrosanct. But there is no point striving for an unobtainable state of being.

Besides, born-and-bred Mexicans struggle with what it means to be puro mexicano too. Luchadores wonder if they are selling out when they fight WWE-style instead of traditionally. Gay men question whether they can still be macho, and therefore Mexican, if they are homosexual. After years of being treated like "aliens" in El Norte, undocumented workers return home to their villages and discover they have changed so much, they actually start to feel like an alien. Indigenous dialects are disappearing throughout Mexico for the same reason so many U.S. Latinos no longer speak Spanish: our elders want to spare us the linguistic discrimination that burdened them. And for every Samuel Huntington* or Pat Buchanan, who fears that Mexicans are altering the (Anglo-Protestant) face of the United States, there is an intellectual or Zapatista fretting U.S. encroachment in Mexico. The former scorns welfare moms, depressed wages, and gangs; the latter dreads Wal-Mart, stripped land, and gangs.

Identity crisis is endemic to the U.S. Latino community as

---

* In the March/April 2004 edition of *Foreign Policy*, Harvard professor Samuel P. Huntington wrote an article called "The Hispanic Challenge," which said the persistent inflow of Hispanic immigrants "threatens to divide the United States into two peoples, two cultures, and two languages . . . rejecting the Anglo-Protestant values that built the American dream." The United States, he warned, "ignores this challenge at its peril." Patrick Buchanan makes a similar argument in his 2006 book *State of Emergency: The Third World Invasion and Conquest of America.*

well. I recently joined Las Comadres, a national organization that networks Latinas from all nations. At practically every meeting, I encounter another caramel-skinned woman who speaks Spanish fluently, cooks arroz con pollo, and salsa dances on weekends, yet *still* doesn't feel Latina enough. This is especially ironic considering that white society created what it means to be Latino in the first place. Colonists diluted indigenous blood through conquest and rape; the U.S. government drew up categories like "Hispanic," "White," "Black," and "Other" and made us choose. Hollywood created the cholo while MTV gave us J. Lo. For generations, we've felt pressured to emulate these role models because they were our only ones.

But poco a poco, we are coming into our own as a people. We're making strides in film, literature, nonprofits, politics, science, music. Creating our own definitions of who we are and who we can aspire to be. Fulfilling the dreams of ancestors who struggled to root (or keep) us here.

I'm driving cross-country again, this time up Interstate 35 with a friend who has graciously taken the wheel. As the Texas hill country rolls into crushed velvet plains and gold prairie, I grow nostalgic. My father was born and raised out here, in a rural Kansas town. He split after high school to drum in a U.S. Navy band, but when I was young, we packed up the van every summer and drove up for a visit. Countless things lured me back here: the crisp, sweet smell of the hay, the enormity of the sky, the tartness of my aunt's cherry pie—but Grandma's stories were what I coveted most. She spun tales of retreating into dugouts after spying tornadoes on the horizon; of battling dust storms and brush fires; of sleigh rides at Christmas. I would sit on her kitchen counter while she mashed pots of potatoes and beg for another story, one about my great-great-grandpa Oliver, who got his arm blown off in the Civil War, or about Scurvy Irv, a hermit who spit tobacco into a potbellied stove.

I grew so distraught while saying good-bye one summer, Grandma suggested that I write a letter whenever I missed her. Our correspondence lasted a decade. I never kept a diary back then: every secret, thought, and dream got mailed to Kansas—until she died of leukemia. The loss so devastated me, I never returned.

Until now. By the time we've crossed the Kansas state line, I've been transported to early childhood. As far back as anyone can remember, Griests have lived here. It is just as much my heritage as Mexico. This realization crystallizes when we park in my cousin's driveway and three kin step onto the porch. I haven't seen them in nine years. They have married, divorced, remarried, raised half a dozen kids. Their mother died. I missed it all. And yet they dropped everything to see me—the long-lost cousin—on a moment's notice. I run into their arms crying, and the four of us embrace on the front lawn. When I step back for a better look, I am amazed to see three pairs of indigo eyes gazing into mine. The physical characteristic that sets me apart from most Mexicans unites me with them.

That night, I research "being biracial" online. A list of seven characteristics pops up, including: "Undergoes periodic racial interrogations; gets attacked for perceived lack of racial allegiance/authenticity; feels most comfortable in racially mixed crowds; experiences identity crisis at some point in lifetime." I fit every description. Something surprising occurs to me: the schizophrenia of being biracial, of straddling two worlds but belonging to neither, might give me my deepest understanding of what it means to be Mexican.

Moreover, the people I encountered in Mexico treasure their mestizo heritage, their blending of bloods. I should too. After all, while my intrepid Abuelita Ramona was braving the Río Grande, my entrepreneurial Grandma Madge and her two sisters ran their own hamburger joint during the war, supporting their families and mother. There is a history, culture, and identity on either side of my heritage. It is time to embrace each. Like the seven million Americans who claimed to belong to more than one race in the 2000 census. That's only 2.4 percent of our nation, but we're growing, organizing, forming committees. Striving to believe that—whatever we are—it's enough.

To live in the Borderland means you
are neither *hispana india negra española*
ni gabacha, eres mestiza, mulata, half-breed
caught in the crossfire between camps
while carrying all five races on your back
not knowing which side to turn to, run
from . . .

—*Gloria Anzaldúa*, Borderlands/
La Frontera: The New Mestiza

NOTES

Chapter 1. Legacies

page

2 Studies show that only 17 percent: Rubén Rumbaut, Frank Bean, and Douglas Massey, "Linguistic Life Expectancies: Immigrant Language Retention in Southern California," *Population and Development Review,* September 2006.

2 Bound and gagged: William Allen, "I've Never Seen Anything Like This Before," *St. Louis Post-Dispatch,* April 16, 1989, 9D.

Chapter 2. Miracle City

page

16 A megalopolis of 22 million: Joel Simon, "Sinking City," in *The Mexico Reader*, eds. Gilbert M. Joseph and Timothy J. Henderson (Durham, NC: Duke University, 2002).

16 It is also sinking: "Thirsty Mega-City Sinks As It Drinks," *The Australian,* March 18, 2006, A15.

16 Last year, some two hundred: Dane Schiller, "Mexicans Demanding a Cure to the Plague of Kidnappings," *San Antonio Express-News,* July 22, 2005, A1.

16 D. F. is a postapocalyptic: Carlos Monsiváis, "Identity Hour, or What Photos Would You Take of the Endless City?" *Mexican Postcards* (London, UK, and New York, NY: Verso Books, 1997).

18 During the 2000: Wendy Patterson, "For Homosexual Men in Mexico, Every Day Brings Threat of Danger," *San Francisco Chronicle,* October 12, 2000, A12.

20 The largest private employer: Statistics taken from www.walmartstores.com, July 2007.

Chapter 3. The Land of Ni Modo

page

28 If there is a party: Octavio Paz, *The Labyrinth of Solitude* (New York, NY: Grove Press, 1985).

33 Comedian Héctor Suárez: Patrick Oster, *The Mexicans: A Personal Portrait of a People* (New York, NY: HarperPerennial, 2002).

33 Writer Octavio Paz: Paz, *The Labyrinth of Solitude.*

35 While 98 percent: UNESCO Institute for Statistics: at http://stats.uis.unesco.org, Education Table 1.

35 Nearly half the nation: Joseph Contreras, "Teens at Work," *Newsweek Web Exclusive,* July 31, 2007, at www.msnbc.msn.com/id/20056614/site/newsweek.

36 In 2004, Mexico City: Mary Jordan, "Poetry in Motion: Mexico City Subway Aims to Elevate Culture by Lending Books to Riders," *Washington Post,* February 4, 2004, A17.

36 Although Mexico is ethnically: Sylvia Schmelkes, "Education and Indian Peoples in Mexico: An Example of Policy Failure," in *Unequal Schools, Unequal Chances*, ed. Fernando Reimers (Harvard University, David Rockefeller Center for Latin American Studies, 2001). Also see Alan Riding, *Distant Neighbors: A Portrait of the Mexicans* (New York, NY: Alfred A. Knopf, 1985).

Chapter 4. ¡Mucha Lucha!

page

45 After hundreds of thousands: Dan Murphy, "Mexico's Wrestling Heroes Give the Smackdown to Vice," *Christian Science Monitor,* August 22, 2001.

45 Luchador Ecologista Universal: Anne Rubenstein, "El Santo's Strange Career," in *The Mexico Reader*, eds. Gilbert M. Joseph and Timothy J. Henderson (Durham, NC: Duke University, 2002).

50 At 522 cups: Sara Silver, "All the Range in Mexico Coca-Cola Is Useful," *Financial Times,* October 1, 2005.

Chapter 5. The Coyote's Wife

page

60 Princeton scholar Douglas: Douglas Massey, *Beyond Smoke and Mirrors: Mexican Immigration in an Era of Economic Integration* (New York, NY: Russell Sage Foundation Publications, 2003).

61 This sums their relationship: Interview with Víctor Guerra, state coordinator of the immigration advocacy group Consejo Estatal de Proteción de Aguascalientes (COESPO).

61 Journalist Cecilia Ballí: Cecilia Ballí, "The Border Is Wide," *Harper's Magazine,* October 1, 2006.

65 It is no small amount: "Remittances Reach US $20 Billion in 2005," *El Universal,* February 1, 2006.

Chapter 6. Malaleche, Spoiled Milk

page

68 Then–Mexican president: "Mexican Workers Since NAFTA," *NACLA Report on the Americas,* July/August 2005, 15.

68 According to the Carnegie: Sandra Polaski, "The Employment Consequences of NAFTA," Testimony submitted to the Senate Subcommittee on International Trade of the Committee on Finance, September 11, 2006.

68 Freak theories abound: Interview with Cecilia Ballí, *Texas Monthly* staff writer.

74 Meanwhile, that same week: Tim Gaynor, "Murders of Women Rising in Mexican Border City," Reuters, March 16, 2005.

Chapter 7. Mexican Road Trip

page

84 Between 1942 and 1964: Rodolfo Acuña, *Occupied America: A History of Chicanos* (New York, NY: HarperCollins, 1988).

84 The United States withheld: Hiram Soto, "Mexico Takes Step to Pay Former Bracero Workers," *San Diego Union-Tribune,* January 29, 2005.

89 Harvard economist George J. Borjas: Stephen Macedo, "The Moral Dilemma of U.S. Immigration Policy," in *Debating Immigration*, ed. Carol M. Swain (New York, NY: Cambridge University Press, 2007).

90 *Fast Food Nation* author: Eric Schlosser, "A Side Order of Human Rights," *New York Times,* April 6, 2005.

Chapter 9. Motherlands

page

97 After buying every single: Helen Kleberg Groves, *Bob and Helen Kleberg of King Ranch* (Albany, TX: Bright Sky Press, 2004). See also Mona D. Sizer, *The King Ranch Story: Truth and Myth* (Plano, TX: Republic of Texas Press, 1999).

97 So he "offered: Don Graham, *The Kings of Texas: The 150-Year Saga of an American Ranching Empire* (Hoboken, NJ: John Wiley & Sons, 2003).

100 After discovering that three: Ibid.

105 Cruillas is so often: Ibid.

109 After the Texas-Mexico border: Ibid.

111 "To cross over: Rubén Martínez, *Crossing Over: A Mexican Family on the Migrant Trail* (New York, NY: Metropolitan Books, 2001).

112 Between 350,000 and 600,000: David G. Gutiérrez, *Walls and Mirrors: Mexican Americans, Mexican Immigrants, and the Politics of Ethnicity* (Berkeley, CA: University of California Press, 1995).

113 Some 6.2 million: Jeffrey S. Passel, "The Size and Characteristics of the Unauthorized Migrant Population in the U.S.," Pew Hispanic Center Research Report, March 7, 2006, http://pewhispanic.org/files/reports/61.pdf.

Chapter 10. Who Killed Octavio Acuña?

page

125 Ten years later: Linda Diebel, *Betrayed: The Assassination of Digna Ochoa* (New York, NY: Carroll & Graf, 2005).

125 According to the Citizen's: Monica Campbell, "Activists Hail Mexico City's New Same-Sex Civil Union Law," *San Francisco Chronicle*, November 23, 2006, A25.

Chapter 12. *Incantations*

page

139 And their demands: Tom Haines, "On the Edge: For Some Indigenous People, a Life of Struggle, Devoid of Basics," *Boston Globe*, December 18, 2005, M1.

139 He began writing: Susan Ferriss, "Mexican Rebel Standoff Becomes a Way of Life," *Atlanta Journal-Constitution*, December 28, 2003.

141 Mexico has had socialized: Jamie Talan, "Mexico's Health Care on a Pedestal," *Newsday*, October 16, 2006.

142 Started in 1997: Eliza Barclay, "More Than a Drugstore: Mexico's Poor Flock to Discount Chain for Medical Basics," *Houston Chronicle,* May 19, 2006.

145 According to journalist: Andrés Oppenheimer, *Bordering on Chaos: Mexico's Roller-Coaster Journey toward Prosperity* (New York, NY: Little, Brown and Company, 1998).

149 Books have a: Interview with Ambar Past, founder of Taller Leñateros.

149 During the Conquest, however: Friar Diego de Landa, *Relación de las Cosas de Yucatán,* 1566.

Chapter 13. Meet Me at the Hour of God

page

156 In the late 1990s: Interview with Miguel Pickard of the San Cristóbal-based Center of Economic and Political Research for Community Action (CIEPAC).

161 They had recently formed: Michael McCaughan, "Facing Mexico's Pain," *Irish Times,* December 4, 1999, 62.

161 For weeks, Zapatista: Linda Diebel, "Mexico's Littlest Victims of War," *Toronto Star,* March 7, 1998, A1.

161 At 10:30 A.M.: Interview with Pickard.

161 At the entrance: Diebel, *Betrayed: The Assassination of Digna Ochoa.*

161 The killings continued: Julia Preston, "Mexico Accuses Policeman of Helping Arm Mass Killers," *New York Times,* January 13, 1998, A8.

162 Ilol, or shamans: Teresa Borden, "Traditional Healers Put Coke to the Test," *Atlanta Journal-Constitution,* April 14, 2004, 1F.

162 To celebrate a baptism: Teresa Borden quoting scholar Jan Rus, "In Chiapas, Cola Is King," *Atlanta Journal-Constitution,* April 14, 2004, 1F.

164 Like Zenaida Pérez: Diebel, *Toronto Star.*

164 A year after the: Diebel, *Betrayed: The Assassination of Digna Ochoa.*

164 But while the interior: Ginger Thompson, "Where Killings Defiled a Church, No Forgiveness," *New York Times,* December 23, 1998, A4. Also see Diebel, *Betrayed: The Assassination of Digna Ochoa.*

165 This strategy was employed: Jan Rus, Rosalva Aída Hernández Castillo, and Shannan L. Mattiace, eds., "Introduction," *Mayan Lives, Mayan Utopias: The Indigenous Peoples of Chiapas and the Zapatista Rebellion* (Lanham, MD: Rowman & Littlefield Publishers, 2003).

Chapter 14. The People with No Place to Go

page

170 The literal translation: Tom Haines, "On the Edge: For Some Indigenous People, a Life of Struggle, Devoid of Basics," *Boston Globe,* December 18, 2005, M1.

181 For remorse, you: Victoria Dawson, "One From the Heart," *Smithsonian Magazine,* February 2003.

Chapter 16. The Strikers

page

191 It wrote reams: "Old PRI Returns to Life in Oaxaca," *Latin American Weekly Report,* July 26, 2005.

Chapter 17. The Resistance

page

207 A *New York Times* reporter: Sam Dillon, "Rebels' Call to Arms Echoes in Rural Mexico," *New York Times,* September 19, 1996, A3.

207 Troubles here began: Francisco J. Sanchez, "Mexican Police Arrest Man They Call Leader of Shadowy Rebel Group," Associated Press, March 19, 1998.

208 Claiming retribution: Susan Ferriss, "Mexican Indians Say They Were Framed as Terrorists, Want Fox to Free Them," Cox News Service, December 20, 2001.

218 Human Rights Watch: Adam Thomson, "Mexico Criticized over Lack of Human Rights Progress," *Financial Times,* May 18, 2006, 4.

218 Torture-induced confessions: Monica Campbell, "Fox Bids to Reform Mexican Justice," *Christian Science Monitor,* April 6, 2004, 6.

218 In D. F., for instance: Kevin Sullivan and Mary Jordan, "Disparate Justice Imprisons Mexico's Poor," *Washington Post,* July 6, 2002, A1.

218 As the martyred Salvadoran: Mary Jordan and Kevin Sullivan, *The Prison Angel: Mother Antonia's Journey from Beverly Hills to a Life of Service in a Mexican Jail* (New York, NY: Penguin Press, 2005).

221 As we eat: Sara Silver, "Mexico Joins Plan for Regional Development," *Financial Times,* July 1, 2002, 5.

222 This $183 billion: Cathy Booth and Thomas Hutto, "The Next Wave in Superhighways, or a Big, Fat, Texas Boondoggle?" *Time,* November 28, 2004.

Chapter 18. Little Zapotec Girl

page

226 This is a fiercely: Marc Lacey, "Guatemala System Is Scrutinized as Americans Rush in to Adopt," *New York Times,* November 5, 2006, A1.

Chapter 19. Valley Mantras

page

233 They explode membership: Solana Larsen, "The Anti-Immigration Movement: From Shovels to Suits," *NACLA Report on the Americas,* May/June 2007, 14.

234 He traveled to: The Handbook of Texas Online, www.tsha.utexas.edu.

237 As homicide has: Kevin Johnson, "Always on Guard in Nuevo Laredo," *USA Today,* May 17, 2006.

237 These unincorporated: Cecilia Ballí, "Bottom's Up," *Texas Monthly,* January 2003.

240 Aside from the military: Douglas Massey, "Foolish Fences," *Washington Post,* November 29, 2005.

241 President Bush will soon: Carolyn Lochhead, "Bush Seeks 'Middle Ground' in Debate on Immigration," *San Francisco Chronicle,* May 16, 2006.

241 That's true: the Congressional: Angie C. Marek, "Good Fences and Such," *US News & World Report,* October 16, 2006.

243 Some 400,000 people: P. J. Huffstutter, "The May Day Marches," *Los Angeles Times,* May 2, 2006, A10.

243 Seventy-two thousand: Anita Hamilton, "A Day without Immigrants: Making a Statement," *Time* (online edition), May 1, 2006.

244 According to the *New York Times*: Julia Preston, "As Pace of Deportation Rises, Illegal Families Are Digging In," *New York Times,* May 1, 2007.

Chapter 20. Rebel Yell

page

257 Located eighteen miles northeast: Ginger Thompson, "Cornfields or Runways? Zapata's Ghost Watches," *New York Times,* July 18, 2002, A4.

257 The Fox government: Kevin Sullivan, "Double-Edged Machete in Mexico Fight," *Washington Post,* August 9, 2002.

258 Most news reports: David Sasaki, "Mexico: Violence and Backlash in San Salvador Atenco," www.globalviolence.org, May 18, 2006.

258 Whatever the case: Interview with John Gibler, Human Rights Fellow at Global Exchange.

259 They have also been accused: John Ross, "The 'Dirty War' Returns to Mexico," Blindman's Buff at www.narconews.com, May 18, 2006.

260 Because this is an election year: Héctor Tobar, "Oaxaca Teachers' Strike Jeopardizes Presidential Balloting in State," *Los Angeles Times,* June 19, 2006.

260 In the predawn hours: James C. McKinley, "Teacher Strike May Influence Mexican Vote," *New York Times,* June 22, 2006, A6.

273 The United States recently: Adam Thomson, "Fox in U-turn over Bill of Possession of Drugs," *Financial Times,* May 5, 2006.

281 The police estimate: Manuel Roig-Franzia, "Lopez Obrador Urges Civil Resistance," *Washington Post,* July 17, 2006, A12.

281 Truckloads of white party: John Gibler, "Designer Uprising," Z-Net, August 7, 2006.

282 In September: Manuel Roig-Franzia, "Partial Vote Recount Ordered in Mexico," *Washington Post,* August 6, 2006, A12.

282 Four Mexicans die: John Ross, "Shooting the Shooter," *Washington City Paper,* August 8, 2007.

283 All told, the conflict: Monica Campbell, "A Killing in Mexico," Report for the Committee to Protect Journalists, April 17, 2007.

ACKNOWLEDGMENTS

Beautiful people inspired, informed, and supported this book. Mil gracias to all of the following:

In Querétaro: Greg Rubio, Raúl, Karina, Jésica and the Ibargüengoitia family, Omar, César, Fabián, Federico, Emmanuel, Noel, Aldo, Nadia Sierra Campos, Piedad and Laura of Malaleche, Lupita Gómez, Mariela Castañeda, Ángel, Alma, Silvia and Goyo, Elsa Doria, Atómico, Bulldog Quintero, Dragón de Oriente II, Lady Black, Luis Felipe Zanidio Burgos, Yves Marceau, Chad Brown, Jen and Barry Girard, Valerie, Manuel Ruzzo, Martín Romero Ortiz, and the valiant work of Octavio Acuña. In Mexico City: Michael Schuessler, Rogelio Negrete and family, Yolande and family, Tito Vasconsuelos, and whoever stole my laptop and had a sudden change of heart. In Aguascalientes: Chuy and Víctor Guerra Ruiz. In Morelos: Víctor, Jumi, Judith, and extended family. In Tamaulipas: Martín Aguilar Cantú, Dr. Octavio Herrera, Oscar López, and Marie Nazaire. In Guadalajara: Miriam Cárdenas Torres and Jorge Ceja Martinez. In Monterrey: Imelda and Tomas, Edna Elizondo. In San Cristóbal de las Casas: Rebeca Gonzalez, Miguel Pickard, Sergio Castro, Ambar Past, Jan and Diane Rus, Margarita Plaza, Rafael, Marta, Roberto at Posada 5, Mitch Anderson, Natalie (and Sulita!), Colin Bossen, Melissa Mundt, las catequistas de Polhó, Francisco and Roselia in Acteal, CDH Fray Bartolomé de Las Casas, Canek Peña-Vargas, and Roger Stoll. In Oaxaca: Juan Sosa Maldonado, Isabel and Luciana Almaraz Matias, Padre Bernardo Murcio, Padre Jesus Seguro, Francisca Pérez Hernández, Claudia, Guadalupe and Ignacio, Ismael Sanmartín Hernández and the staff and vendors of *Noticias*, everyone at Tepeyac in Tehuantepec, Alan Goodin, Lourdes and Ricardo, Centro de Esperanza Infantil, and Henry Wangeman. In the Valley: Hector, Ramiro, and family; and Scott and the Laredo Border Patrol. Deep respects go to the "Other Journalists" who keep us posted on the "Other Mexico": Al Giordano, John Gibler, Nancy Davies, John Ross, and the rest of the gang at NarcoNews, Indymedia, and Global Exchange. Brad Will: may your brave soul rest in peace.

En El Norte: Irene Carranza, Michael Robertson, Sherry Shokouhi, Sonya Tsuchigane, Chuck Whitney and Ellen Wartella, Daphne Sorensen, Irene Lin, Kavitha Rao, Jeff Golden, Rachel DayStar Payne, Tori Langland, Amaya Moro-Martín, Jo Dunkley, Sylvia Smullin, Karla Cosgriff, Lauren Erdreich, Ines Brand, Maria Sacchetti, Cindy Casares, Patricia Rojas, Joy Baker, Amy Schapiro, Neda Farzan, Becky Kroll, Nick Tilsen, Stephen Danner, Jennifer Peskin, Mercedes Gallego, Gerardo Jaime, Sylvia Martínez, Michele Serros, Tyra Robertson, Shea Daugherty, Daniel Doremus, Michelle Herrera Mulligan, Stephanie Emory, Cathryn Calderon, David Farley, Jessie Sholl, Sheryl Oring, Angie Cruz, Paul Stekler, Paulette Searle, Justin Pico, Nora de Hoyas Comstock and all my comadres, Tony Diaz and everyone at Nuestra Palabra, Cecilia Ballí, Mario Tejada, Irma Cantú, Lupita Quintanilla, Michelle and Roberto Alegria, Homero and Letty Vera, Bruce Cheeseman, Tom Kreneck, Lee Byrd and Ligia Arguilez at Cinco Puntos Press, Carlos Marentes, Julia Preston, Tracey Wong Briggs, Kevin Smokler, Henry and Gregory Ramos, Esmeralda Santiago, Mary Morris, Don Graham, Rene Alegria, Alex Rivera, the Texas Book Festival, Austin's Mayor's Book Club, Larry Habegger and James O'Reilly at Travelers' Tales, Marcy Gordon, Roy Rieck, Carmen

Scheidel at MediaBistro, Kevin Hopkins, and my colleagues at the National Coalition Against Censorship: Joan Bertin, Marvin Rich, Svetlana Mintcheva, and Justin Goldberg. Roz Udow: your fiery spirit is sorely missed.

My eternal gratitude goes to the Council of Humanities and Department of Creative Writing at Princeton University for inviting me to spend 2005–2006 on their campus as a Hodder Fellow. Special thanks to John McPhee for his wise and friendly counsel, and to Michael Stone and Deborah Yashar at the Princeton Latin American Studies Department por su hospitalidad.

This book was written in the following dreamy cloisters: The Ledig House at Art Omi International (courtesy of the Geraldine R. Dodge Foundation); Lebh Shomea; the Kimmel Harding Nelson Center for the Arts; and the Writers' Colony at Dairy Hollow. My sincere thanks to Francis Greenburger, D.W. Gibson, Father Kelly Nemick, Denise Brady, Pat Friedli, and Jane Tucker for the gift of time and space to think and create.

Literary angels brought this book into being: my agent Sarah Jane Freymann, editors Wendy Walker and Amy Tannenbaum and Johanna Castillo. Besos to Omar López, Elliot Ratzman, Irene Lin, Miguel Pickard, John Gibler, and Irene Griest for their insightful comments; to Tania García for the aid of her mother tongue; and to Justin Goldberg and Justin Pico for their technical wizardry.

A shout-out to those who propel me forth: my readers and my students. Your letters mean the world. Thank you.

And now for my family: Irene and Dick Griest; Barbara, Alex, Jordan, and Analina Devora; all my tías y tíos (especially Tío Valentine) and primas y primos in South Texas; and the Griest clan up in Kansas. Thanks for your faith and for always welcoming me home. I'd be lost and lonely without you.

Final gratitude goes to the Ancestors for growing the roots.

INDEX